Steve Lowe and Alan McArthur are the authors of IS IT
JUST ME OR IS EVERYTHING SHIT?: THE ENCYLOPEDIA
OF MODERN LIFE VOLUMES 1 AND 2. Their next book
BLIGHTY will be published as a Sphere hardback in October
2008.

THE BEST OF
IS IT JUST ME OR IS EVERYTHING SHIT?

THE ENCYCLOPEDIA OF MODERN LIFE

STEVE LOWE AND ALAN McARTHUR

SPHERE

First published in Great Britain in 2008
by Sphere

A CIP catalogue record for this book
is available from the British Library.

ISBN 978-0-7515-4174-8

Typeset in Palatino by M Rules
Printed and bound in Great Britain by
CLays Ltd, St Ives plc

Papers used by Sphere are natural, renewable and recyclable
products made from wood grown in sustainable forests and certified
in accordance with the rules of the Forest Stewardship Council.

Mixed Sources
Product group from well-managed
forests and other controlled sources
www.fsc.org Cert no. SGS-COC-004081
© 1996 Forest Stewardship Council
FSC

Sphere
An imprint of
Little, Brown Book Group
100 Victoria Embankment
London EC4Y 0DY

An Hachette Livre UK Company
www.hachettelivre.co.uk

www.littlebrown.co.uk

THE BEST OF
IS IT JUST ME OR IS EVERYTHING SHIT?

THE ENCYCLOPEDIA OF MODERN LIFE

A

Ads for Credit Cards

'Don't put it off, put it on.' Let's be clear about this: there is absolutely nothing wrong with putting things off.

'Things get more exciting when you say "YES".'

Your life is not exciting enough, quite simply, because you haven't borrowed enough money. That much should be self-evident. Borrowing money may make you taller. You will have a nicer smile, and have read more books – while still finding time for that all-important jet-skiing holiday. It's possible that, by borrowing money, you can end all wars.

This is the abiding message of ads for credit cards. In 2005, posters for HSBC credit cards bore the slogan 'Magical Christmas Cards'. So that's 'magical' meaning 'running up large debts so that more of your money ends up with the bankers'. It's magic only in the sense that it involves a trick. We should trust our banks: they look after our money and everything. Yes, they make more every month from skanking people with late payment fees than you are likely to earn in your entire life, but that's only fair. With the UK public clearly in the middle of a cash crisis, still the adverts offering more credit come thicker and faster. Anyone would think the only way our economy is remaining afloat is by getting everyone to embrace really quite terrifying levels of financial insecurity – borrowing squillions to buy tat, and driving up house prices and rents with mortgage-mad buy-to-let mania (Britons owe over a trillion in mortgage debt alone). Britain is booming! Don't let your fear of bailiffs spoil it. Do bailiffs give you a new Audi and a spangly top? They do not. Credit does. So I know which side I'm on.

Adult editions of children's books

If you must follow the adventures of a public school conjuror, even though you are a) notionally a grown adult, and b) have probably been to university or at least to 'big school', why attempt to conceal the fact behind a different cover, as if fellow passengers will assume after a casual glance that you're actually reading Thomas Mann in the original German?

Just because the train on the front is black and white rather than bright red, it doesn't suddenly become a harrowing Booker prize-winner called *Harry Potter and the Genocide in Rwanda*.

How do the dinner party conversations go?

'What are you reading at the moment?'

'It's called *The Very Hungry Caterpillar*. It's about a caterpillar who gets really hungry – he just has to keep on eating stuff.'

'I've read it. Marvellous.'

'Oh, don't tell me how it ends!'

'No, I wouldn't. But it's . . . well, it's pretty moving. Oh look, I'm hogging all the Hula Hoops . . .'

Adventurers/mountaineers/explorers

BONG! This is the news: some bloke with more money than sense has got himself lost on a small dinghy in the middle of the Pacific Ocean. Sorry, when I said 'news', I actually meant 'waste of everyone's time'.

The world being largely explored now, is there really any need for a load of posh blokes to try to reach the South Pole living only on roasted peat and using equipment they bought in the Blacks sale? (Note to any posh blokes reading this: that's a rhetorical question – that is, no, there is no need for a load of posh blokes to try to reach the South Pole living only on roasted peat and using equipment they bought in the Blacks sale.) If they do set out over the Pacific in an 8-foot dinghy, risking almost certain drowning, would it be unreasonable to suggest that when they do capsize, rather than expect a multi-thousand-pound rescue operation and media furore, they could at least have the decency just to drown, quietly?

These posh weirdies say things like, 'If you make a mistake in that situation, you're dead.' Well, don't do it then, you twat! Because it's at least feasible that you'll make a mistake! Also: 'If the weather closes in, you're dead.' Well, forgive me, but isn't that what the weather does in the mountains? 'At that point, the weather started to close in!' Of course it did. You were climbing up a fucking mountain.

As recreated in the acclaimed documentary *Touching the Void*, mountaineers Joe Simpson and Simon Yates decided to be the first to climb the treacherous west face of the Siula Grande in the Peruvian Andes. What happened? They made a mistake and the weather closed in.

Simpson fell badly, breaking his leg and forcing the bone through his kneecap causing unimaginable agony. Then, after Simpson fell over a precipice, Yates, thinking his partner dead, cut the rope and his friend fell 100 feet into a crevasse. Pulling down the rope, Simpson realised he was alone and almost certain to die. At this point he cracked and started punching the ice wall, yelling: 'STUPID STUPID STUPID CUNT! CUUUUNT!!! STUPID CUNT! STUPIIIIDDD!!! CUUUNNNTTT!!'

A moment of clarity which, all things considered, he might have had in his living room in England. The stupid cunt.

Advice slips

In what meaningful sense does a receipt from a cashpoint constitute advice? All it says is: 'You haven't got any money.'

That's not advice. It would only be advice if they said: 'My brother's just won some money on a horse. I expect he'd lend you a couple of quid until you get paid.' Or: 'If you turned up to work on time occasionally, maybe you'd get promoted and we wouldn't have to go through this pathetic charade every month.'

'Cash machine' is also a misleading term: it sounds like an amazing mechanical device for the production of free money. It's not though.

Alpha Males

Does your boss sprawl over his chair like he's got two prickly pineapples for testicles? Does he clearly consider murder when faced with a promotion competitor? Does he prowl around believing all female employees are mere seconds from dragging him to the bogs for a short, sharp bunk-up? If so, he probably considers himself an 'alpha male': the kind of business/politics top dog who treats everyone else as his bitch – like the Marquis de Sade with a flip chart.

It's amazing how many people swallow this stuff – that a man's at his best when he's at his most animal – despite the seemingly obvious fact that we are, in fact, humans. In his doomed US presidential election campaign in 2000, Al Gore was implored by image consultant Naomi Woolf to discover the brooding sex panther within. In 2004, John Kerry had to go out and shoot at ducks. If this process accelerates, we'll soon be choosing our leaders by getting two beefy Nazis to have a willy-bashing contest in a pit.

Dominance hierarchies in the animal kingdom were discovered in the 1920s by Norwegian scientist Thorleif Schjelderup-Ebbe. Studying flocks of hens, he noticed how each member recognised its place above and below its peers; the upper echelons got first dibs at the corn (hence the phrase 'pecking order') and peace generally reigned. Clever hens, thought Thorleif Schjelderup-Ebbe.

But applying the same concept to *Homo sapiens* isn't that clever – unless we want our leaders to do head jabs at their opponents' faces before squatting down in the corner for a crap (actually, that might be interesting). In fact, most alpha males are a brain-rotting liability. Look at that Big Bad Wolf of recent British politics, Alastair Campbell, a man so virile he could inseminate a lump of coal. As Downing Street press secretary, he must have reckoned that his rugged rudeness meant all lobby journalists, female and male, fancied the arse off him. When he left – presumably to go drag-racing with Tommy Lee or shark-bashing with Billy Bob – they missed his verbal spankings terribly and only compensated by beating the bollocks out of each other after hometime.

But surely Campbell's alpha male qualifications only ever amounted to graceless egomania, screwed-too-tight menace and the ability to run marathons. You could say the same for Jimmy Saville* and he never moved out of his mum's house. Before *Big Brother 6* began, Maxwell predicted he would be the house alpha male. By Day 11, he was demonstrating his leaderene qualities by instigating a competition with Anthony to see who could be first to pee in their pants. Wondering what stunt they could pull next, Anthony suggested: 'We could shit ourselves.'

That's where trying to be an alpha male gets you. Think on, Campbell.

*See the 2000 documentary in which Saville was caught on camera reminiscing about tying up troublemakers in the boiler room of his club in the sixties. Surveying the ensuing scene, police officers would apparently say: 'You were a bit heavy with those two.' Owzabout that, then?

Amstrad health and beauty

You have to feel sorry for affable *Apprentice*-winner Tim Campbell (who once described himself, rather brilliantly, as 'a very small fish in a big world') when you consider the task awarded to him for scooping the Top Job on the runaway ratings-grabbing show: marketing an Amstrad-branded beauty device that pumps electricity into your face.

'So, you want me to enter the image-sensitive health and beauty market, a smoke and mirrors world where aspiration is all, with a brand name mostly associated with green-screen 1980s word processors and a very gruff man with a stubbly beard? Right. And it pumps electricity into your actual face? Okay. Yes, I understand it's safe, it's not that, it's . . . So that's the actual prize, is it?'

Amstrad cleverly overcame the possible image problems by giving their revolutionary health and beauty product the very Primrose Hill name of Integra Face Care System. And that's going straight into *Top Santé*, surely? Face Care System. Caring. Systematically. For your face.

Sir Alan 'Sir Alan' Sugar, by the way, once sent his wife a birthday card signed 'From Alan Sugar'. Well, we've all done it: worked hard on a heart-rending, confessional message of love before bottling out at the last moment and putting down 'From Alan Sugar'.

He also sent a fax to a videorecorder manufacturer in China which read: 'DEAR MR CHING CHANG CHONG, WE HAVE RECEIVED YOUR VIDEO. IT IS SHIT.' Sugar PR man and *Apprentice* regular Nick Hewer told the *Sunday Times*: 'It was all spelt out in bold. In capital letters . . . His use of language is very explicit, but he has this real ability to communicate.'

There are people out there, right now, all over this land, treating their own faces in the comfort of their own homes.

Anti-Americanism

You cannot escape the point: America has produced a vibrant culture that is the pleasure and envy of millions. These people have given us not only *The Cannonball Run* but also *Love In An Elevator* by Aerosmith. That's right.

But despite all these achievements, a wave of anti-Americanism is sweeping the globe. In Indonesia in April

2006, people rioted against *Playboy* – not because it was porn per se, but because it was American porn. 'Down with Yankee bongo' – that might have been the slogan. Apparently, even Japanese porn was deemed comparatively harmless – which is weird, considering it basically consists of women dressed up as little girls.

In Britain, we have certainly traditionally ridiculed Americans for being clamorous, rotund morons who have to be forcibly stopped from eating the furniture (the latest craze in US supermarkets is to buy paper plates in bulk: so no one has to wash up after dinner – how sick is *that*?). This is all good clean family fun. But now it's getting out of hand with supposedly rational souls seeing Islamists holding up posters proclaiming, 'God is great and America is Evil' and thinking: 'Hey, I'll have some of that. Surely I can harness that enthusiasm for the forces of good . . . Hey, you know what? America *is* a Great Satan. Eight quid – that's what going to see *Big Momma's House 2* cost me . . . the bastards!'

But the Americans need not fear, because leading the charge against the 'they had it coming' hordes, is . . . Tony Parsons. Writing a year after 9/11, he said the US should be hailed for its considered response to the atrocities: 'So a few al-Qaeda tourists got locked without a trial in Camp X-Ray? Pass the Kleenex. So some Afghan wedding receptions were shot up after they merrily fired their semi-automatics in a sky full of American planes? A shame, but maybe next time they should stick to confetti.' ('Pass the Kleenex,' by the way, does seem rather an unfortunate choice of phrase.)

Perhaps there is another way. Perhaps people who just happen to have all been born in the same country are not some strange homogeneous Other. Have they not flesh? (And plenty of it quite often.) Do they not bleed? In the same way that the people of Lower Dicker will tend to despise the people of Upper Dicker (something to do with a drill not being returned), not all Americans feel as One. It's a simple matter of divorcing the idea of the American state going round doing all the bad things from the people who live under it. They aren't the same thing.

So now, more than ever, we must demonstrate our solidarity with this fine (if often quite fat) people – perhaps by watching some Wesley Snipes films while eating floppy cheese. We must remain confident in the potential of the American people. We believe they are deserving and capable of human liberty. If they would just pull their fat fingers out of their fucking arses. I thank you.

Arguments between equally objectionable celebrities

When Jordan calls Victoria Beckham an 'evil, conniving cow'.

Or when Jodie Marsh accuses Abi Titmuss of being a 'whore'.

Or when Christina Aguilera attacks Britney Spears, calling her wedding 'trashy' and 'pathetic'.

Or when Britney Spears calls Christina Aguilera 'scary'.

Or when Victoria Beckham calls Jordan 'vile'.

Or when Jordan claims Victoria Beckham has had breast implants.

Or when Jacques Chirac says George W. Bush 'is so stupid it's amazing he can eat stuff'.

Or when Damien Hirst says that Charles Saatchi is 'arrogant' and 'childish' and 'only recognises art with his wallet'.

Or when Donald Trump brands Richard Branson a 'total failure'.

Or when Victoria Beckham chants 'Who Let The Dogs Out?' at Jordan.

Why don't you all just play nicely?

B

Baby name books

Nobody has ever found a good name in a baby name book because most of the entries are things like Hadrian, Dylis, Mortimer and Binky. Oh yes, and Adolf.

The Collins Gem version genuinely points out under the entry for Adolf/Adolph that 'Adolph and the latinised form of the name Adolphus have never been common names in this country and received a further setback with the rise of Adolph Hitler.'

Setback? I'll say.

Baby pics in newspapers

'Hello, I'm a journalist in my early thirties and I have noticed a terribly strange phenomenon called "babies". They really are fascinating creatures which raise a number of intriguing issues. Interestingly, I myself have just produced one of these "babies" and really think you ought to know more about it. 'Honestly, it's incredible! I didn't know what it was like to have a baby, until I had one . . . You're up all night at first, you know. Actually, here's some pictures of me with my baby. Bloody big ones. Pictures, that is, not babies. Babies are quite small.' The evidence – viz. the fact the human race has not died out – suggests that, of all the things journalists might usefully gen up on on our behalf, babies are probably not one of them. People do generally seem to know what babies are, and even where they come from.

Sure, if you have a baby you're going to talk about it at work – that is, with your friends and colleagues – but only journalists (and politicians) crap on about the fruit of their loins while undertaking the actual work.

Bus drivers don't do it: 'Single into town? One fifty. Look at this picture of my daughter. She's got her mother's eyes.'

Or bakers: 'So, packet of doughnuts, one sliced loaf, one picture of my new baby.'

'No, not the picture of the baby.'

'I love him.'

'Bad boys'

'We know it's wrong, but they're just so . . . so . . . likely to commit random acts of violence! Yeah?'

Aisleyne from *Big Brother 6* revealed she was 'addicted to bad boys'. On meeting Mark Croft, Kerry Katona told *Closer*: 'My new man is a bad boy.' Inside, she revealed he's a 'naughty man'. So what are we talking? Stealing hubcaps? Or just all the Hobnobs? It's not clear.

For today's thrill-seeking chick, a right bad 'un is the ultimate accessory. Essentially, if your man has never been had up for GBH while dealing out crackpipe from his Harley Davidson motorbike, is he even a man at all? BOOOORING! In *Observer Woman* magazine, Meg Mathews (yes, she's still here) revealed: 'Bad boys are always the most attractive . . . When I look back at all my exes, they've all of them either been in borstal or prison or rough-and-ready or rock-and-roll. The last one was in prison for 10 months. I thought it was great. I thought I was in *Married To The Mob*. I used to go on the visits all dressed up.' Dressed up as what, though? On past form, it could be anything from a Phoenician slave-trader to Little Bo-Peep.

Next week: 'My new man is Radovan Karadzic. He's been on the run from the UN War Crimes Tribunal for murder, plunder and genocide since 1996! Genocidal Bosnian Serbs? Saucy!'

Big Brother firsts

There's a first time for everything – even having a wank with a champagne bottle on live telly. Each year, *Big Brother* contestants are encouraged to score more *Big Brother* firsts.

Otherwise, viewers might decide that it's just the same as last year and stop watching, and then where would we all be?

Big Brother 5, for example, saw the first *Big Brother* fight.

Emma and Victor were eventually pulled apart by security guards. It was most exciting. Recalling the scrap on a Channel 5 talking-heads-celeb-clip programme, the editor of *More* magazine declared: 'It was brilliant. I was shaking watching it – anything could happen.'

During *Big Brother 6*, remaining whities Maxwell and Saskia started acting as though they were under siege. Viewers were enthralled by what appeared to be the first *Big Brother* to divide along racial lines. Mmmm, racy! That same year, Kinga famously broke another taboo by seeming to masturbate with that champagne bottle. Viewers were shocked. Susan of

Torquay complained: 'It gives young people a bad name.' Mostly, of course, *Big Brother* gives young people a really good name.

Blackberries

What exactly the fuck do you think you're doing to yourselves?

Cherie Blair

Now, you'd struggle to make the case that Cherie Blair has remained immune to criticism throughout her husband's premiership. But in amongst all the lambastings for New Age freeloading and buckshee election coiffures, she has resolutely hung on to the image, in the popular and media consciousnesses, that she is cleverer and 'more political' than her husband. Eminent left-wing journalists have urged her to stay on in public life. Under that steely, flat- and friend-buying exterior, we are led to believe, beats a softer – or should that be harder? – political heart.

But it's difficult to work out where this reputation for political sharpness and principle comes from. You never hear Cherie Blair saying things like: 'In years to come, may we not hold as an image of these times, Little Ian McCartney, stricken on a hospital bed recovering from two emergency heart operations, quite possibly about to die, being duped into signing documents approving peerages for backdoor big-money loans from billionaire donors. Multicultural billionaires, of course . . . which makes it better.'

Or she might say: 'What a legacy! An Airforce One-style

presidential plane for the PM; political language gutted of all meaning; a PM hocking himself up with £4m of mortgages on the strength of his forthcoming memoirs deal, while also trying to suppress civil servants' perfectly legitimate memoir criticisms of his lying and obfuscation in the run-up to the disastrous Iraq War; the disastrous Iraq War. I could go on.' Then she might go on: 'Packing government committees with unelected business people and policy wonks; creating a situation whereby the richest 1% of the population now receive more of the nation's income than at any time since the 1930s; Byers and Milburn consulting for Iraq and NHS profiteers; a groundswell of support for the far right; a government lushing itself up with cushy pension deals while exhorting everyone else to work until they drop. I could go on.'

Then she might go on: 'David Cameron; the lowest mandate for a government ever; so toadying to the US that we would fly in the face of every single other country on the entire face of the whole planet in refusing to call for an immediate ceasefire in the Lebanon; Labour Party membership decimated, and Labour members' influence ever diminished, even to the point of setting up a shadowy Supporters' Network of people who can only reply to absurdly phrased multiple-choice questions via e-mail making Labour less a political party and more like a fairtrade banana republic.'

But I've never heard her say anything like that. I've only ever heard her say:

'Hello, is that a woman Labour MP? Cherie here – you know, the one with the reputation for shrewd politics. Vote for Tony's war, there's a good girl. Human rights? Yeah, loads of them. I love him, you know.'

'Hey, Tony – sign these Downing Street postcards for me and I'll pop them on eBay.'

'I know the Queen, you know.'

'That'll be $100,000, please' (– to the organisers of a charity book tour of Australia).

'What's that, Silvio, another biscotti? Don't mind if I do.'

'What's the point of holidaying at the expense of a grotesque plutocrat if you can't have a biscuit? Garibaldi? No, he was a bastard.'

'All I did – boo hoo – was get a crook – boo hoo – to buy me a couple of flats. I didn't – boo hoo – know – boo hoo – that there was anything – boo hoo – wrong with being so – boo hoo – grasping. I only – boo hoo – wanted to make – boo hoo, sniffle – loads – whimper – of cash.'

'Gordon Brown is a fat, miserable freak who should have made his move years ago. The twat.'

Except we should make it crystal clear that she didn't say the last one. What with her being a lawyer and all.

Tony Blair

People dislike Tony Blair for varied and sometimes vague reasons. Here, finally, we present The 10 Definitive Reasons Why Tony Blair Is Fucking Rubbish.

1. Ugly Rumours. You can pinpoint the death of rock 'n' roll as a progressive force to the very second the young Tony Blair picked up a guitar and started playing the riff from 'All Right Now'.

2. His magnificent way with members of the public who disagree with him on television Q&As. 'I think if you listened to the case for war you'd find –' he says before repeating his last point, only

more slowly. This is Tonyspeak for: 'Look, prole, the reason you don't agree with me is . . . you're thick!'

3. How he speaks about Healing The World (yes, just like Michael Jackson) before enacting a foreign policy that 'heals' the world by either bombing it or selling arms to it. Heal the 'scar' of Africa? He's done such a good job of healing Burnley that everyone's voting BNP – and Burnley's quite small by comparison.

4. The New Age shit that he and his wife go in for: crystals, Carole Caplin, Mayan rebirthing rituals. Look, mate, if we wanted David Icke in charge of the country we'd have said so.

5. His friends. Tony's best mates include: Derry Irvine, Alastair Campbell, Lord Charlie Falconer and Mandy Mandelson – that's, respectively, a pompous egomaniac, a bullying egomaniac, an egomaniac buffoon and an absolute weirdo egomaniac. Bet it's a right laugh down the pub with that lot. Wonder if Blair says: 'Blimey, me and the missus, last night and every night – doing it and doing it and doing it and doing it and doing it!'

6. The way he exhorts everyone to Think The Unthinkable – unless this means thinking anything he doesn't think himself, which is genuinely unthinkable. What Blair defines as Unthinkable (capital U) are things most of the rest of us think are unthinkable (are you keeping up?). Things that Mr B finds unthinkable (lower case) actually qualify as some kind of Thought Crime. So it's Unthinkable (that is thinkable) to charge tuition/top-up fees to

go to university. But it's unthinkable (lower case) to fund education by taxing the wealthy and big business. So, to sum up, Thinking The Unthinkable means Thinking Thatcherite. But Blair can't say that because it would be honest and unpopular. And that would be unthinkable.

7. The fact he drinks mugs of tea at press conferences in order to look 'relaxed' and 'blokey'. Oh, so it's not meant to make him look like a laser-eyed pixie weirdo with a pole up his bum, then?

8. The invention of 'New' Labour. Or, to put it another way, Old Liberal. You have to wonder why Blair joined the Labour Party, considering he hates it so much. Shame he wasn't around for the Whigs' heyday – now there was a party for do-good lawyers who didn't want to change the world much. In fact, it was to avoid voting for them that people started the Labour Party. Now they're saddled with this great bastard. It takes a special kind of chutzpah to call this progress.

9. Because he will go down in history as 'one of the most popular Prime Ministers ever' despite not being as popular as John Major (whoever he was). In 1997, Labour's 179-seat majority was won with 13,517,911 votes – fewer than the 14,093,007 votes John Major won with in 1992 (oh yeah, I remember – he was the Prime Minister!). Blair's 2001 majority of 167 seats was won with 10,724,895 votes, which is fewer than Neil Kinnock's losing total from '92 (11,560,484). And Kinnock a) lost, and b) went 'oh yeah' at an eve-of-election rally like a pissed-up gibbon.

10. The way he thinks he's doing us all a favour. As a young MP, Blair was always moaning about how much his Islington mates were earning while he suffered on an MP's salary. Isn't the point of going into politics to represent other people's interests, not your own? Maybe we should have a whipround? Oh, look, we've got three buttons and a chewing-gum wrapper with a naughty word written on it. Lovely.

Bling

Louis XIV was big pimping. Imelda Marcos is a powerballin' bee-yatch. Zsa Zsa Gabor? The motherfucking bomb.

By the late 90s, hip-hoppers had abandoned all pretence of fighting the powers that be. Instead, most had become the kinds of cartoon money-grabbing capitalists that could slip neatly into a Soviet propaganda film – except replacing the bushy moustaches and top hats with hos. Once it took a nation of millions to hold them back. Now it takes a nation of millions to hold their coats.

The word to describe this phenomenon was 'bling' – a coinage from New Orleans rapper B.G. of the wonderfully named Cash Money Millionaires collective (hmm, definitely a money theme developing here) to describe light glistening in diamonds. His 1999 US smash 'Bling Bling' portrayed a fantastic world of Mercs, platinum rings, diamond-encrusted medallions, helicopters and drinking so much fine booze that you end up vomiting everywhere (bet you didn't know that was cool, did you?).

Clearly these new capitalists are better than the old ones,

though. They don't get rich off the backs of others – they do it just by being fly. Oh, hang on: ultimate blingster P Diddy – who produces his own custom-made Sean John diamond-encrusted iPods – destroyed his image as a shrewd businessman in December 2003 when confronted by Lydda Eli Gonzalez, a 19-year-old former factory worker from Honduras. She asked him how come the people who made his $50 Sean John T-shirts were paid 24 cents per shirt, were limited to two toilet breaks a day and forced to do unpaid overtime. Puffy said he didn't know anything about it. It's okay, though, he said, he'd look into it and, if what she said were true, he would sever all ties with the factory. Cool. Although a pay rise might have been more use than unemployment. For all but a handful, of course, bling is a glaring lie: 50 Cent's 2003 album *Get Rich Or Die Tryin'* should more accurately have been called *Highly Unlikely To Get Rich, Far More Likely To Die Tryin'*. But, as Public Enemy's Chuck D recently claimed: 'Hip-hop is sucking the nipples of Uncle Sam harder than ever before.' What he failed to report was how P Diddy actually manages to suck the nipples of Uncle Sam and his great mate Donald Trump at the very same time. That makes four nipples. But then, as we know, he is quite a guy.

James Blunt

James Blunt is the perfect singer-songwriter for the busybusy-busy generation who don't have time to consider what a song might actually mean. Literary conceits swallow up valuable minutes which might be spent . . . oh, I don't know, cracking up or having a really massive latte.

Given these constraints, the smartest, sharpest title for a song about a woman being beautiful is surely 'You're Beautiful'. And why call any song that concerns the pain of saying goodbye to a lover anything other than 'Goodbye My Lover'? From this perspective, it's hard to see why anyone gets stewed up about this songwriting game. It's quite straightforward. A fucking monkey could do it.

'Goodbye My Lover' was the emotional core of Blunt's huge-selling debut album *Back To Bedlam*. As the title implies, the song in no way involves saying 'hello' to a lover. The situation departs from the pleasures that come with welcoming a lover almost completely. It could equally have been called 'Farewell My Lover'. Or: 'See Ya! My Lover'.

Blunt – the 'epitome of 21st-century chic', according to the *Mail* – has probably said goodbye to quite a lot of lovers. If the tabloids are to be believed, he can't keep it in his trousers: sort of like a posh-rock Darren Day. But those were merely casual lovers. The lyric of 'Goodbye My Lover' explores the crucifying angst of losing a woman who Blunt apparently 'pretty much considered the one'. Interviewed on *James Blunt At The BBC*, the Queen-guarding balladeer called the story 'very tragic'. And, in many ways, he is right.

The song begins by questioning whether he failed his departed lover, before his thoughts turn back to the early flowering of romance, depicting himself as some sort of victor (that would be the army background, presumably). His powerful presence caused his new lover temporarily to lose her sight. So he decided to take, not forcibly but with a certain righteous zeal, what he considered his property by an everlasting, possibly even divine, covenant. Continuing this reverie, Blunt imaginatively plants his mouth over various parts of his ex-lover's body before recalling how they would both sleep under the same sheets. This is the reason he can then claim intimate knowledge of her physical odour.

In the chorus, he repeatedly bids his lover farewell before revealing she was probably the only woman for him in the world. The implication is that he can never love again. That's it. He is spent. Goodbye to love, perhaps.

The second verse finds the war-hero-turned-singer still urgently envisioning his former girlfriend and imploring her to remember him, too. He has watched her at various times, he reveals, while she was crying, while she was smiling and also while she was sleeping (but not for that long, he also assures her – not so long that it would become fucked-up).

You see, he would happily have sired offspring with this woman and spent all his born days with her. Actually, you know what? If she isn't there, if she has definitely disappeared for good, then he is genuinely unsure about whether he can carry on living. It's not quite, 'Don't leave me or I'll kill myself!' But it's not quite not that, either. Self-harm, possibly? The chorus then repeats the claim that she was his only hope. Everything is ruined. And so on.

We're nearing the end now, but he must still detail the haunted nights; the nights when, lying in bed, he actually feels her hands. Honestly, it's like she's really there. She's not, though, as I hope we've established. At the song's climax, he brings out what we have already surmised: that this heart-rending experience has left him an empty husk. To emphasise this point, he repeats it six times.

The moaning twat.

Body art

Actually, I think you'll find it's called a *tattoo*. When Picasso painted *Guernica*, it was not, as I understand it, a toss-up between a nightmarish pyramid arrangement of horrors in black, white and grey representing the effects of fascist bombing, or a big eagle with 'Mum' written underneath it. I could be wrong. (See also **Tattoos**.)

Boobs specials

How was the March 2006 *Nuts Boobs Special* special? *Nuts* is full of boobs week in, week out, so what's 'special' about an issue of *Nuts* with boobs in it? Boobs it has. Special it is not. The men's weeklies contain roughly 70 pictures of women per issue, around a third of whom are topless. That's twenty-three and a third pairs of boobs. Or 46.66 (recurring) individual boobs. That's a lot of boobs. With such a high boob count, a few extra will make little impact. To stand out as 'special' you'd need to, say, put that many boobs on each and every page. But then the pictures would be quite small. And where would they put all the stuff about John Terry?

Or maybe the *Boobs Special* was a fact-packed public-service extravaganza about breastfeeding, and infant nutrition generally: 'Women – don't feed your baby foods high in salt, sugar and preservatives on a Tuesday.'

It wasn't.

Or maybe it was a fascinating and insightful discussion of boob-politics through the ages, considering how primitive sculptures from ancient civilisations tended to depict full, ripe breasts as symbols of life-giving force, health and wealth. The Egyptian goddess Isis was often portrayed with milk flowing from her breast; the Greek goddess Artemis had a dozen breasts – and you could definitely see how *Nuts* might be interested in *that*.

They might then go into some detail about how it was Christianity that wanted breasts repressed and covered up, comparing it with the polar opposite attitude in periods of freedom like the French Revolution – where Liberty, as per the Delacroix painting, is bare-breasted.

They could conclude by wondering whether they are reversing the gains made by the boob in the 1960s sexual revolution with their mania for very skinny women with unfeasibly big tits ('breasts on sticks', as Sally Feldman put it in the *New Humanist*), created by a combination of plastic surgery and desktop airbrushing: the beauty myth indeed, they might have concluded.

They didn't.

Men's mag editors do like to deconstruct their activities, though, and place them in a wider social context. On the need for soap stars and tabloid babes to bare all, *FHM* editor Ross Brown said: 'When you become a celebrity, you automatically tick the box saying, "Are you prepared to be photographed in your knickers and pants?"' Which could be interesting news to, say, Walter Wolfgang.

Further explaining the high concept behind all the norks-aloud covers, Paul Merrill, launch editor of *Zoo*, said of the trademark shot of the model's breast partially concealed by her hand (devised to keep WH Smith's and the supermarkets happy): 'We call that shot "hand-bra". We use that a lot.' Considering a cover showing a model whose hair extensions cover her nipples, he added: 'This is hair-bra.

'Then we have knee-bra, where she's sitting down hugging her knees.

'And boob-bra, also known as girl-on-girl-bra, where you have two girls' breasts touching.

'Oh, and this is clever . . . [Points to a cover showing two images of Abi Titmuss facing each other.] Look, she's being her own bra [!].'

'When we get really bored, we even use a bra-bra.'

Most insightful. But boobs specials? You want to take your hands off your tacker for five minutes and give Trading Standards a call.

Books on CD (except for blind people)*

I may not know much, but I do know this: books is for reading. Being read is one of the key characteristics of your actual book. If you don't like reading, you're just not the sort of person who wants to get involved with books. And this isn't rocket science: I learnt it in infants' school.

The second most insane example of the audio book is the complete *Ulysses* by James Joyce. Now, this is by no means an easy book. It is a very long book – with long words in it and, famously, a really, really fucking long sentence. Not being a booky type, you may decide it's not for you. Fair enough. But what sort of freak who doesn't wish to read *Ulysses* buys the Naxos 22 CD set of someone else reading it for them? You can't be arsed to read it, but you can be arsed to listen to 22 CDs? Freak.

But the first most insane example is *Finnegan's Wake* (also by Naxos), a book that even people who really like reading get frightened of. Indeed, people who like reading so much they do precious little else, who like it so much they did Double English Literature With Extra Reading at university just so they could do a shitload of reading, have been known to run off down the street when someone produces a copy of *Finnegan's Wake*, shouting 'Stay back! That's too much reading!' For this reason, I firmly believe that all the *Finnegan's Wake* CDs are actually blank.

Botox bollox

The biannual *New Beauty* (according to the *Sunday Times*, 'The new magazine for the Botox generation') has helpfully collected '40 Uses for Injectables'. It's 'highly experimental', but Botox can potentially 'inhibit the nerve impulses that make you feel hungry'. Furthermore, sticking it into the armpit can 'completely shut off the production of perspiration'. So Botox can save you from sweating or getting the munchies. That's right: just like Barbie.

It's not all post-sweat, post-comestible fun, though. High-powered London bankers are injecting Botox to stop looking all frowny and stressed after regularly working eighteen-hour days. One told *Time* magazine: 'It's important to look your best . . . like you can take it in your stride.'

Of course, injecting yourself with bacteria to look like you're not tired when you really are *very* tired would make you a living metaphor for the age. Which is sort of cool. Hopefully, we're on our way to a big-bosomed, non-frowning utopia. Hey, maybe we should all dye our hair blond and put in blue contact lenses, too? Wouldn't that be perfection? When the 'Botox generation' dies, what will its ashes look like?

Bratz

Look, here's saucy leatherclad Roxxi, one of the Bratz Rock Angelz, playing a flying-V rock guitar and showing off her midriff and high-heels. Kind of like when Britney dressed up as a Nazi dominatrix. 'Hi! My name is Roxxi,' says Roxxi. 'My twin calls me "Spice" because I like to spice things up!' Twins, eh? Eh? Wicked!

Bratz are taking over. You might have thought they were just a range of dolls, purple-spangly teenage dolls in 'funky' outfits slathered in make-up. But you would be wrong. The Bratz doll is not a doll. Well, it is a doll, anyone can see that. But it's also, according to Paula Treantafelles, who initially created the range, a 'self-expression piece'.

How this 'self-expression' piece expresses itself is mainly through the prism of having the right trinkets, phones, accessories and shoes. (Without shoes, the Bratz dolls have no feet. It's kind of a metaphor.) They are 'the only girls with a passion 4 fashion!' It's a sort of WAG training course for six-year-olds.

Doll designer Lui Domingo insists: 'We are not making a deliberate effort to sexualise these dolls. We are making them fashionable, and coincidentally the fashions these days are rather sexy.'

Not trying to sexualise them? They look like a series of Hollywood central casting whores made out of plastic! Then there's the passion 4 dating guyz: the 'Secret Date' range of Bratz included a dolled-up doll, plus a mystery date (one of the Bratz Boyz) and – oh yes – champagne glasses! Why not go the whole way and chuck them naked into a jacuzzi? Bubblicious!

Then there are The Bratz Babyz – sort of what babies would be like if they decided to become strippers. And there's a 'Babyz Night Out' fashion pack and 'Brattoo Parlor' playset. Because if there's one thing babies need it's more nightz out and tattoos. They could go out and compare their new markings: 'Look, I've got a spider, what about you?' 'Mine says "Mum".' Bratz Big Babyz (yet another range) have 'Designer Diapers' – lovely frilly knickers, which they set off with these highly peculiar coquettish poses. Oh yes, and earrings. And a bikini bearing the slogan 'I Blow Bubbles'! This is also a coincidence. The fashion among babies is definitely for looking like little sexpots. Oh no, hang on . . .

Even the Bratz Babyz Ponyz have coloured highlights and makeup. So they're sexualising ponies now? Come on – if you're sexualising ponies, you're definitely taking the sexualising way too far. Or is this a coincidence too? Are there slave-to-fashion ponies out there now, right this minute, having their tits done?

Hey, I know! How about a Babyz Self-Harm Kit? Or at least just supply the Secret Dates with Rohypnol. Or is that going too far? How does one judge? Anyway, let us be thankful that children are not generally impressionable or easily led – or we may end with a generation of stifled, consumer-crazed fuckups. Another one.

Britain, Britishness, the British Empire, British citizenship tests, Britishness lessons in schools, the proposed Britishness Day, New Britain, *Little Britain*, Fern Britton, etc.

Britishness is everywhere. Well, in British political discourse it's everywhere – no one else really gives a monkey's. There are new British citizenship tests for people who want to become British, a proposed Britishness Day (a day on which

British people shalt be Exceedingly British), the BBC has been told 'promoting Britishness' might be added to its charter (BBC3 already complies with all those *Little Britain* repeats), and Gordon Brown has nailed the flag to his mast with his adherence to a new, strong, vibrant, albeit hazily defined, British identity. A hazily defined identity he proposes to be hazily taught in schools.

It's devilishly difficult to work out what would be taught, though, because a key feature of the Britishness debate is a refusal to give any specifics and say what 'Britishness' may actually mean. It's as if they have taken French philosopher Ernest Renan's adage that a nation is 'A group of people united by a mistaken view about the past and hatred of their neighbours' and focused entirely on the mistaken-view-of-the-past aspect. (They explicitly play down the whole 'hating the neighbours' side of things. Well, unless they've got oil, or vote the wrong way in the EU.)

In a speech to the Fabian Society in January 2006, Brown made Britishness the launchpoint of his proposed premiership, thereby cleverly reversing another famous maxim, Dr Johnson's one about patriotism being the *last* refuge of scoundrels. 'What is our Fourth of July?' he implored. 'What is our Independence Day? Where is our Declaration of Rights? What is our equivalent of a flag in every garden?'

That summer, of course, much of Britain would indeed boast a flag in very nearly every garden. Just not the British flag. Another flag. Which complicates things.

The job of defining Britishness can, it seems, lead only to a hasty retreat in bloody disgrace – like invading Russia. In his book *The Abolition of Britain*, the somewhat barking (actually positively medieval) right-wing commentator Peter Hitchens defines core British values as 'patriotism, morality, tradition and beauty'. And he comes out strongly against ... central heating. (When it's cold, families congregate in one room; when it's warm, they go off and do their own thing and the edifice of the family fractures. Maybe that's why he's always arguing with his brother?)

So it's tricky. Nevertheless, you would think that someone trying to get us to fall in behind a common notion of Britishness would have the good manners to say what it is. They don't even define Britishness in the citizenship tests: based on the book *Life in the United Kingdom*, the new exam for all immigrants seeking a UK passport ignores history and culture entirely, focusing instead on how we say 'please' and 'thank you' a lot, and what to do if you spill someone's pint in a pub (I'm not making this up).

Some say British values are the best defence against terrorism. When the public voted for their chosen Britishness Day, the winner was 15 June, to celebrate the 1215 signing of the Magna Carta, which brought the tyrannical King John to heel and enshrined such key concepts as habeas corpus (the right to have the legality of your detention put before a court).

Certainly, nothing will ever come between us and these core values. Except Guantanamo Bay. And Belmarsh. But then, those places aren't even in Britain. Except for Belmarsh. Or are we so committed to 'British' values that we must demolish 'British' values in order to protect them? To paraphrase the US commander in Vietnam, maybe we need to destroy the village green to preserve it.

The closest we get to a proper science bit – as opposed to just feeling slightly teary while watching *Blackadder Goes Forth* – is a 2005 Commission for Racial Equality report called 'What is Britishness?'. By focus-grouping almost a hundred people of various ethnicities, they found Britishness included things like:

- Geography – that is, it's something to do with the British Isles. Nowhere outside of this area can truly be considered British. Not really.
- Values and Attitudes – including wholesome virtues like 'a strong work ethic, community spirit, and compassion', which are, of course, completely unknown in other nations (particularly the Germans), as well as 'drunkenness, hooliganism and yobbishness', which are bad virtues also unknown to other nations (except the Irish . . . obviously).
- Cultural Habits and Behaviour – for example, queuing, watching football, listening to the Beatles and Charlotte Church, and consuming 'fish and chips', 'English breakfast', 'curries' and 'beer'.

Britishness, then: it's Charlotte Church playing keepy-uppy in the rain while eating a fried-egg sandwich and listening to 'Tomorrow Never Knows'. Or, to put it another way: it's what the people who live in Britain just sort of bod about doing anyway. Not much of a unifying political vision, is it? Given these findings, and in keeping with the need to display patriotism in our gardens, we present our own British citizenship test – which is, if anything, even more British than the real one:

1. By 1921, the British Empire held sway over:
a) A population of between 470 and 570 million people, approximately a quarter of the world's population, and about 14.3 million square miles, about a quarter of the world's total land area.

b) I am Scottish/Welsh and we never done it. We didn't fight for the Empire, our bosses didn't profit from it, we didn't own our own mines and industries and thus exploit our own, that was the English, blame them, the English did it, it was the English. Not us.

c) I don't know, we only did Hitler at our school.

2. Name three Loyalist paramilitary groups.

3. How many pints can you get down your neck in an hour?

4. In 250 words or less, tell us what you love most about Britain. (Clue: don't mention benefits.)

5. What is the title of Charlotte Church's debut pop single?
a) Crazy Chick
b) Crazy Chicken
c) Funky Chicken
d) Kentucky Fried Chicken
e) Dixie Fried Chicken
f) Chickago Fried Chicken
g) Chickin' Lickin' Fried Chicken
h) Ain't Nobody Here But Us Chickens
i) I don't know, I'm more of a Cheryl Tweedy person myself. Chicken.

British journalists who never got over the end of *Sex and the City*

There is a certain type of British female journalist who never got over the end of *Sex and the City*. Constantly on the search for her own 'Big'-type suit guy, these are the only people in the world who still go on 'dates'.

You're looking for that ideal guy who knows grooming but is also slightly roughed up; who all the waiters know, who deals stocks and also deals art and respects a woman's independence but will also splash out on something to make you look and feel fabulous at the casino. You do this by filling professionally concerned broadsheets with articles about how rich people are great and how expensive stuff is the best stuff.

Now, it's hard to say how much the series' portrayal of the New York singles scene is fact or fantasy without doing more research – and that, frankly, is not what this book's about – but if you transplant this vision to the thronging metropolitan centres of the UK, well, you're screwed.

Look: all the money-raking bachelors around these parts are a braying bunch of yahoos who simply want to a) finish the gak, and b) come on your face. Sorry about that.

So, while it seems churlish not to wish you luck, please don't get your hopes up. Oh, and if you do ever find your own personal 'Big', do you then think you might possibly be able to shut up?

That would be just so fabulous!

Broadband service providers

While broadband service providers maintain the illusion of competition by vying to have the stupidest name, they actually collude in keeping us in a state of roiling panic.

One day, according to their fiendish plan, you might be up and me down. The next day, the situation might be reversed with me on top, cackling with a glass of something nice, while you're down in the pit feeling abandoned like an abandoned dog feels abandoned when it's been abandoned. Fucked, essentially.

It's the broadband whirligig of life that makes weak, impotent pawns of us all. In fact, when Polish sociology guru Zygmunt Bauman formulated his new theory of the 'liquid life', a scary new precariousness that sees the 21st-century individual walking on quicksand, under perpetual siege, while seeking shelter from the storm in Pandora's Box (which is on fire), he had just lost his broadband connection and was being seriously dicked around by the helpline staff.

Or is it even more cosmic than this? Is it part of the divine plan, of which broadband companies are mere fucknutted minions? Is there some kind of karmic payback going on? Do we get the broadband service we deserve? Or are we randomly picked out for this torture because we're completely controlled, both physically and metaphysically, by complete bastards? They send our instructions down the broadband cable. It's possible. Well, probably it is – I don't actually understand how it works.

I think it's all of the above. And more.

Gordon Brown

At the time of writing, Gordon Brown was still the Prime Minister-in-waiting; a brooding, fat-faced Hercules just itching to clean out all the Blairite crap from the Augean stables.

If we believe the script, he's ready and willing to redirect us to The Promised Land. He's Westminster's own Special One. He's Episode IV: A New Hope. That kind of thing. This is, after all, the man who claimed (at the 2003 party conference) that

Labour is 'best when we are Labour', a coded message to the disillusioned hordes meaning: 'Come to Daddy.'

But if Labour is at its best when it's Labour, presumably Labour is not at its best when it's doing things like: promising the CBI 'a light touch' on workplace health and safety inspection; or siding with employers against unions in having people work more hours in a week than they are likely to sleep; or letting public sector workforces be subsumed by privatised McJobs; or relaunching the system of PFI, which means your local hospital wing is built by the same company that does school meals in Baghdad and nothing works quite right because everything's done on the shit and which can all be summed up in one word: fucking Jarvis. Okay, that's two words.

So, who was that letting the side down all those times? Two clues: he's the Chancellor of the Exchequer and he's called Gordon. And he's got a fat face. Okay, that's three clues.

George W. Bush

George W. Bush is much vilified for reasons such as wars, oil, incapacity to eat pretzels without causing injury to himself (the freak), abolishing tax for the rich, stuff like that – but his critics miss the central, absolutely key point: the fact that George W. Bush claims to 'speak Spanish'.

Chutzpah? *Hola! Sí!* Fucking hell, *sí!* You'd think he'd be better mastering one language at a time, and that English would be a more pressing priority. But *no, Señor*.

This Hispanic turn is, of course, politically motivated.

Here's how it works. In Texas there are lots of Hispanic voters. So it helps, if you want to be Governor of Texas, to get

Hispanic people to vote for you. So you 'learn Spanish'. It's unclear if 'speaking Spanish' means he can conduct negotiations with Mexican trade ministers in their native tongue. Or maybe just that he can almost ask his way to the swimming pool – if there's also a mike strapped to his back? But still. As news of his Latin temperament spread, Bush's share of the Hispanic vote rose from around a third in the 2000 presidential election to 44% in 2004. Kerry (whoever she was) still took 53%, but the gap with the Democrats closed from a 36% deficit in 2000, when some bloke stood, to 9% – which, as any seasoned election analyser will tell you, is less. If you did some more sums you could predict by how much Bush would lead in the Latino vote next time if he were allowed to stand, which he isn't, and it would probably make for scary reading, I should expect. *Hola!*

This is why Bush has been sponsoring massive immigration from Spanish-speaking countries – mainly Mexico, which Bush really likes because it rhymes with Texaco, but also Spain itself. That's why Laura delivers leaflets saying 'Come To America' outside Barca games. And why the pair of them often hit the Andalusian coastline to swim naked and free. Which, in fact, now I come to think about it, isn't happening. So, actually, all this stuff about the Spanish thing is wrong and the people who concentrated more on the wars and tax cuts and stuff were right. Sorry.

C

Cafés that charge excessive amounts for a mug of shit tea

A pound? A fucking pound? I *know* what tea costs! I make it all the time!

Cafés that charge excessive amounts for a set breakfast but try to justify it by putting a bit of basil on the tomato

I *know* how much basil costs, too! And it's not the £2 you've just slapped on the price of my breakfast. It's much less than that – slightly over £1.99 less. Why don't you just have done with it and move your family into my fucking house?

Cafés that cut sausages in half down the middle

Does *anyone* believe they're getting two sausages, rather than one bad sausage sliced down the middle, with the curved sides pointed upwards to momentarily create the illusion of two bad sausages? Anyone at all?

Cafés that offer you butter but then give you marg

It's the lies I can't stand.

Cafés that refill Heinz/HP bottles with cheaper sauce

You're not fooling anyone.

Cafés whose idea of a sausage sandwich is to cut a cooked sausage into very thin slices lengthways, then deep fry that cooked sausage for a considerable period of time, then put what are effectively sausage crisps – that is, crisps made out of sausage – between two dry slices of Value bread

There's a reason why sausage crisps remain excluded from the exhilarating new wave of crisp-style snacks, root-vegetable crisps, bagel chips, all of that. This is because sausage crisps – that is, crisps made out of sausage – are a very stupid idea. A very stupid idea that will attack your heart with a heart attack.

Cafés without toilets

Basically, what they're saying is: 'We've had your money, but we've not got a pot for *you* to piss in – now buzz off. And once you have buzzed off, go and fuck yourself.'

Calamity porn

The 2006 documentary *The Falling Man* was built upon the premise that we cannot bear to look upon the image of the mid-air mystery man jumping to his doom and so end up censoring the image. This was good because it enabled everyone to print the image again, really big, just to prove that we are now brave enough to face the image. Look, here we are: facing it.

Photoshopped images of a future London after some future flood? Horrendous, yes. But also quite cool. After all, didn't New Orleans look dramatic? The picturesque hobos, the battered streets, the martial law surrounding the chain stores . . . and what a soundtrack: between all the blues and all the jazz, nature could not have wreaked havoc in a more culturally enriching setting.

'Disaster movies will never be the same again' was one verdict, in the *Guardian*, on *United 93*. Oh, good. So they didn't die in vain. If nothing else, at least we can point to 9/11 as having revived a moribund movie genre.

At the time of writing, anyone hoping for a revival in fortunes for the cop buddy movie would be slavering in anticipation of Nicolas Cage and Michael Peña in Oliver Stone's *World Trade Center* – two men bravely fighting an evil even worse than Joss Ackland in *Lethal Weapon 2* (and he killed Patsy Kensit!). Hopefully, other moribund movie genres will also get a twenty-first-century calamity boost: personally, I can't wait for the first weird weather sex comedy. Or the first post-Guantanamo caper flick.

'There's such a lot on at the moment. What do you fancy? There's the Twin Towers film or the New Orleans film. Then there's *Fast and Furious: Nightmare in Najaf*. Oh, and *The Taleban Terminator*, about the British sniper in Helmand Province. It's apparently a bit like *Phone Booth* – only they haven't got a functioning telecommunications network.'

David Cameron

Here is the first draft of an appeal from Conservative leader David Cameron to 'The Kids' . . .

Dear The Kids

Hi! It's David Cameron here. Dontcha just love the environment? Big up to the biosphere. That's what I say. Like, totally.

Up the gays! I mean it!

So here are my new priorities as the new leader of the new Modern Compassionate Conservative Party:

1. Kiss Muslim babies.

2. Bring hope to the poor. I love the poor. I mean, the less financially engorged. In particular, I like sullen young men in hoodies. I like to touch them. Jesus – not in that way! I mean reach out to them, give them belief. With the substitution of one little letter I will bring understanding to these poor, deluded, feral children. Not hoodies – but goodies! Less knifing each other; more making tea for oldies. Goodies!

3. Institute the use of Smythson's stationery. My wife's a director, you know. Smythson's of Bond Street – for all your posh paper needs!

4. Go blue. No, green. Vote blue, but go green. Don't go blue, that would be awful. You'd be like that Blue Man Group with its stupid mime drum act bollocks. And nobody wants that. In fact . . .

5. Deport the Blue Man Group. I'm going to send those bald drumming bastards straight back to Vegas. No messing.

But don't let that give you the idea I'm prejudiced. Another aim of mine is to get ethnic and lady. Nine out of 10 Tory MPs is, like me, a white man. I consider myself ideally placed to sort this out, having been intimately involved with Black Wednesday.

Free Nelson Mandela!

The all-new New Tories are so new it's like we never even existed before. Maybe we didn't? I myself am so shiny and new that I had nothing whatsoever to do with the last Conservative manifesto – the one with all the NHS privatisation and sending the buggers back home. Nothing at all. Except I wrote it. I was Michael Howard's right-hand man – his writing hand, the one writing all the stuff about sending the buggers back home. Aside from writing the 2005 manifesto, though, I couldn't have had less to do with it. Apart from, as I say, writing it. That was me.

New! I'm new! Can't you read?! New!!!

With me, what you see is what you get. And what you see is a man riding a bicycle being followed by a chauffeur-driven limo that you pay for.

Coal not dole!

And I care. I really do. I often weep openly for Gaia. I'll do anything for the environment, and have written a special New 'Compassionate Conservative' (yes, just like

George Bush) New Programme to Renew the Old Environment. Here are my pledges for you to cut out and keep.

1. I will recycle plastic bottles.

2. I will take short-haul flights to glaciers to talk to journalists who have also taken short-haul flights to hear me talk about how important the Earth is. And it is.

3. I will use both sides of the excellent paper marketed by my wife – Smythson's of Bond Street, available to buy in the shop or via the website (Smythson's – for all your posh paper needs).

4. I will go 'aaaah' if I see any pictures of seals, and will become quite stern if I think for any significant period about carbon dioxide.

5. I will regulate and tax the rapacious big business interests who are raping the Earth for their filthy private gain. What? Shit. No. Not the last bit. Sorry, I was copying some points out of a Friends of the Earth pamphlet and did the wrong bit. I mean it about the seals, though. Just look at them! Aaaah. It's all about balance. About balancing your concerns about the environment with not actually doing anything. Regulations, man, who wants to be tied down with that shit? Hang loose – that's what I say.

Basically, I would say this to you: if the traditional ideological barriers between left and right have broken down, why not just vote for the right? Or, as you Kids would say: whatever.

He was the future once. But tomorrow belongs to me.

Peace, y'all.

Dave Cameron

Carbon offsets

The wonder of carbon offsets shows that there really is no problem you can't solve by throwing more money at it, even if that problem is born from having money. Honestly, it's like a little miracle.

So Coldplay can feel OK about the CO2 emissions of their super-success enormo-gigs by funding the planting of 10,000 mango trees in India. In this way, a recent broadsheet interview can proudly report the band flying 'by private jet to Palm Springs . . . The band can now afford to fly wherever possible.' (Of course, pretty soon there might not be any palms or any springs when they fly to Palm Springs – but that won't be their fault!)

In such ways, even an utterly atomised populace can change the world. Any problems? Well, only that it's largely bollocks. landscape historian Oliver Rackham has compared the practical effect of carbon offset tree-planting to drinking more water to keep down rising sea levels. Even Friends of the Earth, who fucking love trees, say it's 'not a solution'.

In culinary terms, it's like living on a diet of doner kebabs and thinking that's all right because you've also got the slice of lemon, lettuce and pickled chilli in there.

The message is simple: the planet cannot survive on a diet of kebabs.

Jimmy Carr

The real reason that charmless, podgy-faced careerist ex-ad man Jimmy Carr – who is famous for his gut-churningly shite-hawk jokes about women being fat and ugly and is NEVER OFF YOUR FUCKING TELLY – is pathologically unable to turn down work, however nuts-dissolvingly awful it is, is that he single-handedly cares for around 35 elderly neighbours.

He pays for all their heating through the harsh winter months and, as soon as he's finished filming, he's off delivering them their dinners with those metal lids keeping them warm.

Not really. He's just a grasping cunt.

Casualty

Far be it from me to let the fact that I haven't seen this programme since the mid-1990s stop me from pointing out the following differences between this silly, makeweight BBC 'drama' and a real casualty unit:

1. On *Casualty*, the staff aren't all ripped to the tits on stolen prescription drugs.
2. In real life, no casualty unit has ever treated a small boy who's been electrocuted after his kite drifted into electric power lines, let alone an average of three per series.
3. On *Casualty*, they haven't contracted out all their major services to the people who do the cleaning.

What I have seen is *Casualty* spin-off *Holby City*, which is *much* better. The doctors are all called things like Zuben, Rick

Griffin and Mr Campbell-Gore, names that could proudly do service for a motorcycle display team or a circus. And everyone's always shagging each other. Now *that's* drama.

CBI, the

Talking in *The Times*, CBI director-general Sir Digby Jones said there was a general perception that 'Everyone hates businessmen.' However, this is not because of businessmen. It's because of the media.

Digby complained that TV programmes like *Blackpool* and *The Office* portrayed managers negatively as 'greedy' or 'bullying'. Digby even complained to ITV about the *Coronation Street* plotline involving a serial killer businessman. When you start seeing Richard Hillman as an agent of anti-boss propaganda, you're clearly feeling touchy about something or other.

In reality, of course, all bosses are lovely. And none are more lovely than Digby Jones. But every time you hear about his organisation, it is in headlines like 'The CBI says more staff appear to be skiving off with faked illnesses', or 'Sickies cost businesses billions, says CBI' or 'The UK's minimum wage should be frozen at £4.85 an hour until 2006, says CBI', 'CBI says CO2 limits suicidal for competitiveness' or 'CBI demands the retirement age be lifted to 70'.

In summation: the CBI reckons workers are wasters who are always only inches from stealing the computers and shitting in the cupboards. Bosses, meanwhile, are great. So you'd better back off or we'll pick up our balls and fuck off to Taiwan. So, not 'greedy' or 'bullying' at all, then. It's certainly a moot point what kind of image the modern businessperson Digby Jones believes he is projecting. Hoping to colour in some of the many blanks of this enigmatic figure, we sent a questionnaire to the CBI's Centrepoint HQ asking Digby Jones:

1. The CBI/Real Finance FDs Excellence Awards dinner at a Park Lane hotel in April 2005 – 'a night of celebration of the role of the finance director' – would have cost a business £2044.50 for a table of 12 plus wine, travel, accommodation, etc. Which is over five grand. Prudent spending by business?

2. The morning after the dinner, how many of the guests woke up with a head cryogenically frozen by booze and then called in with a special 'stuffed-up nose' voice? Have you ever done this, Digby Jones?

3. Digby Jones: you are a proud member of the National Trust. But isn't the National Trust just a load of old communist toss? If stupid old buildings can't pay their own way then they should be blown up. You're getting soft, man.

4. In the middle of all these corporate galas, regional dinners and minor awards ceremonies, do you ever think, 'Oh my stars, this is tedious. What am I doing here? I'm pissing my life away'? And idly dream of the day that man may be free and the whole squalid business is replaced by a life of beauty and equality and freedom? Or aren't you that fucked?

5. Where the bloody fuck do you go to get your hair cut, man? You're out there representing the Best of British and your hair looks like shite having a bad day.

Sadly, Mr 'Stop The Shirkers' never bothered his arse to reply. Lazy sod.

Celebrity fragrances

Have rubbish names. There's Lovely by Sarah Jessica Parker; David Beckham's Instinct; True Star Gold by Beyoncé; Britney Spears' Fantasy and Britney Spears' Curious.

Britney Spears 'personifies daring . . . Curious by Britney Spears represents the young woman that pushes boundaries and revels in adventure.'

Yes, Britney Spears is indeed fairly curious, although not in the sense that she might suddenly, say, get really into botany. She's curious in a different way. And she's getting curiouser and curiouser.

True Star Gold sounds like one of those obscure petrol stations you only ever see in the countryside – like the ones in Sussex with a logo that is almost exactly, although not quite, the same as the European Union's, if the European Union had produced its logo on a Commodore 64 and superimposed the British isles over the top.

Sean John's scent is Unforgivable.

Celebrity magazines

'She's too FAT!' 'Wait, she's too SKINNY!' 'Or is she so utterly FANTASTIC it's not true?' 'No, she's a SLAPPER! With sweat-patches!' For fuck's sake, at least make your minds up.

'Change Yourself Today!' culture

Understand this: there is something deeply adrift within your personality. Be prepared to chuck it away and start again. The urge to start afresh seems particularly strong in the New Year. A few hours after the bells have chimed, anyone remaining unaware that they are polluted rotters will soon be disabused of this by shelves crammed with books by Paul McKenna offering to Change Your Life in Seven Days. Or possibly Make You Thinner. Or Turn You Inside Out if You Fancy.

Newspaper headlines urge you to 'Change Your Life for 2006: Be happier, be healthier, be richer. The experts tell you how in our special guide' (*Independent on Sunday*). Why are these writers so obsessed with cleansing their souls and starting afresh? What did they do over Christmas to mire themselves so thoroughly? Did they find themselves shouting racial epithets in the middle of an orgy?

In March 2006, the self-helpish magazine *Psychologies* included a special dossier called 'Get Ready to Change'. It had the headline 'Are you ready to CHANGE?' Plus bullet points: 'Your life map: what needs to change?', '"How I got a new life"' and 'Test: how will you handle change?' A subliminal message arguably emerges here. And it's not: stay exactly the same as you already are.

A change, it's often said, is as good as a rest. I prefer a rest, myself, but there you go. The self is a tricky concept that has been the subject of anguished debate since time immemorial. Maybe the autonomous individual has a burning core of consciousness from which all else exudes. Maybe this is a myth to enforce positive feelings about ourselves and engender the illusion that we can determine our own way in the world.

Perhaps we are merely the sum of our socio-economic relations with other human beings. Or simply the totality of all the words we ever speak and think. Alternatively, we could just be a set of genetically pre-programmed desires designed to propagate the species, a trillion mindless robots dancing . . .

Whatever, it's clearly a tangled affair. So thank the Lord we have Paul McKenna to sort it out.

Charity, tits out for

On occasion, all the diseases and disasters, the billions afflicted by worldwide poverty, the endless oceans of distress, the maimed unfortunates desperate for some kind of relief, fill one with the need to help in the only way that's appropriate. That's right, folks, it's bikini carwash time!

This is, after all, a fitting way to raise money for Cancer Research UK. How better to highlight the hardships of all those middle-aged women undergoing intensive radio- or chemotherapy on their breasts than to parade some healthy, pert, soaped-up jubblies around a supermarket car park in Surrey? How very thoughtful you all are.

Nothing moves us to give like a good dose of smut. And so there are charity calendars featuring *Casualty* babes in naughtily revealing medical drapes, Chippendales-style charity thongathons, Macy Gray going starkers. After the World Trade Center attacks, some lapdancing clubs were even moved to lay on special nights collecting money for the families of the victims. Now that's really bending over backwards for others.

So, come on everyone – let's really pull together this year. What about the starving in Sudan? Who's up for a Charity Soapy Tit Wank?

Charity, trips of a lifetime for

There you are, an Inca, sitting on your Trail, appreciating the view and munching on a coca leaf, generally enjoying the atmos, when along come 30 bored computer programmers from Bristol, having the time of their fucking lives 'raising money for cancer'. It's okay, though – it's 'for charity'. Because charity does not begin at home: it begins on holiday. Previously, people booked a holiday and paid for it themselves. You didn't say to your workmates: 'I fancy two weeks in Ibiza, getting ripped to the tits on Ecstasy tablets and contracting an STD: fancy chipping in? Go on, if you all put in 50 quid I can go for sweet jack nix.'

Now, though, people are quite happy to say: 'Go on, it's only 50 quid and it's for disabled kiddies.' But then they mumble: 'Except half of it pays for me to go camel trekking in Mongolia.' And when you ask them to repeat the second bit louder, they show you a picture of a child who's been blown up by a mine.

Other similar gambits might include: 'If you pay for me to go to the pub tonight, I'll put your change in the charity box – go on, it's for lifeboats, you stingy cunt.'

Some people do pay the travel costs of their charity holiday themselves, but it's still fucked up. Cancer research, care for the elderly, orphaned children: what happened to the idea that society should fund these things, what with it being stinking rich and all? Instead, it's the cue for everyone to start cycling along the Great Wall of China (which, by the way, you can't see from space – that's just a barefaced lie. If irrelevant . . . but still, you can't).

Charles, Prince of Wales

He might believe that cancer can be cured by daily coffee enemas, but the heir apparent does make a nice sausage. Maybe this is because those freely ranging Duchy of Cornwall pigs spend the summer months on the Highgrove estate rolling around in 'cooling mud baths'. Sometimes, when schedules allow, Charles even finds the time to join them (that's after he's stuffed half a jar of Gold Roast up his arse). Now, some people might say: look, he doesn't exactly make the food himself, he gets some farmhand to do it all for three lumps of coal and an orange at Christmas and what's he doing owning a whole fucking county anyway isn't it the 21st century now he's decided he hates science too the fucking freak and if people shouldn't be getting above their station why doesn't he try a bit of agricultural labouring himself the thick fuck and anyway if he really loved his people he'd give all the biscuits and sausages away for free the usurious cunt. That is what some people might say. But not me. I like the sausages and let that be an end to the matter.

Other than that, though, I haven't got a good word to say about the loony feudal shithead jug-eared parasite bastard.

Chefs' families

Start off by frying the garlic and the red onion in a touch of extra-virgin olive oil. When that's sizzling, drop in the chillis and the ground spices. After a couple of minutes –

Look at my kids! Look at them! My kids!

Now this is the crucial bit. Get the pancetta and wrap it round the chicken breasts. Make sure you have a little bit left over – we'll be needing that later for the dessert. Stick it in the oven at about –

Mum! Here's my mum. Taught me everything she knew – shit at cooking, mind. Only joking, Mum. I love you really. You old tart! Only joking. Freak.

Now mix the chocolate with the whipped cream until you form a marble effect. Make sure not to overmix. Before adding the Radox, just –

Uh-oh, Dad's here. 'The Colonel', I call him. Put *me* through my paces, I can tell you. But now I'm Mr Moneybags and he comes on *my* show. So there you go . . . all right, Dad? I'm fucking minted.

At this point, you'll need to coat the strawberries in liver.

Add them to the pan and let them gently frown –

Look! At! My! Kids!

Now, aren't we a family? One big happy family? Except when we're all shouting at each other, but we even do that in quite an animated kind of way. Think of this as not just a cookery programme, but also a lesson in how to be more Italian. We're so Continental, it's mental!

At this point, I like to stuff my face with grated Parmigiano, feast on the family pet (look at it!), pour a southern Burgundy that tastes of appley snails over my head, and then cackle in the summer rain as I luxuriate on top of a roasting hot barbecue. Yeah!

Look! It's my kids! Look again! Kids! My!

LOOK AT MY KIDS!

Che Guevara merchandise

Let's not be negative about this: Che Guevara did help put in power a Stalinoid dictatorship which locks up gays and trade unionists – but, you know, fair's fair, he did also have a cool beard. And Cuba can't be proper Stalinism, like in Eastern Europe, because it's really sunny there, whereas Eastern Europe is cold. Brr.

Che is everyone's favourite facial-hair-motorbike-stood-for-some-stuff-but-I-don't-know-what-it-was-and-don't-really-give-one-check-out-the-beard-man revolutionary. Ace. The sort of revolutionary you can safely put on T-shirts, clocks and candles – yes, Che Guevara candles are available from a firm called Rex International. They also do candles with Elvis on them. Same difference. Che's real name was Ernest which is perhaps not so cool, but who cares when you factor in the whole motorbike thing?

Or maybe the kids really are into vague, trigger-happy yet hippyish developing world guerrilla vanguard revolutionism tinged with Stalinism? Either way, buoyed up by Rex's success, other companies are trying to float similar products, including a chain of North Korean restaurants full of images of Kim Il-Sung (provisionally called Yo! Rice), and a range of sportswear called simply Gulag.

Rex are responsible for Che coasters and the Official Che Guevara calendar. How the red blazes do you get an *official* Che Guevara calendar? Presumably, there is a Guevara estate somewhere sanctioning all this crap? In fact, we've got hold of a tape of the chat between Che's relatives and a Rex representative where the historic coasters decision was made:

AUNTIE FLO GUEVARA: It's what he would have wanted.
UNCLE DAVE GUEVARA: Yes, yes. He was always drinking fluids from glasses and mugs, but not all in one go. He needed something to rest the glass or mug on, so as not to mark the surface of the table.

AUNTIE FLO GUEVARA: He was very considerate like that.

UNCLE DAVE GUEVARA: Yes, he was a considerate boy: he always left his machine gun in the hall.

AUNTIE FLO GUEVARA: Yes. And his motorbike.

UNCLE DAVE GUEVARA: Yes, the motorbike also.

AUNTIE FLO GUEVARA: How much money were you going to give us again?

UNCLE DAVE GUEVARA: Yes, we need to pay our gardener in the Maldives. We haven't lived in Cuba for years – it's shit. They lock up gays, you know.

AUNTIE FLO GUEVARA: Yes, and glasses and mugs – they just put them on the table. Just right on the table: they don't even care if it makes a mark!

UNCLE DAVE GUEVARA: They're animals. Cigar?

Dick Cheney

Sometimes, one may have doubts about whether it's right to demonise one man as the figurehead for all gas-guzzling, planet-raping, profiteering bastardry. We might momentarily wonder whether such a complex individual can really be so baldly drawn as the pure, living embodiment of bug-eyed Republican evil. Then, for a relaxing day off, he gets pissed up and shoots another man in the face.

Dick Cheney hunts pensioners – releasing them into the Texas scrubland, then letting off 260 pellets of leaden injury right in their faces. Still, at least it gets him into the outdoors – his previous exercise having been confined to climbing greasy poles and counting his money.

Cheney has often been called the architect of the Iraq War (however, an architect would have made a plan – so let's just say it was 'his fault'). Even people supposedly on his side (Lawrence Wilkerson, a former aide to Colin Powell) have openly wondered whether his propensity to ignore UN conventions makes him a war criminal. His enemies, however, *really* don't like him.

After the shooting, Cheney took a while to take responsibility for pumping buckshot into hapless Harry Whittington. It was a full 14 hours before the cops were called. Earlier, the local sheriff – alerted to the incident by the call made to the ambulance service – had been turned away from the estate by security guards who 'knew of no incident'.

According to our sources, the full 14 hours were taken up with an in-depth debate on how to play the issue. Cheney argued that if he could get Whittington classified as an 'unlawful enemy combatant' then he could not only shoot him in the face but also torture him. 'Let's waterboard the fucker,' Mr Cheney is reported as saying. He then suggested the excuse 'An Arab did it.' Ultimately, his final gambit that he should 'privatise responsibility' having fallen on deaf ears, he was persuaded to go on the telly and claim to be 'a bit sorry'. Even then, he managed to turn his admission that he shot an old man in the face – 'I'm the guy who pulled the trigger that fired the round that hit Harry' – into a piece of sing-song circumlocution in the style of 'There Was an Old Lady Who Swallowed a Fly'.

I don't know why she swallowed a fly. But I strongly suspect part of the reason why Dick Cheney didn't alert the police until 14 hours after he had pulled the trigger that fired the round was because he was an old man who had swallowed a beer. Followed by another beer. Possibly to catch the first beer. Who knows?

Chick-lit

Competition: Three of the below chick-lit titles are real chick-lit titles and two are not real but made-up chick-lit titles. Can you spot the not real but made-up ones? (Answers below.)

1. *Dot.Homme*: Mid-thirties singleton Jess is sent by friends into the world of internet dating – with unexpected results!
2. *The Ex-Files*: Take a soon-to-be-married young couple, four 'exes', mix with alcohol, and stand well back. Boom!
3. *Virtual Strangers*: Fed up, frustrated and fast approaching forty, Charlie suddenly thinks she may have finally found her perfect soulmate – via e-mail!
4. *The Mile High Guy*: Twentysomething Katie is a flight attendant thrown head over heels by a handsome, wealthy first-class passenger. Emergency landing!
5. *Old School Ties*: Tracey is 32, married and bored. Then she spies an advert for a reality show on a perfect school reunion. Friends – and enemies – are soon reunited!

Answers: sadly, there are no answers.

Chinese Communist Party, the

Plimsolled peasants, the blind tide who have floated down re-routed rivers: hanging off girders a hundred thousand stories high. Everything everywhere expanding like a great big expanding thing that moves very quickly. In 1998, 16 of the world's 20 most polluted cities. We must build more. Build more and capture the last few places until the buildings eat the sky. Wonders accomplished far surpassing Roman aqueducts, Gothic cathedrals, the Burj al-arab. No one can breathe. It doesn't matter.

Everyone must live in a pod hotel and eat out. All the restaurants in China full – all the Chinese restaurants full of Chinese people, which, as we know from our dads, is 'always a good sign'. Now, 24 million chickens eaten a day. It's not enough. Soon they won't be able to wait, and will just eat the eggs. Everything laced with agricultural chemicals and animal hormones: women buying tits; men growing them. 'Western' technology bought or taken. A resplendent Olympics showcasing the all-new Re-education Through Labour event.

Beijing sites of English public schools churning out Chinese public schoolboys. Polo. Party princelings and the rich renew their organs from slaughtered-to-order cultists and Christians. Power-brokers chasing 'wild flavours' gorge on SARS-carrying civet cats from the wild animal markets of southern China. Businessmen's prandial panda penises wreak disease and pestilence in foreign financial centres that are no longer houses of finance but merely houses of whores. Kids sent away to see how estate agents live. Kids who now can read but cannot read their history. *Teen Vogue* swearing allegiance to the Party. No longer an iron smelter in every garden – steel plants for all that want them, dismantled and labelled piece by piece and shipped in from Germany. Motorways upon motorways – leading inevitably to motorway service stations; corrupt officials skimming off the top to leave potholes and cave-ins for unwary capitalist roaders. Families hitherto forced to work at opposite ends of the country now can work at opposite sides of the globe. A mature society, with proper vast inequality between the supra-rich and the super-poor.

They will solve the problems of the countryside by abolishing the countryside. All will be a constantly renewing urban sprawl, an end of days of peasants starving while they feed the cities; now they can starve in the cities – cities leaping through stages of development and redevelopment. And again. A billion five-car families buying widescreen refrigerators. A billion coal-fired arms dealers propping up revolving African despots. Socialism which you cannot eat becoming state capitalism which you cannot stop eating. Obesity: growth measured with a tape measure around the waist. Production producing product-producers nestle everywhere, settle everywhere, establish connexions everywhere.

The cheap prices of Chinese commodities are the heavy artillery with which the new system batters down all Chinese walls, bringing home brands as souvenirs. Baby milk. Toys and tractors. Soft war by penicillin production. If only we could make the West wear its shirt-tails a half-inch longer; the mills of China would be working round the clock. The world gorged on cheapness. Tesco and Wal Mart merrily marking up mark-ups that merely mark the end. The West desiccated and ruined – everyone reduced to surviving by selling one another their knick-knacks on eBay and servicing each other. The rest of the time is spent falling down manholes, the iron caps melted as scrap by kids to send East. Kids once more display posters of Mao. Snakeheads smuggling people in. The only good goods the Chinese goods.

Fish, wood, logs legal and illegal. Oil. Wood for wood; wood to make way for soy beans. 20% of the population; 7% of the arable land. Raw materials sucked in from the globe like a giant fishing factory-ship draining all the oceans at once, commodity prices trebling even in the instant that they are sold.

Norwegian men fight in the street like dogs, over tree

saplings. The West morally outraged by the combination of low wages and environmental degradation. The very idea! Taiwan purchased. A yo-yo of African despots, misery revolving; cash loans and ivory palaces bestowed upon the new dictators. China Radio International broadcasting as Radio Not Free Nairobi. But starvation-waged copper miners listen instead for accidents. More Chinese in Nigeria than the Brits ever had. Hard power. Oil wars. Chinese fiefdoms in the Middle East – Mad Max beyond the Terrordome. Mel Gibson strung up on an oil derrick like Christ.

Jailed journalists fail to report the unveiling of the statue of the Google founders – 1,989 feet high at the gates of the Forbidden City, next to the mural of Mao. Under it, the Google motto – now the organising principle of the Communist Party of China – 'Do No Evil'. Kids jailed for internet searching 'Tiananmen'. Twenty years for throwing an egg. Shi Tao – jailed for 10 years for emailing abroad how the paper he worked for covered the 15th anniversary of the slaughter in the Square. Yahoo helped identify him. Yahoo/Google/Microsoft: will you let me search 'police informants' or 'accomplices to repression'? Murdoch: he knows a ruthless money-hungry elite when he sees one. Seek truth from facts – even if you have to make them up. Party and nation fused; run by arse-lickers, nepotistic yes-men and old-fashioned bastards. Lawless local government mafias getting fat on the wages of migrants; siphoning enviro-cash to build coal-fired coal burners, just for kicks, state loans disappearing in a puff of sulphurous smoke. 170,000 party members found guilty of corruption in 2004 – just the careless ones. Grasping at the organs of the living – imprisoned for the fear of funny-exercising Falun Gong. Churches putting party before God in their screeds. The organs of Christians (body organs, not big music ones with pipes – that would be stupid). The organs of the trade unionists. The organs of those jailed for having a picture of the Dalai Lama: look, he's 'Tibetan'. Tiananmen? An 'incident'. The Cultural Revolution? A couple of mistakes may have been made. 30 million dead of famine? I couldn't possibly comment. We prefer to be called the ruling party, as if someone else might get a go.

Acid rain already falling in Canada reaches all the way around the world and comes back. But it cannot be enough. Overproduced stock piles of baby clothes tower. Pauperised paupers pauper their pauper. Workers handed the shitty stick – and are then struck with it if they strike. The iron rice bowls are empty. A communist state which is not as 'socialist' as Germany – spending less than half the share of GDP on its people. 120 million migrant workers with no welfare. Housing sold off. Mass state redundancies. Releasing private firms from the commitment to fund healthcare and workers' kids' education. But it cannot be enough. Private and public blurred, with CP fingers over every sticky pie. Nobody knows where the join is. The CP keeps the water and energy costs low; they'll turn a blind eye to piracy and environmental destruction and twat anyone who gives you jip. Beating back social movements like bashing moles with a mallet. No one can stop this? There are 1.3 billion Chinese who need to consume like Americans. There is no alternative? The Three Gorges Dam – the world's most costly construction project, its opponents disappeared? 'It is not enough! I want a bigger dam! Get me more gorges!'

Onwards. Driving up commodity prices until you have to pay to stand in the breeze. Driving down prices to the point that they actually pay you to take pirate copies of VW Golfs off their hands. Everyone is eating everything, and everyone is being eaten. Everyone waiting for the Chinese Elvis. But she is in the army. The galleries have been closed. They are coming for the backward elements who do not shop at Accessorise. A billion boys and girls, no longer aborted, playing video games continuously for days on end. Once, kids denounced their parents. Now, parents bottle pressure up in kids. The kids lose themselves in online games; generations jump from buildings, believing they can live and die and live again, as in a game. But you cannot repair nature. The air is like sewage. But what do you want? Scenery or production? All relationships are burst asunder except relations to money and relationships to the party. Ancient traditions prove futile to resist, and are swept away. New traditions are ratified unanimously by the National People's Congress. All that is holey is propaned. A man stands stripped bare in a dry riverbed, clutching a pirate Harry Potter with an alternative ending. Everyone is melting. Well, that's one school of thought, anyway. Who knows? Maybe sense will prevail. Or they might just run out of oil or get a bit tired out or something.

Chuckle Brothers, The
Disturbing.

Church billboards with trendy messages
In a bid to woo trendy young groovsters inside their doors, churches put up boards bearing messages that incorporate topical events or 'street-yoof' language. But this can be confusing. I once read a billboard saying: 'Jesus is dead good.'

Which, unfortunately, was printed in such a way that casual passers-by would read: 'Jesus is dead. Good.'

'Christianity – less a religion, more a relationship.' But Christianity is clearly more a religion than a relationship. It's the whole weekly meetings giving thanks to an invisible deity at a communal place of worship that gives the game away.

Citybreaks

Spend half your prized three-day break getting there and coming back; struggle to reach your 6:30 a.m. flight at an airport that calls itself London but is actually in Norfolk, to get somewhere that calls itself Venice but is actually in Switzerland. Then realise you have seen everything in the first hour.

The travel agent literature for Bruges claims: 'Throughout the year streams of tourists photograph its beautiful buildings and wander in and out of the chocolate and lace shops.' As anyone who has wandered in and out of chocolate and lace shops will tell you, it doesn't take very long; and once really is enough. After spinning out your stroll to the point that you hit The Wall and start burning your own body fat, you realise that there's nothing else to do for the remainder of your stay except drink heavily and/or row with your travelling partner.

You might become so desperate for variety that you're persuaded by the guidebook's intriguing descriptions to explore a picturesque suburb where the real city dwellers, possibly even vibrant immigrant communities, live out their lives drinking insanely strong coffee in colourful gambling dens. On arrival, you find yourself walking down an empty street where the silence is punctuated only by the bark of a dog and the distant chink of cutlery from behind shuttered windows. An old man's vacant stare seems to ask the question that's already forming in your mind, pounding at your forehead: 'What the *fuck* are you doing *here*?'

CNN, NBC, etc.

Who would have thought, when the concept of the global media first appeared, that what they meant was the whole globe getting *American* media? Really, *who* could have predicted that?

And why are they always called Bob? The bloke doing the piece to camera in Washington? Bob. Who hands back to the studio – to Bob. Sometimes it's women. But mostly it's Bob.

I once saw this on CNN:

BOB: A flood in Indo- Indo- ... how do you say that, Bob?

BOB: Inda Indakinesia.

BOB: A flood in Indostania has left 400 people dead with another thousand so far unaccounted for. But first, let's go back to Minneapolis to get an update on that dog up a tree. She's a real cutey, too. Bow wow, Bob.

BOB: Bob. Bow wow.

When I say I 'saw' this, I had been drinking so it might not have happened. In case you were going to use it in an essay or something. Or work as a lawyer for CNN.

They definitely did call forces fighting the US in Fallujah 'anti-Iraqi forces', though. And you can check that. You can't fucking touch me for that one – so don't even try. I was on my holidays. It was August 2004. Not sure which day it was. They had CNN where we were staying. You might wonder what I was doing inside watching CNN when I should have been outside in the sunshine enjoying my holiday. But it was the evening.

Colours of the season

Who actually decides the new colours of the season? Is it God? No, it's not. It's actually a global network of analysts and trend forecasters in organisations like the Color Association of the United States (CAUS) and Pantone Inc. who together form a kind of new black Bilderberg Group. They meet in secret, possibly in Davos, possibly in a hi-tech base built into a volcano, and usually let the weakest link in the group – possibly the one with a distasteful penchant for lime green – take their chances down the shark chute.

Their forecasts influence designers of shirts, paper products, candles, cars, tiles, paints, silk flowers and lipstick. When they say 'Aqua', the rest of the world says, 'How high?' These people know about colour. The CAUS website boasts: 'Pinks and fuchsia were everywhere in spring 2003; CAUS members knew this in spring of 2001.' That's some serious knowledge. But predicting colours is a strange pursuit – a bit like predicting cows. Basically, they're just kind of there; not really getting any better or worse with the passage of time. This partly explains why, describing their recent aqua-blue ranges, designers Narciso Rodriguez and Michael Kor could only really claim inspiration from seeing – surprise! – some blue water.

'Colour is always out there,' pointed out Leatrice Eiseman,

executive director of the Pantone Color Institute, to *Time* magazine. 'We just have to determine where it's coming from at any given time.'

Beware of flying colour. It's 'out there'.

Comedy clubs

In every comedy club chain, the compere always kicks off with the lie: 'We've got a great bill for you tonight.' His icebreaking banter involves asking the audience where they have come from. Perhaps inevitably, the answers rarely provoke high comedy so the conversation very soon starts resembling distant relatives who haven't met for many years exchanging pleasantries at a funeral: 'So where did you come from?' 'Doncaster.' 'Great.'

The first act begins by explaining that he's 'trying out new material'. Sadly, though, somewhere in his mind the phrase 'new material' has become entirely disassociated with the concept of 'jokes'. Fairly soon, it goes so quiet you can hear people pissing in the toilet.

After a few more minutes of 'no jokes', a stag party starts yelling: 'Fuck off, you're shit.' 'No,' the comedian shouts back, 'you fuck off.' When this has finished, the host returns to try simultaneously to convey the two sentiments 'You were a bit nasty to that chap, don't do that or I'll have to get stern' and 'Please, for the love of God, do not turn on me.'

This pattern is repeated three or four times until the arrival of the headliner – or, rather, the pseudo-headliner, the actual headliner having cancelled (a fact advertised by a small handwritten note stuck on a wall behind a curtain). The stag party's 'fuck offs' will grow in intensity until you realise, as they trade unamusing insults with another bastard working through their 'issues' by inflicting their paper-thin personality on people who have never done anything to hurt them, that you have paid good money to sit in a dark room listening to people bellow 'fuck off' at each other.

Then there's a disco.

Cool brands

'Perhaps you had dreams of becoming an adventurer like Indiana Jones [when you grew up],' reckons a huge pullout ad for Diesel's 55DSL brand in the pages of *Dazed & Confused*. 'Or a world-class ballet dancer, maybe even an ace fighter pilot. Perhaps you wanted to be all three at the same time! Either way, you probably wanted to do something a little more exciting that what you do right now . . . 55DSL is looking for two young and gifted individuals to join our new Kick Ass Department. This isn't a joke, we really do have a Kick Ass Department and we really are looking for someone to fill our Junior Lucky Bastard position.'

Not joking, but really having a Kick Ass Department: how cool is that? The winning (junior) lucky bastards get to see cool stuff, film cool stuff (films are cool), blog about cool stuff (blogs are cool), supplying the content for DSL's new 55 Seconds campaign . . . Making someone's ads for them? Now *that's* cool. Diesel is cool. Not the fuel – although some maintain it's more environmentally friendly than petrol, as it's more efficient. No, Diesel the clothes.

The best brands are always on the hunt for cool. Cool-hunting: it's like fox-hunting, but cooler. Cool brands are not afraid to let cool kids show them the way to cool. If you can get them to do your advertising for you for free, then you're on to a double-winner.

And if you can't get the kids, then best rely on style journalists who, as we know, can always be relied upon to dance for beans. Cool brands get these cool consultants to show them how to be cool. These people are the consultants of cool. In return, they write about your brand and place it in photoshoots. So it's sort of like a bribe . . . only cooler.

Cool Brandleaders, a Brand Council initiative, saw a judging panel of cool people deciding which brands were the coolest. Among the chosen brands were the London Eye (Standing in queues for hours? Totally cool) and Coca-Cola (Diverting water supplies from Indian villages? Way cool). One of the prime factors the judges identified was that cool brands never actively try to be cool. They never ask, 'Are we cool?' And they definitely don't say, 'We are cool.' According to photographer (and *Dazed & Confused* publisher) Rankin: 'If you have to try then you've already failed; if you want it too bad you're just chasing your tail.' Tails are not cool.

But brands must also work hard to keep their cool. Not abandon their original purpose or personality for the sake of cheap profit. Rankin's advice here is to 'stay focused'. So brands must stay focused on being effortless. Which might be the same as staying unfocused about making an effort. You mustn't make an effort at being focused, anyway. Are you following all this? Or are you just not cool enough? 'Cool has nothing to prove/Cool dares to be imperfect,' claims Isabella Von Bulow of the Institute of Practitioners in Advertising in a cool poem she contributed to a cool book called *CoolBrands: An insight into some of Britain's coolest brands*. After noting that cool is 'visionary' and 'selfish', von Bulow concludes that cool 'fills a need'.

Poems about cool? How cool is that?

Sofia Coppola

The portrait of the babbling airhead Hollywood star in *Lost In Translation* was reportedly based upon writer/director Sofia Coppola's first-hand experience of Cameron Diaz.

I would personally be very keen to see Cameron Diaz make her directorial debut with a movie that featured a supercilious rich-kid indie *auteur* who does pseudo-profound confections that people initially twat themselves over but which, on second viewing, are the cinematic equivalent of non-flavoured rice cake, with comedy scenes that are not especially funny, endless 'arty' shots of the Tokyo skyline filmed out of hotel windows and dialogue that is only naturalistic in the sense that it possibly took as long to write as to say, and which are considered original only by people who have never set eyes on any other footage showing characters suffering from exquisitely well-turned neon-lit urban ennui like Wim Wenders directing a crap U2 video in 1993.

And she was shit at acting.

Cornish nationalism

Palestine, Kurdistan, Cornwall – a roll-call of trapped nations and oppressed peoples. The latter, shamefully, a country so close to our own. Kicked to the floor by the jackboot of the Blairite junta; a fetid bog of poisoned nationalist aspirations and fudge, oppression crashing on to their cliffs like the sea, gradually rendering their spirit unto sand.

Such is the view of political and intellectual heavyweights like Lisa Simpson of *The Simpsons*. In a special edition of the show, Lisa ran round the family home waving a Cornish flag, shouting, 'Rydhsys rag Kernow lemmyn' ('Freedom for

Cornwall now') and holding a placard saying, 'UK OUT OF CORNWALL'. Mebyon Kernow (the Party for Cornwall), meanwhile, refers to the proposal for the Plymouth unitary authority expanding ever so slightly into east Cornwall as 'an invasion of Cornwall, a violation of its territorial integrity which must be resisted at all costs'.

The UK has an incredibly cunning way of being 'in' Cornwall – by overtly occupying it for only three months of the year, lying prostrate, eating clotted-cream ices or bobbing about on novelty inflatables. This is not occupation as we understand it from, say, Iraq. Certainly, if the Coalition had 'done a Fallujah' on Polperro I think I'd have noticed. Maybe High Command decided they'd never get the tanks up that steep hill near Liskeard on the A38? (It is *very* steep.) To find notions of Cornwall as anything other than just another English county – albeit quite a handsome one; I mean, don't get the idea we're just taking the piss here – you have to go back to medieval times.

One of the very last mentions is from Italian-born scholar Polydore Virgil. In the introduction to his *Anglica Historia*, first published in 1535, he wrote: 'The whole Countrie of Britain . . . is divided into iiii partes; whereof the one is inhabited of Englishmen, the other of Scottes, the third of Wallshemen, [and] the fowerthe of Cornishe people, which all differ emonge them selves, either in tongue . . . in manners, or ells in lawes and ordinaunces.'

'Thee Cornishe,' he added, 'do devilish maketh fudge. But they can patenteth not pasties, which they didn't invent. Alleth of the isles eate stuffe in pastrie; not just them; just because they were popular with tinne miners, it doesn't mean they invented it or have exclusive rights. It's not like champagne, which is clear-cut. They can't even agree whether you put swede in or not. And most of them are knockede up by Ginster's in a huge factorie usinge ingredients bussed in from all over the country. So I'm not taking that claim at all seriously.'

And what's this Spirit of Cornwall obsession with being Celtic? Cornwall, they remind us, is one of the 'historic Celtic nations' – that's historic as in 'ages ago'. If the Cornish do want to be a bit Celtic, best of luck to them, but it does seem a tad random. The Celts only arrived in 500 BC, after the Bronze Age. Long before that, in the fourth millennium BC, Cornwall saw the arrival of Neolithic tribes from mainland Europe – as did the whole of Britain. Before the Neolithics, there were just wandering tribes, wandering about. So if getting tribal is the thing, let's go back to that.

Sadly, all of these options breach the useful rule of thumb that, if your political views are fundamentally and inextricably based on something that happened before, say, 1700, you probably want to take a long, hard look at yourself. Perhaps we could draw a line a bit later – say when the Great Western Railways came with their amazing steam horses? This rule goes for the Balkans, the Middle East and Yorkshire, too; otherwise things just seem to get silly.

Incidentally, Rick Stein's not Cornish; he's from Oxford. He is Judge Jules's uncle, though. That's a fact.

Cosmetic surgery gone wrong as televisual entertainment

Permanent scarring: now *that's* television.

Couples' columns

Here's a chance to look back fondly at everyone's favourite must-read column, 'We Hate Each Other's Guts', soon to be published in book form . . .

Her story

To begin with, it was pure, full-on hysterical attraction. Our appetite for each other was prodigious, as it was for many things: going to the cinema, cakes . . . And we were always at the centre of everything. We loved getting a crowd of friends over for food, wine and gossip round the kitchen table. We were like the Liz Taylor and Richard Burton of our scene. People loved us. But, even more than that, we loved us. Our philosophy, on life and home, was to reflect the individual in each of us. To be diverse. Plus we complemented each other work-wise: we both wrote about our latest relationships for the gratification of others.

It's hard to say why things started to go bad. In retrospect, the strain started to show when he wrote a column headed: 'She's smelly, and has many annoying habits'. From there on in, I started developing sudden feelings of rage. I thought I was a patient person, but I found myself increasingly wanting to snap his fingers off backwards and shove them up his arse. This made me sad.

I wondered where this anger came from. Was I a bad person? Was I a stupid person? I didn't know any more. I explained these feelings in a new weekly column called 'I'm Seriously Considering Getting Out'.

At that point, he became worryingly unhinged. One morning, I woke to find he had left me the message 'DON'T FUCKING LEAVE' by scorching the grass on the bit of Hampstead Heath behind our garden flat with the hot coals left over from the previous night's barbecue. This was a sweet, romantic gesture of the kind that reminded me of our early days together. But deep down I had already realised that by nature I am a nomad. I love change, just to keep up my spiritual energy. So I moved out to live with our daughter's trampolining instructor.

I still think we were soul-mates. We were just soul-mates who grew to hate each other deeply. In a way, we sort of turned our mateyness into hatiness. We became soul-hates. We had to have the good times to get to the bad times. That's what I think, anyway.

His story

Mutual friends always said we had to meet. They realised we were very alike, that deep down we were both people of substance. I often feel like that: that we were both completely full of the same substance.

When we moved in together, our house was an open house. Everyone was welcome day and night. People came and went. They stayed for a drink or supper or perhaps tea or a cold drink and, because they felt so at ease, they often stayed longer. Sometimes, they came and went, and then came back again – after leaving, they'd soon realise they couldn't stand to be apart from us much longer. Always the people and the coming and the going. Always.

But nothing lasts, does it? I started to have my doubts about our relationship when I read an interview with a Sunday magazine in which she said: 'I'm starting to realise that I'm married to a prick.'

Then, later that week, I was listening to my iPod in the bath when I opened my eyes and saw her trying to pull the lampstand through from the hall to throw into the water. Luckily, this ill-thought-out murder attempt failed – although, ironically, I was the one always saying we should get a longer lead! But from then on, I knew we would never find that freshness or innocence of the early days.

Not long after, my book *I Feel so Much Hate towards My Wife and, Indeed, All Women* was published, which some took as a fictionalised account of our marriage. Thereafter, she seemed increasingly distant. When I burned the words 'DON'T FUCKING LEAVE' on to the Heath for her to see out of our window, I thought that would convince her to rethink, but it only seemed to heighten her feelings of insecurity.

Deep down, I think she was scared of how happy I could make her feel. In a funny way, I think I was *too* good as a lover and as a friend. There was so much goodness, she didn't know what to do with it. There was a surfeit. I fulfilled her too much. To the point of over-filling her. There was spillage.

I still think about her all the time. I would say that, yes, I'm obsessed, but not in a way that stops me getting on with my life. I don't just prowl around her neighbourhood in the early hours of the morning. There are many other neighbourhoods I prowl around in the early hours of the morning, too. But that's life, isn't it?

Crabtree & Evelyn

Don't even get me started on those bastards.

Creative industries, the phrase

Funny how you never hear novelists or painters say they work in the 'creative industries', but only squalid little advertising people. How could this be?

J. Walter Thompson, the world's oldest ad agency – founded in 1864, they currently handle Ford and Unilever – tell us on their website: 'We believe: in influencing the world to think more creatively.' Provided, presumably, only if that thought is 'must – buy – more – stuff'.

If you listen to advertisers, you'd think they're the fucking Oracle and that for a fee they'll slip you The Answer. They are obsessed with being seen as 'creative', but what they do seems rather to be 'parasitical': pinching cultural innovations and using them to persuade people that they want stuff. So there's a dilemma right there for us all to think 'creatively' about.

JWT also believe in 'raising the creative bar as far as it will go. Then jacking it up a notch after that.' However, having already raised the creative bar as far as it will go, further notching up the creative bar will cause the creative bar to break. The creative bar will be completely fucked. That's just physics.

J. Walter Thompson further believe: '90% of the world's surface is made up of ideas. The rest is water.' A brief look at an atlas or infants' school geography textbook could have disabused them of this errant fallacy. Creative? Maybe – after all, they have completely made it up. But certainly not 'industrious'.

Leo Burnett (who do Heinz and McDonald's) are also into 'belief': 'We believe Disney, McDonald's, Nintendo, Heinz and Kellogg's are some of the world's most valuable brands because people have gone well beyond merely buying them. These are brands people believe in. When people believe, they buy more, pay more, stick with a brand more and advocate the brand to others. And so belief is the ultimate brand currency.'

Instead of all this gibberish about creative bars and making wine from water, really to convey the essence of their activities they'd all be better off with just one page of flashy swirly graphics, fading in these four words:

We
    are
        cack
            wizards

Critical reassessment

Yes, for fuck's sake. By which I don't mean yes, as in 'the affirmative'. I mean no – to Yes.

In their lifetime, the prog-rockers were critically reviled and were held in particular derision by the punk movement. There was a reason for this: they were so bad they made your ears want to die. However, having tried to wreck completely all music by making really bad music is no barrier to critical reassessment, the process in which rock critics look for a date on a CD, see 1973 and think: 'Hmmmmmmm, interesting . . .'

The criteria for critical reassessment reflect the high critical standards traditionally exercised by the music press. The criteria are:

- You must once have put a record out.
- Erm, that's it.

You might imagine reissuing Jeff Wayne's *The War Of The Worlds* in a lavish 7-disc box set (including the best club mixes from 1979–2005, rarities, outtakes and a 'making of' DVD) has scraped through the bottom of the barrel into the dark, dirty ground.

But even now a few neglected cases are still, in our humble opinion, ripe for rediscovery:

- Solo albums by members of Roxy Music that aren't Brian Eno.
- 'I Eat Cannibals'-era Toto Coelo.
- U2.

Culture of praise, the*

As in, when describing an unremarkable work of artistic creation, the application of words like 'magnificent', 'unbelievable', 'an awesome achievement' and 'If you don't think this is unfathomably great, I'm coming back with my rifle and the two of us are going to teach you some sense.' Are these bringers of hyperbole being paid in sacks of gold? Or are they the subjects' mums in disguise?

According to these throwers of garlands, we live in an unparalleled age where a new masterpiece is being created by another genius roughly every 20 seconds as opposed to, say, every other year. The very week it was announced that *Top of the Pops* would be demoted to BBC2, presenter Fearne Cotton followed a piece about the *Magic Roundabout* film, saying: 'Kylie?! *The Magic Roundabout*?!?!? Genius!!!!' Really? Is this genius as in Leonardo da Vinci? Or better?

If a book reviewer likes a book they've been given, they often claim it is 'hard to put down'. Has anyone else except book reviewers ever noticed this phenomenon? Some books are even 'dare-to-put-me-down' books. Soon we will be faced with 'if-you-put-me-down-I'll-rip-your-fucking-feet-off' books. And then where will we be?

Actresses like Kate Winslet often find themselves referred to as 'brave'. When recently asked by veteran CBS reporter Tom Fenton about being 'an uncompromising, very brave actress', Winslet replied: 'Being brave is very important because sometimes, you know, you can find yourself in scary situations at work, you know, when there are scenes that are difficult to do. And you can't run away from it, so you just have to go headlong into it.'

We must all applaud Kate Winslet's ability to cope with scary situations at work. But, we must also wonder, how brave is she really? It would be intriguing to see how she'd hold up faced with the challenge of, say, a burning orphanage.

Watching her go headlong into that would indeed be 'awesome'.

* Dr Jonathan Miller has called this entry: 'Truly stupendous – a work of unparalleled greatness. It actually made me aroused. I'd be very surprised if the authors didn't cure cancer. Just by looking at it.'

D

Daily Express

The World's Greatest Newspaper. Particularly, or indeed only, if your main interest is in who killed Princess Di.

Daily Mail

The *Mail* is very keen on tradition, heritage and 'never forgetting' all sorts of heroic British endeavours. Unfortunately, the great publishing institution appears to have accidentally forgotten one particularly heroic aspect of its own heritage – viz. their wholehearted support for the fascism of Hitler, Mussolini and Oswald Mosley. How terribly absent-minded of them. Acclaim for Oswald Mosley's British Union of Fascists kicked off on 8 January 1934 with the unequivocal headline: 'Hurrah for the Blackshirts!' Some *Mail* staff even wore black shirts to work. Lord Rothermere, the paper's owner, wrote of the BUF in the 15 January 1934 issue that they were 'a well organised party of the Right ready to take over responsibility for social affairs with the same directness of purpose and energy of method as Hitler and Mussolini displayed'. Oh, good.

Rothermere and the *Mail* broke with Mosley in June 1934, when the Blackshirts brutally suppressed (that is, kicked the shit out of) Communist Party supporters who disrupted a BUF meeting at the giant Olympia hall in Kensington, London – although not before investing (and now losing) £70,000 in New Epoch Products Ltd, a business arrangement with Mosley whereby the Blackshirts were to sell cigarettes made by Rothermere.

Towards Mussolini, meanwhile, the *Mail* was 'always friendly' (S. J. Taylor, *The Great Outsiders: Northcliffe, Rothermere and the* Daily Mail). In November 1926, Italy's fascist supremo dropped a hand-written line to G. Ward Price, the paper's Chief Correspondent, congratulating him on his appointment as a director: 'My Dear Price, I am glad you have become a Director of the *Daily Mail*, and I am sure that your very popular and widely circulated newspaper will continue to be a sincere friend of fascist Italy. With best wishes and greetings, Mussolini.' (On my photocopy of the letter there is a PS – 'How's the bunions? Up the Arsenal!' – although, to be fair, I did pencil that in myself.)

Through the 30s, the *Mail* was 'the only major British daily to take a consistently pro-Nazi line': it 'stuck out like a sore thumb' (Richard Griffiths, *Fellow Travellers of the Right: British Enthusiasts for Nazi Germany 1933–39*). Rothermere penned a July 1933 leader, 'Youth Triumphant', praising the Nazi regime for its 'accomplishments, both spiritual and material'. True, he admitted, there had been 'minor misdeeds of individual Nazis', but these would certainly be 'submerged by the immense benefits that the new regime is already bestowing on Germany'. So complimentary was the article, the Nazis used it for propaganda.

Rothermere eventually struck up a friendship with Hitler – or 'My dear Führer' as he invariably began his regular correspondences – and visited him numerous times. Rothermere and Ward Price were among only three or four foreigners invited to Hitler's first ever dinner party at his official Berlin residence. Rothermere, ever the gent, presented the Führer with some Ferrero Rocher. Probably.

In 1937, Ward Price – who 'was believed to be Rothermere's mouthpiece not only by the public but by Ward Price himself' (Taylor) – published a chatty memoir about his great mates Hitler and Mussolini entitled *I Know These Dictators*. Last revised and reprinted in August 1938 – when fascism's dark intents were obvious to even the most ardent reactionary – the book called Mussolini 'a successful man of the world who is expert at his job and enjoys doing it' and spoke warmly of Hitler's 'human, pleasant personality'. The chapter 'The Human Side of Hitler' (not a phrase you hear very often) revealed that, alongside his affection for kiddies and doggies, the great dictator was also partial to the odd chocolate éclair: 'Naughty but nice', as the Führer used to say.

Price urged readers of *I Know These Dictators* to keep an 'open mind' on fascism. Of Hitler's initial wave of repression on gaining power, he wrote: 'The Germans were made to feel the firm hand of their new master. Being Germans, they liked it.'

The concentration camps – about which 'gross and reckless accusations [have been] made' – were just full of dirty Reds. The Night of the Long Knives, when Hitler took on his party rivals – by killing them all – was a sensible bit of forward planning avoiding the need for lots of silly arguments later on. Overall, 'in every respect of the German nation's life the constructive influence of the Nazi regime [was] seen'. The only people who suffered were a few troublesome 'minorities'. Like, for instance, the Jews.

In the chapter 'Germany's Jewish Problem' (the title's something of a giveaway), Price explains how the Jews only had themselves to blame as there had been too large a Jewish immigration to Germany following World War I: 'The cause of this migration was the collapse of the German currency, which gave the Jews of neighbouring countries a chance after their own heart to make big profits.'

Lord Rothermere last visited Hitler in May 1938. While other papers condemned the regime's brutality and oppression, the *Mail* still claimed Germany was 'in the forefront of nations' and that Hitler was 'stronger than ever and more popular with his countrymen'. On 1 October 1938, after the signing of the Munich treaty in which Britain and France appeased Germany's invasion of Czechoslovakia's disputed Sudetenland region, Rothermere sent a telegram to Hitler: 'MY DEAR FUHRER EVERYONE IN ENGLAND IS PROFOUNDLY MOVED BY THE BLOODLESS SOLUTION OF THE CZECHOSLOVAKIAN PROBLEM STOP PEOPLE NOT SO MUCH CONCERNED WITH TERRITORIAL READJUSTMENT AS WITH THE DREAD OF ANOTHER WAR WITH ITS ACCOMPANYING BLOODBATH STOP FREDERICK THE GREAT A GREAT POPULAR FIGURE IN ENGLAND MAY NOT ADOLF THE GREAT BECOME AN EQUALLY POPULAR FIGURE STOP I SALUTE YOUR EXCELLENCY'S STAR WHICH RISES HIGHER AND HIGHER.'

Oddly enough, 'Hitler the Great' never did become a popular figure in England or, indeed, any other part of the British Isles. When war was finally declared in September 1939, Rothermere reportedly uttered just two words: 'Ah' and then 'Bugger'.

Ward Price finally broke with Hitler following the March 1939 invasion of Czechoslovakia. Only a 'foreign policy issue' (Griffiths) could provoke this shift in his opinions: 'Germany's internal policies, even at the extreme moment of the Kristallnacht Pogrom, could never have had such an effect.'

Strangely, though, that's not how he remembered the whole thing afterwards. In his 1957 memoir, *Extra-Special Correspondent*, he 'recalls' how he always thought Hitler was weak and neurotic. Saw through it all from the start. Never even owned a black shirt. Some of his best friends, etc., etc.

Price was clearly suffering from an affliction still rife at the paper today: a version of false memory syndrome that makes you forget you used to be a bit of an old fascist.

It can only but make you wonder what would have happened if the Nazis had won the war. Presumably in the newly fascist Britain they would soon have found a collaborator in their old friend Rothermere. Then we might have ended up with a *Daily Mail* pouring forth reactionary bile against immigrants, gays, trade unionists, asylum seekers, women . . .

Dead prostitutes

Why are all telly crime thrillers centred around dead prostitutes? Jesus, prostitution must be fairly tough already, without some hack bumping you off every ten minutes. I'm surprised there are any left. And it's not even enough for them to be 'dead'. Most of them also have to be 'mutilated'.

Prime Suspect alone, which begins with the identification of the brutally murdered corpse of prostitute Della Mornay, racked up six. And that's just the first series. *The Vice*? The name's a right giveaway: wall-to-wall dead tarts; they might as well put a counter in the corner of the screen marking the time until the first one goes toes up.

And it's not just on the telly. Glance at any crime/thriller book reviews and you'll find: 'Dr Tony Hill is a clinical psychologist whose assistance is often sought by DCI Carol Jordan, with whom he conducts a hesitant waltz of the "will they/won't they?" variety. The mutilated body of a prostitute has been found.' Has it? No shit.

Right next to this, in the *Guardian Review*, 31 July 2004, we find: 'Maverick American director Johnny Vos is in the city to make a film about the Belgian surrealist painter Paul Delvaux, but his female extras (recruited mainly from the red light district [check!]) start turning up dead [check!], their mutilated bodies [check!] accompanied by videos of Kumel's films.'

That Lynda La Plante alone gets through more ladies of the night than Wayne Rooney. If you're a prostitute and you see La Plante coming – and, let's face it, you're not going to fucking miss her, even in the dark – run for your life.

Not content with icing hookers, La Plante's very aura seems to bring danger to staff of her own production company. She told the *Observer*: 'The darkness is all around us. It's very easy to see. It's down there in the street. We just had a guy screaming abuse, stark naked, trying to knife somebody over there in broad daylight. We've had four rapes in this street. Every single girl in my office has been mugged and burgled – sometimes repeatedly. It is life.' Where is this office – in a crack house?

Alain de Botton

Whatever the subject, 'popular' 'intellectual' Alain de Botton will wade in with the most fatuously expected thing possible. Ask him about cooking duck and he'll say: 'Very fatty.' Ask him about Les Dawson's piano playing and he'll say: 'To play the piano that badly, he actually had to play the piano really well. I've read loads of Proust, you know.'

De Botton makes a handsome living from variations on a single phrase: 'Ah, but does it?' So, for the Art of Travel, he will say: 'Travel broadens the mind, they say. Ah, but does it?' And for On Love, he will say: 'Love makes us happy, they say. Ah, but does it?' Throw in a few banalities, raid philosophy and literature to reduce some of the greatest endeavours of human thought to a self-help soundbite, lunchy.

Sadly, as a small child Alain never grew any hair down the central dome of his head. This meant that he grew up with the nickname Alain 'Head As Smooth As A Baby's Bottom' de Botton. This is partly why he is so interested in the concept of status anxiety.

Ah, but is it?

Delicatessen counters at supermarkets

The pakoras piled up in that quaint earthenware bowl are, of course, produced by the Indian matriarch up to her elbows in ghee out the back, merrily crushing her own spices while joshing with the French peasant dropping off filthy cheese in his 2CV.

Either that, or they've been mass-produced, loaded into plastic containers, transported across the country in a big lorry, removed from the plastic containers and placed into said earthenware bowl to seem just ever so slightly more appealing than the absolutely identical ones in vacuum-sealed plastic multipacks on the shelves.

Pasta salad? They've just cooked some pasta and then let it go cold.

I will not take a number. I am a free man.

Design classics that by common consent don't work

The Alessi Juicy Salif lemon squeezer has, according to one retailer, 'earned its place in the Olympus of design. It now stands among the divine.' If you make even a cursory survey of modern design – inquisitive to decode everyday objects, or just wanting to translate some of the conceited consumerist jabber in the back of the colour supplements into English – you will almost immediately be confronted by this divine, Philippe Starck-designed juicer. It is indeed The Law with design books/exhibitions/critics that they must worship at Starck's lemon-squeezing altar, if not pop a picture of the citrus-related masterpiece on the cover.

It's a stone-cold design classic, retailing for around forty pounds. And it doesn't work.

The aluminium lemon juicer, which resembles a tall, skinny, angry spider, has been hailed by *Culture of Design* author and academic Guy Julier as 'beautifully dysfunctional' – that is to say, it doesn't work.

Two-for-one lunchy/design guru Sir Terence Conran said of the Juicy Salif: 'It's intriguing, tactile and desirable, and even though it squirts juice all over your shirt, it's fun to use.'

Fun? What if it goes in your eye? Is that fun too? Why don't all these crazy design gurus just spend all day squeezing lemons straight into their eyes? Or would that just be stupid? Stinging-eyed freaks.

Certainly, Starck doesn't seem to have been entirely on top of his brief. Apparently, company supremo Alberto Alessi was 'surprised and intrigued' when he received the lemon-juicer design from Starck: 'Not [just] because the design was exceptional, but because he had asked Starck to design him a tray.'

Starck said: 'My juicer is not meant to squeeze lemons, it is meant to start conversations.'

Conversations that presumably go: 'Why have you got such a shit lemon squeezer?' 'I don't know.'

Did I mention that it doesn't work?

Dyson vacuum-cleaners, meanwhile, have attained – certainly in the popular consciousness – the hallowed status of all-conquering saviours of British design, the object that proves We Can Still Do It. Workshop of the world? That's us, that is. (Via Malaysia.)

Dyson purchasers are three times more likely to be loyal to the company than those of any other vacuum-cleaner manufacturer. They're yellow and you can see some of the bits inside, so it deserves some loyalty.

It's novel, certainly; like a small Pompidou Centre that cleans your house. But on closer inspection the legend crumbles into dust. Dust you might have to clean up with a different brand of vacuum-cleaner, because *Which?* magazine has found Dysons 'unreliable'.

Anthea Turner, the housework freak, said of the Dyson 'The Ball' DC15: '[It] looks like the Early Learning Centre on wheels ... Just because some bloke designed this, doesn't make it good.'

According to exhaustive consumer tests, the Germans make the best vacuum-cleaners. Damn them to hell!

Designer baby clothes

NEW DAD: Hey, here's an idea – let's get the baby a Daisy & Tom cardie for 50 quid that it'll probably grow out of tomorrow afternoon.

NEW MUM: Great. Do they do ickle baby socks in, like, gold thread? That'd be good.

NEW DAD: Yes, it's so important to dress the baby right – you know, to dangle wealth off it.

NEW MUM: Mmm. Otherwise, what's the point?

NEW DAD: Maybe we could get a head-to-toe outfit from Moschino? Is that what Tim and Candelabra got for little, erm, baby? Or was it DKNY?

NEW MUM: Tricky. What would Gwyneth do? Oh, and then there's I Pinco Pallino! They're Italian, so that's some educational value right there.

NEW DAD: And what about those £1000 Silver Cross prams? I WANT ONE!! I mean . . . the baby wants one.

NEW MUM: Fucking wicked, yeah!

NEW DAD: We could pimp it up real good – jack up the wheels, get some 26-inch tyres on those babies, some leopard skin goin' down . . . Cristal, pick up some bitches . . . ooh, yeah! I'm all excited . . . I think I'll put the Groove Armada CD on.

NEW MUM: Um, darling, you know what? I've been thinking . . . I'm actually quite bored of the baby now – I mean, we've had it for, like, eight weeks or something. Maybe we could drop him off at a charity shop or something? Like with shoes.

Detox socks

Detox rocks. And no form of detox rocks more than detox socks.

These socks hold on detox patches through the night so all

the toxic nasties can pour out of your feet. You then wake up with socks full of tox.

Maybe these can then be sold on as tox socks. Because all the detoxing that modern life offers must also require you to do an awful lot of toxing. Otherwise, you won't feel the benefit.

Pete Doherty blood paintings

Romantic rock rebel and poet Pete Doherty speaks to his generation. And what he mainly says is: 'Give me some money so I can go and buy some crack with it. I'm literally crackers – for crack!'

When Doherty was imprisoned for his various cracky crimes, newspapers ran extracts from his prison diaries: 'I'm an innocent man. Wiggy only goes and gives me a stretch in chokey! Oh, my stars, the curdled days of toil and distress – lay me down my rivers of blue chalk and tears. And that.' Doherty's inchoate ramblings were due to be published in 2007 as *The Albion Diaries*; 'Albion', of course, being one of his big ideas – the name of a ship sailing to a utopia called Arcadia, a place without rules or authority. And there will be lots of free sweets on the boat and jelly and ice-cream and lashings of ginger beer! And crack.

Doherty has famously broken down the historic barrier between musician and fan. Sometimes, he does this by removing blood from fans' veins with which he then produces useless paintings for his website. In response to pictures of him seeming to inject an unconscious girl with heroin, he revealed that he was only taking blood from the girl's arm for another painting – kind of the blood painter's equivalent of nipping down to WH Smith's for some more watercolours. He wrote on his website: 'The photos are stolen from my flat so . . . upsetting and personally catastrophic . . . how rude, secondly it's a staged shot and what a fucking liberty to suggest I'd bang up a sleeping lass.'

Yes, how rude. Says the man who went down for burgling his best friend's flat. Of course, removing someone's blood while they lie on the floor for a blood painting is the height of modern etiquette.

Doherty has famously built back up the historic barrier between musician and fan by failing to turn up to many of his own gigs. Asked about this by the *NME*, he explained: 'Yeah? In what sense did I miss gigs? Missed them as in fondly missing them? I didn't miss any fucking gigs.'

When the *NME* pointed out that he'd 'missed' them in the sense of 'not turning up', Doherty countered: 'And who did? Who did? Who did turn up? Let them show their faces. What do they want, blood?'

Well, we know he's got some.

Dough balls

Executive version of overpriced toast. (See also **Toast, overpriced**.)

Downsizers

Jennifer Lopez recently told *Cosmopolitan* she was jumping aboard the downsizing bandwagon. 'You get to a point where you want to strip down,' the singer-actress explained. 'I'm going to sell that big museum-type house and get a nice cosy house, and I'm going to have one car and trade the others in. I want to go back to something simpler.'

It doesn't matter how many rocks she's got, she's just Jenny the former marketing executive from Islington moving to a croft on Stornoway.

Clearly, there are many ways of being less tosserish in life. But, surely, one of those ways involves not farting on and on about how much your standard of living has improved since you 'cut out all the crap and left all that mess behind'. It's no big deal – you are, after all, probably just living around people who never upsized in the first place; in the process, pushing up the property prices to the point that they too have to 'downsize', to a tent.

These burnt-out escapees could even develop some vague self-awareness that, with their 'opting out of the system' one-upmanship, they are actually another kind of 'cutting-edge taste-maker', colonising outposts and alerting marketing departments to profit possibilities.

Remember that last little trip to Starbucks you made before you left for mid-Wales? They put a microchip in your neck and are monitoring your movements, planning to use the data to locate new store-opening opportunities. They do the same thing to those Thai travellers who only carry one sock at a time and call everyone else 'tourists'.

Incidentally, Downsizer.net offers sound advice on how to survive without a delicatessen nearby. 'Try foraging for your food,' it suggests. 'The hedgerows, fields and woods have a surprising amount to offer.' Doesn't the countryside have enough problems without burnt-out stockbrokers digging around for grubs?

Dubai

I've seen the future and it works! Well, with the help of slave labour it works, anyway.

Through a combination of ambition, sunshine, not levying tax and old-fashioned lunacy, Dubai has turned itself into the fantasy-world holiday destination of the age, offering ample parking, shopping and money-laundering opportunities on the side. There are underwater hotels, the world's tallest building, and the whole thing is being run off slave labour. It's what Vegas would be like if it had any kind of gumption at all. Richard Branson has an island there; Gordon Ramsay has opened a new restaurant; Michael Owen and David Beckham have villas; Jim Davidson now lives there. This dusty, quite deserty garden of earthly delights has become our closest terrestrial equivalent to those casino-planet pitstops the Starship *Enterprise* was forever stopping off at in the original *Star Trek*; a place where all species can kick back and where Captain Kirk's eye will be caught by a woman with big hair and blue skin before the façade cracks to reveal the kingdom's dark secret . . .

In Dubai, being big is big. The most famous landmark is the sail-shaped Burj al-Arab hotel, the world's only self-styled *seven*-star hotel built on its own man-made island with a helipad on the 28th floor. Everything is covered in gold. It's the last word in luxury. (I once saw Anthea Turner and Grant Bovey staying there for a show on Channel 4, which should give you an idea of quite how clean it is.)

When finished, the five-billion-dollar Dubailand theme park will be the world's biggest, bigger even than Manhattan. There's the world's biggest mall, commonly called The Mall, soon to be supplanted by an even bigger mall inside the world's upcoming tallest building, the Burj Dubai. The world's largest indoor ski resort will be supplanted by another, which will feature a revolving mountain (great news for all those who see a mountain and think: 'Hmm, if only it revolved').

Not having much real coastline, Dubai has built more: the man-made island shaped like palm fronds, called The Palms, adds another 120 kilometres. Soon to arrive will be an archipelago of 300 man-made islands, roughly reflecting a map of the world, called The World. This World is a funny old world: Rod Stewart has reportedly already bought up Britain; and there's no Israel.

So how does it all happen? Well, through a kind of magic: an ancient form of magic called serfdom. Workers (largely Muslims from the Indian subcontinent) hand over their passports, work twelve-hour days and live eight to a room, then send home their wages to families they don't see for years at a time. Work is supposed to stop whenever temperatures top 100°F, which they do often, but that never seems to happen. This is because of one of the truly magic aspects of the Magic Kingdom: whenever it exceeds 100°, there is officially 'no temperature', so work continues. 'Hot, you say? I grant you, it might *feel* hot. But to be off the scale would require a scale to be off. And today, there is simply no temperature, scaldingly hot or otherwise. Even though we are, as you say, sweating like a pair of bastards.'

Poor workers enslaved by the forces of kitsch: it's very much the future! 'Can I have my passport back so I can see my family again?'

'No! You must finish building this water park made from gold . . .'

Of late, there has been a spate of workers committing suicide by walking into traffic. (If their deaths are deemed to be accidents, their families back home receive their pay packets.) In Dubai, even suicide isn't really suicide. That's postmodernism for you

Dustmen refusing to fund free education

One of New Labour's key arguments used for crapping student grants out of the window and introducing top-up fees was: 'Why should the dustman of today pay for the lawyer of tomorrow?'

With the average student debt now running at £18,000, perhaps it's time to revisit that argument to see if, on closer inspection, the dustmen really could be contributing a bit more here. Because, you know, they're shirking their responsibilities on this one a bit, and that is not the New Britain way.

Among the money-raising ideas dustmen might take up are:

- Putting a big jar in the staff room that everyone can pitch their coppers into.
- Sponsored walks.
- Cleaning up stuff out of the bins and selling it at a booty.
- Taxing the rich. No, NOT taxing the rich. That is stupid. DO NOT try to tax the rich. Not now. Not ever.

E

Early in/late home
Wrong way round. Surely?

Noel Edmonds' relationship with the cosmos
Noel Edmonds needs to be on television. When he is not on television, the cosmos is actively out of kilter. This is why the cosmos was so desperate for him to get back on television. The cosmos has great affection for Noel Edmonds. Perhaps it grew up watching *Swap Shop*.

As we now know, the cosmos is responsible for resurrecting Noel Edmonds from the TV dead. His adherence to cosmic ordering has changed his life from one in which he wasn't on television to one in which he is on television – almost every day. It's the latter he prefers, most definitely.

The method, garnered from the bestselling self-help manual *The Cosmic Ordering Service: A Guide to Realising Your Dreams* by German writer Bärbel Mohr, is a little like ringing up for a take-away. But this is ringing up the cosmos for a takeaway. And it's not just good for a nice green curry or those hot Thai salads with beef. It's good for houses, too. From his six wishes, the cosmos first gave Noel a holiday home in the South of France. 'I got it two months early,' he said. (He paid for the house, obviously.)

Two months later, he was again serviced by the cosmos: his order for a 'challenge' was answered when a TV executive called him asking him to front *Deal or No Deal*. 'Spooky,' he reckoned. Bärbel Mohr claims she gained her dream job, the ideal man, money, health and, finally, a castle. Key phrases she advises adopting include: 'There is no evil! You are perfect, just as you are' and 'The most loving person is the person who is self-centred.' You can see why Noel Edmonds, who always seems like one of the most 'loving' people imaginable, finds this philosophy appealing.

Since adopting its methods, Edmonds has appeared on television with stars and rain clouds on his hands and has become a rabid proselytiser for the belief system. In a recent interview, he said: 'You'll think I've gone away with the fairies – but it's fantastic.'

And he now has a taste for all things spiritual: 'I have faith. I don't know what shape it is. I feel uncomfortable to think it's purely Church of England, and I'd like to learn more about Islam.' (Noel Edmonds learning about Islam. Could this be the cosmos telling him to save the Middle East? Let's hope so.) I've always wanted a castle, too. Although I wouldn't want the cosmos to spring one on me unawares. I'd want some preparation time before being in receipt of a castle. I'd get some meat in. Probably oxen, and calf.

8th Habit, The

Seven habits must surely be enough, even for the highly effective? Certainly they were highly effective enough to make Stephen Covey a highly effective billionaire with many highly effective dollars.

But following the initial 1989 list in *Seven Habits of Highly Effective People*, he discovered another one. And so, in 2004, he published *The 8th Habit: From Effectiveness to Greatness*. This doesn't inspire confidence. Say I wanted to become highly effective myself, how could I be sure they won't find a ninth habit, or maybe even a tenth?

I'm not even up to speed with the first seven habits of highly effective people (although I imagine it's things like getting up early and never finding yourself on a Tuesday evening at closing time with someone saying, 'Let's go on somewhere else'). But start adding further habits, and very soon you are verily swimming in 'habits'.

And now we've crossed the Rubicon, where will it stop? This adding of habits could become habit-forming. He might start introducing, say, complicated ways to cook fish. Or ceroc.

Tracey Emin

In 2004, the Tate picked, of all the Sensation-al Young British Artists to preserve for 'The Nation', Tracey Emin, awarding her a room (to display work in, not to live in) at Tate Britain, where they keep the proper olden-days paintings.

This is fair enough, because Tracey Emin is as important an artist as Picasso. This is the view of at least some authorities on modern art. Such as Tracey Emin. She told Sue Lawley on *Desert Island Discs*: 'As an artist, to get some kind of notoriety or some kind of credit or fame, then you have to make a seminal piece of work, or you have to change the face of what people understand as art . . . I've done that with two pieces . . . I've done it with my tent and I've done it with my bed. Picasso did it with cubism.' Of course.

Perhaps Tate boss Nick Serota is simply trying to make the Tate accessible. Beds, bits of sewing, a feature film, a forthcoming book *all* tackle one fairly simple theme: how Emin had a bad time as a teenager in Margate and thus feels pain. This couldn't be more the case even if she just wrote 'I had a bad time as a teenager in Margate and thus feel pain' on a piece of paper and exhibited it. Which she probably has done.

But what next? Now that Tracey Emin is in the pantheon of treasured British artists, is there anywhere left for her to go? Is there anything she has not yet done to express her pain? When *i-D* magazine asked her if 'there [is] anything that's too painful or personal to become art', Emin said: 'Yes, of course. I had to have a camera up my bottom and, afterwards, the hospital insisted on giving me the film because I am an artist, but I passed out just looking at the screen. It wasn't that I hadn't had anything up my arse before, but I doubt whether I'd ever use the film in my art.'

So visitors to Tate Britain should rest assured they will only see the metaphorical, and not the literal, inside of Tracey Emin's arse. And for that, at least, may 'The Nation' be truly thankful.

Estate agents 'going to war' for their customers

If your estate agent seems slightly edgy, it is perhaps no wonder. They are foot-soldiers in perpetual combat. We realised this when a BBC undercover reporter working at Foxton's discovered that owner Jon Hunt's mantra was: 'Our clients expect us to go to war for them!'

Maybe this is why they feel the need to parade around their chosen patch like Field Marshal Haig, if Field Marshal Haig was always fiddling with his flies.

Estate agents showing people around houses on telly

ESTATE AGENT: So, here's the bathroom.
PERSON ON THE TELLY: Okay . . .
ESTATE AGENT: And, uh, the second bedroom – quite a nice size . . .
PERSON ON THE TELLY: Mmm.

It's amazing how often you can see estate agents showing people around houses on telly.

Ethical consumer scams

Spotting liberal soft touches from a distance of 40 miles, supermarkets have been known to mark up Fairtrade goods to make them more profitable than non-Fairtrade items. So the small coffee producer is getting slightly more for his goods. The conscience-driven consumer, on the other hand, is getting fleeced to fuckery. This is 'ethical', apparently.

Even if you don't buy your Cafédirect in a supermarket, world capitalism is not exactly quaking in its Jimmy Choo boots. Clearly a few small producers getting more for their coffee beans is not a bad thing, but Fairtrade accounts for only 0.001% of world trade. Even in areas where Fairtrade is strongest, their market share is puny: 3% of the UK coffee market and 4% of the banana market.

Meaning that, as a strategy for changing the world and challenging the structures of global power, 'buying coffee' is possibly not the most effective.

So . . . thank fuck we've got those wristbands as well.

Ethical living

Throughout our history, we have wrestled with the complex web of emotions and reason and social relations and aspirations and power and freedom that define us.

Plato, Ayer, Nietzsche. Liberals, Christians, Muslims, Marxists, Jonathan Porritt – all of them addressing two questions: 'How should I live, what actions ought I to perform?' and 'What sort of person should I be?' In essence: can we be good? How should we be moral? What is right?

And all of them could not see the truths that were staring them in the face and which now we hold to be self-evident.

What sort of actions ought I to perform? Buying Fairtrade coffee, hemp Frisbees and 'Give Peas a Chance' organic baby-gros. What sort of person should I be? Smug.

The salvation of humanity lies through the judicious purchase of ethical goods. You can even buy stuff you don't want or need – it all helps.

Let us now take a moment for reflection and self-congratulation – crack open some Fairtrade Sauvignon Blanc and enjoy our Ethical Rightness Awards for the Ethically Right (Not Wrong).

1. The eco-clutter couple. Pete May and partner Nicola,

one of the authors of *Save Cash and Save the Planet*, cut down on waste being dumped in toxic landfills by, in large part, keeping their own and other people's rubbish in the confines of their own actual house: piles of Tetra Paks and padded envelopes patiently await recycling that WILL NEVER HAPPEN. The subject of a major broadsheet photo feature, the couple do at least prove that ethical living need not mean having to go without stuff. As long as it comes out of a skip. They keep chickens, and have made an 'eco four-poster' by attaching bits of twig to their bed. Their garden seats are made of reclaimed logs, there's old orange peel on the boiler because 'it smells nice', a 'lavender harvest from our garden is drying in the fireplace', there are 'free-range stick insects ... roam[ing] the kitchen', and 'segments of indigenous hedgerow' are growing *inside* their fucking house.

Possibly they mistranslated Aristotle's notion of the flourishing human being living 'the good life' as meaning 'living like you're in *The Good Life*'.

2. The residents of BedZED. The Beddington Zero Energy Development in Sutton, south London, is the world's first eco housing estate: the dwellings have solar panels; the materials are renewable; there are dual flushes; allotments; all of that. The occupants are true pioneers – taking self-regard to hitherto uncharted levels. One told *Time Out*: 'You are saving the planet just by living here.' Another told the *Observer*: 'I live with a clear conscience and I haven't had to give up a single thing.' What they have done: lived in a house. What they have not done: solved the Israel–Palestine

question; explained *The Da Vinci Code*; made wine out of water (drinking your own water doesn't count).

3. The ethical earl. Fred Lambton, the future Earl of Durham, advertised his Ethical Network website with a 20-foot Union flag banner on the side of his massive London house. 'BOYCOTT SUPERMARKETS', it said, 'THEY ARE KILLING BRITAIN'. A massive 20-foot Union Jack? That wasn't doing wonders for the visual environment. So the council made him take it down. Fascists! Oh no, hang on. Fred's thinking about going into politics. Really, your Lordship, please don't bother.

4. Jeremy Paxton is the '46-year-old former water-skiing champion, publishing tycoon and, now, eco-millionaire' behind Lower Mill, a gated eco-retreat for the truly minted at Somerfold Keynes in the Cotswolds. According to the *Sunday Times*, Sol Campbell has commissioned a 12-million-pound glass-and-limestone mansion on the site; John Travolta has also expressed an interest – attracted by nearby Kemble Airfield, where he can land his eco-private jet, the Scientologising freak. Paxton himself is passionate enough about the environment to fly everywhere in his Hughes 500 Combat helicopter, 'even once to pick up Gloucester Old Spot sausages at the local farm shop'. Lower Mill even features 'designer allotments', where, says Paxton, 'We do the work, then you can do an hour's weeding and take your Brussels sprouts home.' Cool: sort of like the pretend farm at Versailles so beloved of Marie Antoinette. Let them eat organic veg!

5. Hugh Sawyer. At the time of writing, Hugh Sawyer was camping out in the woods in Oxfordshire – sleeping under a piece of tarpaulin stretched over a frame made of tree branches, cooking on an open fire, freezing his eco-nuts off. He was commuting daily by train to his job in London, where he works at Sotheby's. Hugh said: 'Once I arrive [at work] I pick up my suit – I have hanging space in the office – and use the showers. My desk drawers have been taken over by clothing and personal equipment. I'm also slowly taking over a filing cabinet – no one's said anything yet.' Why does he do this? To raise money for the Woodland Trust (hoping to raise a whopping £8,000 in a year) and also because 'I guess, having spent my formative years with trees, I have empathy for them.' Hugh explains his typical day: 'It's nice to have the woods to go back to – especially when there's a lot going on at work . . . I get into bed around 10 and only leave the fire burning if it's really cold – otherwise it's a waste . . . I try to cook something good once or twice a week. The meal I'm most proud of was my Christmas dinner: venison in an earth oven . . . It was beautiful. But on a normal night I might have soup or sandwiches. I've been ill a couple of times from not cooking meat properly, and being careless with filtering water from the stream. I also had bronchitis. But it's an adventure . . . I often end up in the woods with suits hanging from the trees.' He lives in the woods. He works in London, but he lives in the woods. In Oxford. He lives in the woods.

You don't have to live in the woods – although,

clearly, that would help. Just buy as much ethical stuff as you can carry.

But is it enough? Sadly, the answer is: balls, no. The top five big polluting companies in the UK produce more CO_2 than all the traffic on all the roads. Individuals can, of course, make a small difference – yes, use farmers' markets if you can afford to; don't be wasteful; recycle ... It's all to the good. But it's dwarfed by the day-in, day-out destruction casually wreaked by industry. So anyone who thinks living la vida eco makes them a saviour is off their organic nut.

It's like looking at the coming Apocalypse and saying: 'I didn't do it. It wasn't me.' Yes, like a prissier, more self-regarding, eco-version of Shaggy. Like Shaggy with plant pots made out of old Ecover bottles.

And, do you know, I think he did do it on the bathroom floor. It *was* him. He was guilty as hell.

Exciting developments in advertising

In 2004, Baz 'Moulin Rouge' Luhrmann made a five-minute, $12-million advert for Chanel No. 5 starring Nicole Kidman. Except he didn't – because, according to some quite major authorities such as Luhrmann's publicist, it was not an advert but a 'film'. This 'creative first' was, he said, 'the film to revolutionise advertising'.

Many others commented on how this 'film' radically broke down the barriers between commerce and art – which it did. It broke down the barriers between commerce and art by the commerce side kicking the barriers to pieces then lumping the art side with a tyre iron.

Meanwhile, plans are afoot in the US for interactive technology to let viewers instantly purchase products they see being used by TV/movie characters in product placements. Just to be absolutely clear about this, Baz: that's a bad thing.

Exercise videos

Here is a fun quiz. Which is the weirdest exercise video of them all? Is it:

- *Ultimate Results with Beverly Callard* (aka Liz McDonald from *Corrie*). This is THE video for all those people whose 'ultimate result' is looking like a startled ginger giraffe.
- *Anna Kournikova's Basic Elements*. Combines a workout with an elementary chemistry lesson.
- *Patsy Palmer's Ibiza Workout*. Which shows you how to get fit by necking lots of Ecstasy tablets and contracting an STD. Possibly.
- *Davina McCall's The Power of 3*. How to get fit while using a video mobile.
- *Daniella Westbrook's Better Body*. Includes those all-important nose exercises.
- *Lynne Robinson's Pilates with Fern Britton*. Now, I don't in any way want to denigrate someone for their physical appearance, but I'm saying if you're marketing a range of exercise videos, Fern Britton is not really the image you want to project. If you were marketing a range of biscuits, maybe.
- *Tantra t'ai Chi Fitness (Adult Educational)*. Eh? Eh? I'll say.

- *Kate Lawler's 'Kate's Cardio Combat'*. In which the *Big Brother* winner takes on the seemingly unbeatable Russian monster Drago to avenge the death of her friend Apollo Creed. Actually, no, now I come to think about it, that's *Rocky IV*.

F

Faith schools

At 1996's pre-victory Labour conference, Tony Blair declared that in power he would prioritise three things: 'Education, education and education.' What he should have said was: 'I'm one serious Christian right here.'

God helps you learn stuff. Everyone knows this. If God's there glaring over your shoulder, it really focuses the mind on understanding how glaciation works. No one can put the fear of God into you like God. Don't think He can't see you drawing a penis on to Henry VIII's forehead in that textbook. He's a big bugger too, so watch out.

In 21st-century Britain – a place where people think more about John Leslie than about God – a quarter of all schools are now allied to a faith. The nation is blessed with Anglican schools, Catholic schools, Muslim schools, Sikh schools, evangelical schools, Seventh-Day Adventist schools; in Hereford there are even plans for a school that worships Thor, the Norse God of Thunder, where pupils can specialise in bolt-throwing, beard maintenance, warmongering and, of course, thunder.

In Parliament, Tony Blair even defended one school's right to teach Creationism alongside evolution, claiming that 'a more diverse school system will deliver better results'. In a sense, this is correct. Creationism and Darwinism are both simply theories on how the human race came into being. But where Darwinism is a theory that allies itself with logic, Creationism is a theory that allies itself with making stuff up and pretending it's true.

In C of E schools around Canterbury, teachers have been instructed on how to induce a state of hypnotism – or 'guided meditation' – in five-year-old children by lighting candles, closing curtains and asking them to close their eyes before lullingly evoking images of the Last Supper.

The teacher tells the children to imagine an old-fashioned room with a big bowl of 'delicious-smelling stew'. They are carrying this receptacle into another room where long-robed men are gathering. As everyone sits down, the children must envisage Jesus entering through the front door and ask themselves: 'What does he look like? . . . Is he clean-shaven or bearded? . . . Happy or sad? . . . Everybody greets him, including you . . . Jesus takes the bread that you set out and breaks it in half and says: "Take this and eat, because this is my body" . . . How does he look? . . . The bread comes along and everybody breaks off a piece and eats it . . . What does it taste like?'

Erm, like bread? The diocesan schools adviser does admit this process can 'produce deep emotions'. You can say that again – I've just lost my fucking lunch.

Britain's most worrying new educationalist is evangelical second-hand car magnate Sir Peter Vardy. At his flagship Emmanuel College in Gateshead, pupils have to carry not one but two Bibles, which, even if you're quite big on the whole Bible thing, does seem excessive.

So how does God influence the teaching? This was spelt out in a controversial document – now removed from their website – called 'Christianity and the Curriculum', which reckons science classes should show how 'the study of science is not an end in itself but a glimpse into the rational and powerful hand of the Almighty'. Art classes should show how art can 'serve the glory of God and celebrate the complex beauty of His creation'.

At which point, even the Scouse bloke who does *Art Attack* on CBBC starts feeling his intelligence being insulted. The document went on to say – and this is genuinely not made up – that History lessons could usefully consider whether, during World War II, Britain was saved from Hitler by God intervening to halt the Nazis at the Channel. Meaning that maybe the Battle of Britain film classic *Reach For The Skies* could more accurately have been called *Reach From The Skies With A Big Fuck-Off Finger Saying, NOT SO FAST, MR HITLER!*

I personally think it's a crying shame that no school in the land teaches my own theory of creation: that this whole grand enterprise is merely an imaginative figment of my Uncle Mick, who smokes a pipe and seems to live entirely on toasted sandwiches. I firmly believe that he dreamed the whole thing up one afternoon while watching the Channel 4 racing, which he loves, and the moment he gets bored, that's it, we're all toast, just like one of Uncle Mick's delicious sandwiches.

I was going to set a school up, but I couldn't be bothered.

Fashion journalism

Words to go with pictures of people wearing clothes written by boarding-school girls with misspelt first names (so many 'z's) and double-barrelled second ones.

At heart, fashion journalism isn't about clothes; it's about being so Now that by the time you've finished typing the word Now it's too late, because by now you're Then. Among fashion journalism's key linguistic traits are:

- Sentences that resemble complicated Google searches: 'the Kate Moss/Jade Jagger/Sienna Miller school of Primrose Hill bling-meets-boho laid-back high-chic'. Keep up, ugly losers.
- Casually dropped French terminology – *'au courant'*, *'de la saison'* – in the style of popular sitcom character Delboy Trotter.
- Weird boasts. Like 'I'm a fashion innovator,' 'I take classic Armani pieces and wear them in a modern way,' 'I'm an accessories freak.' These are good things, presumably?
- Hyperbole. 'Oh Jesus, bite me on the arse these bags of the season are making me so high, they must be a gift from God!'
- Referring to people you have never met by their first names: Kate, Mario, Lemmy.
- Deification of models. Not just models modelling, but interviews with models about modelling too! Here's Karolina Kurkova, a model, on what it's like to be a model: 'It's not just about being cute. It's about creating something through light and clothes and expressions. It's like theatre.' This woman was the highest-paid model in 2003, but we should feel very sorry for her: 'Modelling looks glamorous from the outside, but sometimes I have moments when I cry.' Yes, me too.

Sometimes fashion journalists get paid to write novels, like Plum Sykes's excruciating *Bergdorf Blondes*, a book which has apparently become 'a Bible for the fabulously wealthy, the inner circle elite'. And which proves, decisively, that you should never read books by anyone named after a fruit.

Fast-food chains marketing themselves as 'healthy' (and feminist)

'Hi – we're McDonald's, a great big company that would love to come round to your house and tell you about how we're changing.'

In the 1950s, French artist Yves Klein invented his own colour, International Klein Blue, which he believed represented *Le Vide* (the void) – not a vacuum or terrifying darkness, but a void that invokes positive sensations of openness and liberty, a feeling of profound fulfilment beyond the everyday and material. Standing before Klein's huge canvases of solid blue, many report being enveloped by serene, trancelike feelings.

I feel something very similar looking at the pictures of salads in the window of Kentucky Fried Chicken. Or that surreal meal deal with the plastic bowl of rice. You wouldn't actually order these items, but their very existence expresses that corporation's painful identity crisis faced with a shrinking market. Mmmm. Lovely.

I get similar buoyant sensations by reading the McDonald's Corporation's 2004 pamphlet '(We thought we'd come to you for a Change'), posted through letterboxes across the land, which bravely reconfigures McDonald's as a health-food restaurant and general harbinger of world peace. The tone of a spurned lover who treated you wrong and now sees the error of his ways pervades the whole document: 'Hi – we're McDonald's,' it begins, 'a great big company that would love to come round to your house and tell you about how we're changing. But there are a lot of us and it takes ages to get organised.' That's a joke (no, really) to show us they have a Good Sense Of Humour.

'We've knocked the booze on the head and got a job. We've moved out of our mum's and got a flat: it's not much, but it's a home. It could be *our* home.' I made that last bit up.

The pamphlet desperately bids to woo everyone back to their formerly favourite restaurant: there are pictures of cute black children, pictures of cute moo cows, parents lovingly clasping their children's hands and a cute child on a swing – all brimming with salad-derived vitamins. In keeping with the identity crisis theme, there's also a picture of some paunchy blokes watching the football in a pub to reassuringly convey the message: yes, we do still sell shitty burgers that chew your guts up something rotten.

Another section, which contains some of the most remarkable prose ever written, aims to reposition McDonald's at the head of the feminist market (this is not made up). Headlined 'You go girls', the empowering passage claims that 'spending time away from the boys is a rare and precious thing. Make the most of it while you can. Take a shopping break, put the bags down and find somewhere fun to eat.' Because, this says, being a carer to men and shopaholic (which, of course, is the very essence of womanhood) is hard work. But where could you possibly have this break? 'Yoohoo! – we're over here.' Ah yes, McDonald's.

The text – and if you don't believe this actually happened, you can check it out: I've donated my copy to the British Library – ends like this: 'Girls, before you know it, you'll be back home and showing the things you bought to the boys, and unless it's got cars or footballers on it – they won't care. So have a great day, have a great salad, and sisters? Do it for yourselves.'

Faux swearing

Strolling past The Shop Formerly Known As French Connection, have you ever been driven to splutter, giggle, tap your companion's shoulder and exclaim, 'Look, look – it almost says FUCK!'? I rather think you haven't.

Similarly, when you hear a panel show called *Stupid Punts*, there is unlikely to be a mass gasp of shock and exhilaration. Maybe some old people would be shocked – but they're unlikely to be watching BBC3. (Actually, most people are unlikely to be watching BBC3, but you take my point.) During the fox-hunting debate, there wasn't a news source in the land that could resist a cheeky play on the word 'fox'. The silly fucks.

There is nothing big or clever about pretending to swear. If you want to be big and clever you need to call your shop Spunky Fucking Tit-Monkey's Arsing Cockarama and Co. Now *that's* swearing.

Hugh Fearnley-Whittingstall

The whole River Cottage 'experiment' was just amazing. Surviving for a whole year only on what he can grow from the soil or barter. With nothing to fall back on but the enormous royalties from a best-selling book and hit TV series. Amazing.

According to a bloke I met in a pub, what people don't know about Fearnley-Whittingstall is that to facilitate the manoeuvres of the TV crew he had a three-lane motorway put in leading right up to River Cottage, totalling a vast expanse of natural beauty and causing the extinction of some species. And, following his trips there to get crabs and stuff, West Bay has now become so popular that Starbucks and McDonald's are planning to open branches there and British Nuclear Fuels are going to dump toxic waste in the water. This bloke had been drinking heavily, but still . . .

Incidentally, I'm surely not the only person to feel rather perturbed whenever I come across the phrase 'Hugh Fearnley-Whittingstall's Meat'? I'm coughing and spluttering in shock even before I've noticed this meat-based cookbook's price tag: £25.

In his romantic willingness to embrace the extremes of Nature, Hugh is turning into a Kurtz-like figure whose questing spirit puts him beyond the limits of human society. If he doesn't start reintegrating soon, there might be no hope of a safe return. Reconnaissance crews will be sent down the M3 to Dorset to find him dressed in cowhide and taking daily baths in goose fat.

£25? Think of all the meat you could buy with that. You could have it hanging around the house like Christmas decorations.

50 Cent

In April 2005, Reebok launched a TV ad campaign showing 50 Cent sat on a box in a burnt-out warehouse, snarling at the camera and counting to nine while the screen turns slowly red and a crackly newscaster reminds how 'he's been shot nine times'. Oddly, some thought the ad made getting shot look cooler than it often turns out to be.

It's certainly not his clever rhyme skills, so the fact that 50 Cent is now among the world's biggest entertainment figures apparently derives almost entirely from having got himself shot up nine whole times – something he doesn't like to talk about. Oh no, sorry. I was getting mixed up with the singer from Athlete. 50 Cent loves talking about shooting and getting shot up; he's regularly pictured wearing body armour, pointing massive shooters at the camera lens wearing an expression saying 'I'm gonna shoot you up.' He called his last album *The Massacre*, always starting beefs with other rappers about who is best at shooting and getting shot up. And so on.

All his bullet wounds were actually attained in one incident, but his image rather portrays someone who has trouble visiting the local shop without getting himself shot up: 'Honey! I got shot up again . . . Oooweee, this one's a biter . . . got any Band-Aids left or did we run out after last week? Oo!'

Reebok responded to the complaints by claiming the 50 Cent ad campaign was a 'positive and empowering celebration of his right of freedom of self-expression'. And not his 'right of freedom' to get shot right up.

Filming gigs on phones

You are at the gig. You don't need to film it. You can DOWN-LOAD CLIPS LIVE RIGHT NOW – with your eyes and your ears. It is literally right in front of you. They really should put up some signs: NO PHONE-CAMERA TOSSERS! NO! NO! NO! AND ALWAYS! NO!

Film warnings

What's a childhood without a few sleepless nights spent haunted by the memory of a grim celluloid bloodbath? Kids love it. Waking up in the middle of the night, sweating, feverishly recalling a zombie axeman hacking at some poor unfortunate's innards? That's the magic of childhood, that is. Sadly, however, some people don't see it that way and want to deny any potential for trauma with film warnings that seem to get more convoluted by the month.

But really, what kind of person would want to stop anyone seeing a film that 'contains mild peril'? There are, according to some estimates, only seven basic storylines in all human art, all of which contain at least some peril. It's what makes them stories. And even 'mild peril' sounds fairly pathetic; like 'mild action violence' or 'mild sensuality'. If a film is going to include peril, action violence and sensuality – and, clearly, it should – then ideally the usage should not be mild. At the very least, it should be 'moderate'.

Who demanded such stultifying detail? There surely don't exist people who read the cinema listings and think, 'Oh dear, no. We can't go and see the new Spiderman film, it's got one use of strong language and mild sensuality – if little Daisy sees that, she might die.' Or is this, perhaps, America's familycentric right extending its icy influence over the listings in your local free paper? Hell's teeth, it's even got 'thematic elements'! To be truly sensitive to a young person's individual fears, we should probably detail everything that may cause offence: 'One scene takes place in a kitchen, which features a major heat source . . . plus there is one use of a staircase – down which someone might potentially fall. Also involves moderate use of hair and teeth.'

Fish symbols on cars

Early Christians used a fish symbol to identify fellow believers during times of persecution. These days, to let people know they are really into Jesus, many Christians stick a fish sign on the back of their car. Like Baby On Board stickers – but with God-knobs on.

In the US, these symbols have caused belief-system-related mayhem. This is because the symbols don't just mean 'I'm the nice sort of Christian who sometimes distributes hot soup to the homeless,' but are more likely to mean: 'Science is witchcraft and you're all going to hell.' To underline the hard-right/anti-science/anti-abortion intent, some fish contain the word 'Bush' inside indicating that George W. is 'doing God's work'.

Incensed, humanists created their own bumper fish symbols with the word 'Darwin' inside hoping to irritate the Christian right. It worked. They didn't like it. It got nasty. Chris Gilman, the Hollywood special-effects whizz who apparently invented the Darwin fish, said: 'Here's a religion about forgiveness, peace, and love, but I can't tell you how many times I've heard about Darwin fish being torn off of cars and broken.'

The Christians retaliated with a bumper sticker depicting the Darwin fish being swallowed by a larger 'Jesus', or 'Truth', fish.

The humanists shot back with a reversed version of the sticker.

Then the Ring of Fire website produced a sticker depicting the Darwin fish and the Jesus fish forming 'what Shakespeare jauntily termed the beast with two backs' (they were at it, like knives).

Nothing will wind up a right-wing Christian more than piscine penetration faith denigration. And so it proved, with yet more car park/highway altercations.

Actually, this is possibly a good way finally to settle the evolution/creation debate: a demolition derby on the highway with the loser ending up bleeding in a ditch with bits of car stuck in them.

If the Christians won, they could shout back at the twisted wreckage: 'What's that you said about survival of the fittest? I CAN'T HEAR YOU!!!'

Food advice

There is some useful food advice: 'Eat Your Fucking Greens Or You Will Die.'

But for many this is simply not self-absorbed enough so they send cash to strange nutritionists in exchange for magic beans and kelp.

The main problems with the nutritional advice of 'food experts' are that:

1. Even supposedly sound advice reverses every two months. Don't go to work on an egg any more; an egg a day will make your arteries swell up like hose pipes (hose pipes full of cancer). Fish? Well, of course. Oh, but maybe not fish that's been pulled from our polluted seas. Or fish that was reared on a fish farm. Oh hell.

2. They turn healthy eating into the kind of task that would make Hercules say: 'Bollocks to that for a game of soldiers.' Fruit for breakfast is great – but not oranges or orange juice. Orange juice is bad for breakfast! You might as well just eat cancer. If you opt for grapes, don't mix them with anything else. And don't eat spinach unaccompanied by vitamin C or your body won't absorb the goodness. Getting the body to absorb 'the goodness' is petrifyingly difficult: we're all living on a knife edge here.

3. Many nutritional 'doctors' received their Ph.D.s from the Quacky-Duck University, Land of Make-Believe, and so are about as real doctors as Dr Dre or Dr Fox. Dr Fox isn't even a real fox.

4. Because many people have already heard about broccoli and tomatoes, the experts justify their existence by recommending alternative foodstuffs that don't resemble food. Even if you wanted to, you can't buy these items – 'ayurvedic cleansing tri herb combination Triphala' – anywhere in the world except on their personal websites. Even seemingly rational books recommend 'incorporating paprika into your diet – it's a very good source of Thiamin and Magnesium'. How do you

do that then? Make paprika pie? Sprinkle it on chips?

5. It's not just kelp that the eager disciple must learn how to swallow, it's self-help bullcrap as well. Gillian McKeith recommends inhaling and exhaling (which is, to be fair, sound advice) while repeatedly saying 'I love me' (which is more like tosspot advice). Plus, there's her 'little secret': five minutes jumping up and down on a trampette. While, presumably, screaming: 'I give myself the horn! I give myself the horn!'

6. All nutritionists try outdoing each other to be most foam-flecked fundamentalist of them all. Dr John Briffa (who, amazingly, is a real doctor) said: 'Breakfast cereals such as Weetabix, All-Bran and Alpen have had generally good publicity from the dietetic establishment, but I have my doubts . . .' Oh, so you have your doubts about bran-based cereals? And are these serious doubts? Public-health-warning-level doubts? Or the kind of doubts that nobody really needs to hear about? Silly twat.

7. All proper food advisers see dinnertime as a Manichean struggle between good and evil. Red meat? Hear the demons hissing. Alfalfa sprouts? All the birds have started singing. Lovely, isn't it? Except that, confusingly, the forces of 'good' are represented by Gillian McKeith cackling away on her trampette with bundles of wheatgrass stuffed into her ears.

8. Even the government's advice is fairly peculiar: eat five to nine pieces of fresh fruit or veg a day.

What happens if you have 10? Do they all start jostling each other inside your system, the berries ganging up on the bananas and having drive-by shootings inside your stomach? Certain combinations of fruit were used in the war to produce bombs, and if eaten will cause instant immolation.

9. Where were we?

10. Oh yes, and they really are total freaks (let's be clear about this). Gillian McKeith's book *You Are What You Eat* has a whole chapter on the wrong kind of stools – some people, apparently, even suffer from 'FOUL-SMELLING STOOLS'. Imagine that! Every member of the public who appeared on her programme had to undergo an enema, the results of which would then be studied with interest by McKeith. Weirdly, at no point in the series did anyone say: 'Hang on, I'm on national telly letting a freak prod around in my poo. What has become . . . of *me*?'

Food halls

Dishes from the four corners of the world! Left half-eaten, on paper plates, stacked up, on Formica tables.

The food hall, or food court: the most monstrous part of the already desperate shopping centre 'experience'. It's like a horrible accident at an MSG factory.

And always, as well as the usual suspects, there are outlets that you never see anywhere outside of food halls. Singapore Sam Express. Quizno's Sub. What is that? Who is this

Quizno? What is this for? Who are these people? WHAT DO THEY WANT FROM ME?

Football buyouts

Here is a fun quiz.

Where did Roman Abramovich get his money? Did he:

a) Find it on a bus. He handed it in but after an investigation no one claimed the money so the bus company said it was 'morally his'.

b) Marry John Kerry's wife, the one with all the Heinz beans money.

c) Pull off a 20p, 128-horse accumulator, including the famous Glorious Goodwood victory of 250–1 outsider Horsey.

d) Get it by 'talking gullible workers out of their share vouchers, making billions out of rigged privatisations, associating with share dilution coups and the like', and by 'slashed wages' for Siberian oil workers and 'shameless, albeit legal, tax avoid[ance]' (Dominic Midgley and Chris Hutchins, *Abramovich: The Billionaire from Nowhere*). Thus Abramovich has accumulated oil-barrelsful of lolly as one of the most enduring Russian oligarchs – the breed of ruthless free-marketeers summed up generally to Midgley and Hutchins by a seasoned 'Moscow Watcher' thus: 'All these guys are kind of barracudas'.

Marshall I. Goldman says that of all the Russian oil companies' efforts to avoid being taxed, it was always Abramovich's Sibneft that 'paid the least' (Goldman, *The Piratization of Russia*). Sibneft controls the vast Siberian oilfield, which is the size of Wales; Yeltsin offloaded it to his mates Abramovich and former mentor Boris Berezovsky in an 'auction' where the only bidders were companies owned by Berezovsky and Abramovich 'for less than $200m [a fraction of its true value] . . . by the end of 2003 [it] was valued at $15 billion' (Midgley and Hutchins). The Siberians who might have thought they were going to benefit from that mineral wealth, what with having put up with Stalinism and all, may well wonder what it's doing running around a south-west London football stadium in a blue shirt. Tax avoidance ruses have included, once Abramovich became Governor of the oil-rich province of Chukotka, registering lots of his companies there and then using his new powers to 'grant large tax breaks' to them (Peter Truscott, *Putin's Progress*). 'Tax cut, Mr Abramovich?' 'I don't mind if I do, Mr Abramovich . . .'

However one evaluates the vagaries of the Russian tax system, it is undeniable that the money Abramovich throws about on yachts, jets, Kensington mansions and enough world-class players to, as Jose Mourinho commented at the start of the 2005/6 season, field two equally good whole teams who could defend the Premiership title, came from publicly owned resources bought for nix in a country of immense poverty. All in all, we might concur with Will Buckley in the *Observer*, précising a BBC documentary that attempted to unpack the Russian doll structure of Abramovich's empire (companies inside companies inside companies), that Abramovich's dealings at the very least 'lack . . . transparency'.

Personally, I find Chelsea fans being led by John Terry and Frank Lampard in chants of 'Roman Abramovich! Roman Abramovich!' to the tune of '*La donna e mobile*' when they won the title as depressing as them chanting their appreciation of privatisation. Or Putin. Or barracudas (not the fish).

Now complete this tiebreaker: 'The Premiership is a load of stitched-up dogs' cock because . . .'

Football gofers

'Some people describe me as a Jim'll Fix It,' says Manchester United's player liaison officer Barry Moorhouse. 'I call myself a gofer. If [the players] want something done, I organise it.'

A more succinct definition would be 'servant'. Apart from ensuring players don't miss dentists' appointments and important promotional photo shoots, football gofers arrange houses for them, golf matches, flights, plumbers or – for foreign players moving to the UK – a National Insurance number, TV licence and bank account. They even go round and change lightbulbs. Also they iron players' newspapers (or copy of *Zoo*) and wipe their shitty arses with swan feathers. Probably.

When Fernando Hierro moved from Real Madrid to Bolton, gofers Matt Hockin and Sue Whittle not only put his kids into a local private school, they got adjoining flats for his family and his housekeeper (his personal bodyguard said he didn't need a flat, he'd sleep in the garden and eat moss (possibly)). They also had the premises furnished and sent a van to pick up a fridge-freezer from Comet. Plus they got Hierro an iPod and a laptop, and sorted him out with a bank account and council tax payment book.

The Spaniard still had one more request, says Hockin: 'He wanted to know where he could buy fresh fish and meat, so we took him to Bolton Market one day and said, "Here you go." He speaks English, so he's gone back since on his own and been absolutely fine.'

So, a grown adult 'managed to buy some fish'. He can buy fish *and* do a sliding tackle? Truly, he is a prince among men.

Except, even with the gofers, he is not treated as a prince. In fact, the whole gofer concept often falls woefully short. Do the gofers actually bow and scrape? (How does one actually scrape?) And do they refer to the player by his correct title – viz. 'my liege'? Are the players carried about in sedan chairs? And, if not, why not? These are busy people – busy, busy, busy. They have to run around for almost two entire hours of a morning. And they have to work on Saturdays.

Premiership footballers are also, objectively, better than the rest of us – like a 4-4-2 formation of Platonic philosopher kings. Are their shorts of purest silk and their boots of finest gold? Have they each an army of mighty and ruthless vassals sent into the local community to beat the locals and extract due tribute in the form of coin? Why fucking not?

And what of the constitutional issues? At the moment, the constitution places the Queen as ultimate arbiter of power. In theory, as head of the government and the judiciary and commander- in-chief of the armed forces, this feudal relic can dissolve Parliament and impose her will on her subjects. But has the Queen ever curled a free kick in from 30 yards? I've never seen her do it. I think it would be more satisfactory all round if Frank Lampard had the job.

For Lampard and St George! Or that goalie everyone called Safe Hands.

Football pundits

At the 2006 World Cup, Martin O'Neill took the *Mumbling-Idiot Football Pundit Rulebook* and ripped it to bits – as befits a man who drinks petrol for fun and spent his downtime stalking the studio like an avenging justice, casually breaking stuff and seething with barely suppressed bestial rage at an ignorant, heartless world.

O'Nails, officially the world's hardest man, rocked the *Match of the Day* universe by seeking to pass on genuine knowledge and insight. He also eschewed the cardinal rule of exhibiting a general, false bonhomie; instead he seemed actively to despise his colleagues.

The former Celtic and now Aston Villa manager was never happier than when taking former England captain Alan Shearer to pieces on live TV. Toying with the ex-Toon striker as the gods are wont to do with men, O'Nails said Shearer's name had 'cropped up' at his recent interview for the job of England manager. 'Have you worked with Shearer?' asked the FA. 'Would you consider doing so?'

'I said no. Now that I have [worked with you], the answer would still be no.'

At half-time during the Germany–Portugal play-off for third place, O'Neill recounted Hollywood screenwriter William Goldman's famous remark that 'nobody knows anything'. Not seeking to alienate viewers, he was careful to explain exactly who Goldman was – mentioning his most famous screenplay, *Butch Cassidy and the Sundance Kid*. Lineker and the two Alans looked a little shellshocked. Shearer said the story was as boring as the game's first half. O'Neill shot back with the veiled but tragically unfinished: 'Well, maybe you should spend more time watching films and less . . .'

When Ian Wright interrupted O'Nails as he was explaining the finer points of a Holland v Serbia & Montenegro game with, 'So, you like to talk about S&M? Eh? Eh?' O'Neill looked a small step away from chinning him.

As a manager, you could imagine him stamping his authority on the dressing room by freaking out the players – by standing up in front of the chalkboard and arguing . . . with himself. 'You want to spend more time watching football and less time shouting at yourself . . . Yeah? Well, fuck you.' And so on.

Where was I? Oh, yes – with the exception of O'Nails, pundits are generally idiots. Football punditry is a world where Peter Schmeichel, asked to explain why a Blackburn Rovers player received two yellow cards but was not sent off, will oblige by repeatedly shouting throughout the action replay: 'Look at that! Look at that!'

The same standards applied to other areas of media punditry would have financial reporters on *Newsnight* saying: 'The Bank of England, though, you've got to say, they're a different class. They've got everything. Interest rates. Pace. Lots of money. Sensational.' Or authors turning up half-cut on *Start the Week* and saying: 'Books? Yeah.' (Actually, in the case of *Start the Week*, that would be an improvement.)

Ian Wright, for instance, loves England like only a nutter loves England. He made his name as a pundit during ITV's coverage of the 1998 World Cup, where he spent England's rollercoaster second-round defeat to Argentina sulking (1–0 Argentina); jumping up and down while grinning (1–1); jumping up and down while shouting randomly generated vowels (1–2); standing with both hands wedged firmly into his armpits, refusing to speak (2–2); sticking his bottom lip out like a six-year-old (England defeated on penalties).

His greatest moment at the Beeb was his reaction to England's first defeat in 473 years to Northern Ireland. Asked for the in-depth analysis he was paid to give, he just said: 'I don't want to talk about it.'

In Germany, he was rarely used for games not involving England. Presumably as he'd only say things like: 'You'll have to ask someone else because I don't give one. Come on England!'

Foot spas

According to a recent survey, by October 2004 Britons had spent £450 million on foot spas. One in five adults owned one – but not a single one had ever been used (probably). Don't ask me who the fuck works this out or why – maybe it's what the people who set pub quizzes do in the daytime? – but it was in a newspaper so possibly a fact.

But at what point did these people feel they might need something full of hot water to put their feet in that wasn't the bath? Or, if you must, a bowl? It's like using the normal sink to wash your hands but having another, special basin just in case you fancy giving your pits a bit of a rinse.

Other useless items filling up people's cupboards include sandwich toasters and breadmakers. We've got £3.1 billion in useless goods under our collective stairs. What amazing fucking idiots we are. Stick that lot on eBay all in one go and we could probably bring down the economy.

Three-quarters of adults admitted having spent an average of £73 on such items. Presumably the other quarter are the ones who sold it to them and are sitting on a beach in the Maldives laughing like drains. Also, that's the average: so, if, say, 40 people only wasted a fiver, some poor bastard's got £2720 of shitty, useless tat to deal with. That's a lot of trouser presses.

Sandwich toasters are foul, Satanic tempters. They seem like a great idea right up to the point you produce your first cheese toastie and the cheese is hot enough to kill you and melts a hole in your hand.

Breadmakers are just complete and utter bastards. You assemble the eight trillion ingredients and leave it overnight as instructed – to be lulled to sleep by what sounds like someone being beaten senseless by a marine all night long. Look, it was a fucking present, all right, and we smashed it with a hammer and threw it out of an upstairs window. I'd advise you to do the same.

Free CD gunk

What is it? Where do they get it from? Is it bat-sperm? Is it hellspawn? Is it mined by infants? What is it?

'Funky', the word, as applied to anything except a musical genre

A Cityboy being shown around a sleek urban bachelor pad, on spying a particular 'feature', will say: 'Yah, funky. Okay.' A stripped-pine bar-club filled to bursting with vacuous ball-aches will call itself The Funky Monkey. A new handbag with a slightly unusual buckle? That's funky. So too is a reasonably colourful mug.

So forget any earlier associations (adj. from the French *'funquer'* meaning 'to give off smoke' through to 'being enticingly odorous' and on to 'being rhythmically badass'). Now we must presumably imagine James Brown backsliding across some varnished floorboards holding a chrome cafetière and going: 'Urrgh!' With Funkadelic all sitting on little stools behind the breakfast bar.

And how 'funky' is that?

David Furnish getting tough on crime

I want to love David Furnish – he's a professional hanger-on who loves indie, which is cool. But then he must start with all the talking.

When *ES* magazine asked him, 'What would you do if you were mayor [of London] for the day?' he replied: 'I would take a much harder line on crime.'

How hard a line he might take was left undisclosed. Maybe Mayor Furnish would stalk the streets of London in body armour, tracking down drug-dealers and giving them a taste of justice with his cold .38. I now always imagine David Furnish laughing ferociously into the night sky as he aims a flamethrower at the villainous vermin of the streets – perhaps muttering: 'How's this for a candle in the wind, you fucks?' But maybe that's just me.

G

Gadget bores

William Morris said you should have nothing in your home that is not either beautiful or useful. So I wonder what he would make of boring bastards crapping on about their new sat-nav handheld spazz-top.

GADGET BORE: Look, it shows you all the streets and tells you where to turn.

WILLIAM MORRIS: But you've been doing that journey every weekday for four years. You already know the way. Also, this wallpaper's a bit shit.

GADGET BORE: Shows you where the nearest shoe shops are. You know, for if you need, erm, laces. Do you want to see my iPod playlist?

WILLIAM MORRIS: Cobblers to your iPod playlist. That IKEA table? It's bollocks.

If further proof were needed that electronic gizmos are just a way of filling the void, it is that the magazine for gadget bores is called *Stuff*. That's not even a proper name. What are you interested in? Stuff. That's just stupid.

Mecca for gadget bores is Akihabara in Tokyo – or 'Electric Town' – which the guidebooks describe as a dense maze of neon straight out of *Blade Runner* with electronic widgets so amazing you will probably want to sign up to be turned into an android.

However, if you go to Akihabara, you will find it's more like a really, really big branch of Dixon's where everything is in Japanese. The mutating neon could usefully all carry the slogan NOTHING TO SEE HERE. New mobile phones that aren't out here yet? Guess what: they look just like mobile phones that are out here yet. That is, not, at the end of the day, when it comes down to it, very interesting at all.

Later, emerging into a dimly lit sidestreet, you will almost be run over by what looks like a Japanese Nick Cave driving the smallest car you have ever seen.

George Galloway, unfair pillorying of

George Galloway has been the victim of woeful aspersion and mighty deprecation. He has been sore detracted with muck-raking, mudslinging obloquy and scandal. The mockers have mocked their mock of mockery like mocking mocksters of mock. There has been calumny and also smear. But leotard me no more leotard. I say: ENOUGH!

For, as Galloway himself was keen to point out in an interview in the *Oldie*, he always, *always* gives of his best. 'So if you're asked to be a cat, be the best cat you can.' So he licked at Rula Lenska's hands like a submissive, like he was her lick-spittle, licking? What of it? He gave it a good go.

And who – what sort of curmudgeon – cannot draw pleasure from an evening watching 'Gorgeous' George Galloway in his jim-jams, puffing on a stogie while Jodie Marsh chats about fisting? *Who?*

He was only doing his best. If you're going to take a dislike to Preston, do your best. Don't just mumble some mealy-mouthed nonsense about his silly little ska tunes. Call him a 'plutocrat'. You know, like Stalin. Oh no, hang on, Galloway called the collapse of Stalinism 'the greatest catastrophe of my life'. Which must make Preston worse than Stalin. Preston out of the Ordinary Boys is worse than Stalin. Preston out of woeful mod-ska also-rans the Ordinary Boys – they of the execrable 'Boys Will Be Boys' and the jumping up and the jumping down – is worse than Stalin. Now, *that's* making an effort.

And if you want to denounce Iraqi trade unionists, do your best. Others may see people who risked their lives opposing the murderous Ba'ath regime – brave, principled people who are now being murdered by Islamist/Ba'athist insurgents – as enemies of religious reaction. No matter. You should focus on the small minority who supported the war, and denounce them all as 'quislings'. What of it? If you're going to take issue, take issue. Really get stuck in there. And if you simply must have a go at Galloway, do your best. Don't go on about the cat thing – it doesn't matter. Don't criticise his low attendance at the Commons – he's quite justified in saying that the impact he can make there is limited.

Don't keep making vague accusations of financial impropriety you can't prove. That's just stupid – and, ironically, it's making him rich on the libel winnings.

You would probably want to focus mainly on his support for despotic regimes. And don't just lazily accuse him of toadying up to the indefatigable Saddam Hussein. Do it properly: point out that he toadied up to *all* the Husseins. Including Uday, the man Egyptian President Hosni Mubarak labelled a 'psychopath'. (Well, he had just seen him murder his father's personal valet at the dinner table: first beating him repeatedly with a cane, then finishing him off with an electric carving knife.)

Here is George chatting to Uday at a meet and greet in Iraq:

GALLOWAY: Your Excellency, very, very nice to see you again.

HUSSEIN: (*replying in English*) Nice to see you.

GALLOWAY: It's almost one year since we met. How are you?

HUSSEIN: You seem in very good health.

GALLOWAY: I lost weight, I'm very happy about that.

HUSSEIN: (*replying in Arabic*) Yes, I see you've lost some weight, so I think it's better.

GALLOWAY: It's good, but unfortunately I'm losing my hair also.

HUSSEIN: Yes, I've noticed, especially on the left side. But I'm one step ahead of you, I've quit cigars, you are still smoking.

GALLOWAY: People of good taste either used to be, or still are, smokers of Havanas.

HUSSEIN: That's why we have opened this subject so we can call you to quit smoking.

GALLOWAY: I'd like you to know that we are with you until the end.

He was as well. So you shouldn't accuse of him of lacking stamina or being disloyal.

Geographically inaccurate racism

At school, pop sensation Darius would get called 'Saddam'. In fact, his father is Iranian – only one letter and one very long war away from accuracy.

Radio One Asian DJ Nihal once got sent a charming picture with the words 'Go back to India' written on with an arrow pointing to the Indian in the picture. The picture, carefully snipped from a magazine, portrayed a Peruvian Indian.

If people do have to be racist, do they also need to be so droolingly braindead that they can't tell which ethnic group they are rabidly insulting? Maybe they should make special racist maps.

Ginster's Buffet Bars

The Ginster's Buffet Bar purports to be a bar of buffet, a buffet in a bar, but it's nothing but a bar of cheap lies.

Unless, somewhere out there, there are people being heartily satisfied with a buffet whose sole foodstuff is coleslaw mixed with creamed cheese.

I'm not saying Ginster's could or should put everything in there that you would expect to find at an adequate buffet. All I'm actually saying is: if you don't know what words mean, DON'T FUCKING USE THEM.

Or you could get a dictionary.

Global warming sceptics

If you're worried about global warming, you must be some kind of pussy. The ice caps aren't melting. There aren't more forest fires or old people dying in heatwaves. The seas aren't getting substantially warmer – and even if they are, which they aren't, the fish are absolutely loving it!

We know this because of a small cabal of scientists who believe in big business more than life itself and who, funnily enough, often receive funding from ExxonMobil.

These 'sceptics' get everywhere: by the President's ear; near to big business; on news programmes keen to stir up 'debate' and show they're not biased against frothing nutjobs.

In 2004, Myron Ebell, a director at the Competitive Enterprise Institute, told Radio 4's *Today* programme that global warming fears were 'ridiculous, unrealistic and alarmist' and that European countries were 'not out to save the world, but out to get America'.

In 2005, White House official – and former oil industry lobbyist – Philip Cooney was found to have filed reports on the link between greenhouse gases and climate change with dozens of amendments that all exaggerated scientific doubts. That was before he left the White House for a job with . . . ExxonMobil! Could you make it up? Probably, but there's no need.

All this despite the fact that virtually all other climatologists – the ones without links to the fossil fuels industry – now predict that even a conservative rise of 2.1 degrees will probably result in tens of millions of people losing their lives. Even a suppressed Pentagon report warned of a danger that far outstripped terrorism, mega-droughts, famine. Thankfully, President Bush responded immediately.

By standing proud alongside the British PM and declaring: 'We need to know more about it.'

More about what? You can see how this thing will develop in years to come . . . But Myron, I've just put a page of A4 paper in sunlight and watched it spontaneously combust. 'Sheer alarmism – we've always had hot days!' But Myron, a herd of gazelles has just elegantly pranced past the window of our London studio. 'Er, yes, they're mine. I brought them along with me especially. That big one – he's called Dave and he likes crisps.'

And Myron, now you're being swept into the skies by a freak tornado. 'What a funny thing you are! I see nothing extraordinary in this turn of events . . . It's great up here! Hi George, good to see you! Pretty breezy, I know! You what? You want to know more about it? It's okay, I'm on it!!'

Zac Goldsmith

Great news: we've got Zac on board! Following the lead of Cameron's Tories, we too have realised the need for some wafer-thin green credentials. So, great news: we've got Zac on board! *Is It Just Me, or Have We Got Zac on Board?* That's what this book should have been called.

Handsome, dashing, good-looking and very, very, very rich, he's the playboy gambler with the cruel, weird father who shouted, 'OUT! OUT! OUT!' into David Mellor's face like a pissed Trot student after standing against him in the 1997 election. Honestly, he's so exciting, I almost feel like writing a series of novels about him – like Horatio Hornblower, but campaigning against leaving the lights on rather than against Napoleon. (Although I bet Napoleon was a leaving-the-lights-on kind of guy anyway.)

Of course, *Ecologist* editor Zac is less an actual person, more a big sign saying, 'We care about your future.' For this reason, David Cameron has got Zac to head up his new environment and quality-of-life policy group. Of course, the Tory Party has historically regarded the environment as something to cover in tarmac and then privatise. But people can change and, luckily, this renowned environmental campaigner would not simply let himself be used as a tokenistic figurehead for that lot. He's better than that. Just look at him!

Oh no, hang on. That's exactly what he would do. But then, Goldsmith's environmentalism is not really of a stripe to make the Tory heartland shudder and shake. In a recent *Times* piece, he was asked how he thought we should do our bit. 'It's not about living like a monk,' he assured us. 'The single most important thing is to buy local food.'

Bloody wow! How easy is that? No wonder Cameron's such a fan: when it comes to saving the planet from environmental collapse, the absolute number-one priority, the single most important factor, above everything else, is visiting a farmers' market.* I thought things were scarier than that; I thought the Earth was melting and WE WERE ALL GOING TO FUCKING DIE. But clearly I was wrong. We just need to buy courgettes with the soil still on them.

*Oh, and also not letting the kids eat junk, as expressed by Zac's ex-model wife Sheherazade in a gushing portrait in a glossy newspaper supplement: 'I'm not fanatical. One of the children might occasionally eat a KitKat at a party.' Only one of the children, mind – let's not go crazy. Couldn't they have a finger each?

Good and evil as demonstrated in the marketing of automotive transport

Now, more than ever, we need a firm moral compass to guide us through our treacherous age. Let us be thankful, then, for car ads.

Some cars are repositories of goodness that make you feel honest, real and true – like getting emotional about the memory of *Brokeback Mountain* while sitting in a hedge.

Other cars, very different cars, make you feel dark, cruel and sleazy, like you're eating a dirty burger for breakfast in preparation for a day's gunrunning.

Very much in the former camp, the new Nissan Note understands that having kids is the greatest adventure in the world (it's not, though – skydiving is: it's over quicker, and people don't clam up when you talk about it). Billboards show this vehicle of virtue speeding through the French countryside with a kite flying behind in the clear blue skies.

Alternatively, if the idea of going on holiday with children makes you feel nauseous, there's Joss Ackland's doom-laden voiceover and 'Antichrist Superstar' Marilyn Manson creaking out the Eurythmics' 'Sweet Dreams' (it's an ironic cover – it's not about having sweet dreams at all!) as the new Fiat Punto bursts through some weird, gloopy glass walls in a spooky nocturnal cityscape. The subtle message is: you'd better be one sick puppy to drive this baby. This Fiat Punto. Or you might prefer something more in keeping with Cameron's Britain. 'Go Beyond,' says Land-Rover. Appreciate nature, the hills, the dales, the misty moors . . . by driving across a misty moor, in a Land-Rover! Because the Land-Rover is the only off-road vehicle that naturally occurs in nature. Land-Rovers are actively beneficent – like sharing cherries with an Eskimo would be good. Maybe the Eskimo has never had cherries before, and you'll laugh and laugh and laugh.

Or you might prefer to fuck that shit up. In which case, here comes the Predator Jeep – less a vehicle, more an abattoir on wheels. Recent billboard posters showed a pair of these dark beasts standing with quite alarming amounts of menace in some shadowy, rubbish-strewn arches in the dead of night. This image appeals perfectly to everyone who wants their vehicle to carry really quite strong connotations of assault.

With its 'beyond the clouds' campaign, Volvo claimed, somewhat controversially, to be 'For Life' – which is very sweet of them. As though anyone would claim to be 'For Lingering, Painful Death'! Oh no, hang on: here's Audi. TV ads for the RS4 portrayed the new model as a black widow spider bleakly devouring rival cars. Explains Bill Scott, Audi's business director at creative agency BBH: 'The car was described as a predatory animal, one that shows no sympathy, no mercy . . .'

So the choice is clear: you can drive a car that's truly at one with the cosmos, that will make you feel like the Buddha on a mellow tip. Or you can drive the trenchcoat Mafia's crackmobile. At least until these two eternal opposing forces come crashing together in a final titanic struggle that will see the skies rent asunder, the ground shake and the seas get decidedly choppy.

At this point, the lamb will lie down with the lion. The shepherd will lie down with his flock. It will rain cats and it will rain also dogs. The beetles will lie down with the monkeys. The Green will lie down with The Black. Everyone is lying down. Brm brm.

Gravity-defying cream

Clinique's Anti-Gravity Firming Lift Cream is marketed to women as preventing the inevitable downward effects of the ageing process: 'A lightweight oil-free formula [it] helps firm up skin instantly and over time [helping] to erase the look of lines as it tightens. Anti-Gravity Firming Lift Lotion by Clinique restores supple cushion to timethinned skin.'

Of course it does.

Things known to science to defy gravity: aeroplanes, missiles, space rockets. Things known to science to not, generally speaking, defy gravity: magazines, biscuits (not even very light wafers), trousers, cream.

Gravy train, the

Transport laid on for bastards by The Man.

Not to be confused with: the gravy boat, which is laid on by Your mam; 'Love Train', which was laid down by the O'Jays. To be confused with: Virgin Trains.

Philip Green

All business reports concerning 'the high street' have to mention Philip Green at least twice. Why do I know who Philip Green is? He owns BHS. So what? He may buy M&S. Or he may not. So what?

At the end of the day, he's just some rich bloke who owns a lot of shops: but this is not interesting. Neither is it news: 'BONG! Rich bloke owns shops.' See? Rubbish. For some reason, though, the media is obsessed with telling us the behind-the-scenes action on the high street, as if it were a soap opera or remotely interesting in some way. Christmas 2004 saw us constantly updated on whether today was a 'good' or 'bad' day on the high street – as if Christmas would be utterly ruined for us all if Debenhams' profits were slightly lower than expected.

Sainsbury's dip in the share of the groceries market also provided endless fascination, with company spokespeople obliging media efforts to make the dull interesting by referring to their efforts to sell some more stuff as a 'dogfight', as if they were just a hair's breadth away from launching a squadron of Lancasters to fire-bomb Morrison's.

The thing is, who fucking cares? Even if one high-street chain does close, so what? Another will open in its place. There is not going to be any shortage on the high street of bastards hawking tat – of that we can be fairly sure.

If you are interested, there is a readily available source: the *Financial Times*. But really, don't bother, it's incredibly tedious. Quite considerately, they even print it on different coloured paper so you don't wander into a newsagent's and mistake it for something interesting.

Guinness Book of World Records

The Guinness world record for holding the most Guinness world records is held by Ashrita Furman of New York – including Longest Milk Bottle Head Balancing Walk. This fucking freak walked 130.3 kilometres with a fucking milk bottle on his empty fucking head.

Furman also holds the Milk Crate Balancing On Chin record, the Fastest Pogo Stick Jumping Up The CN Tower record, and the Orange Nose Push – Fastest Mile record (24 min 36 sec. Woo! Woo!). Since the 1970s, he has set more than 80 Guinness world records. As of November 2004, he held 20: this means that people see these pointless records and then aspire to break them; presumably saying things like '434 games of hopscotch in a 24-hour period? Ea-sy!'

Ashrita puts his amazing success down to his daily meditation regime. After discovering the spiritual teachings of Sri Chinmoy, he renamed himself Ashrita in 1974. His real name is Keith (you couldn't actually make this up). guinnessworldrecords. com explains: 'Ashrita is on a spiritual mission and uses his inner spirit to perform the record-breaking feats. Under the instruction of his guru he says he's been able to attain a new level of self-transcendence – meaning he can overcome the physical pain and mental anguish of his testing record attempts.'

Didn't fancy using your 'inner spirit' and 'self-transcendence' for, say, the attainment of world peace then, Keith?

The book – the highest-selling copyright title of all time, at more than one hundred million copies (haven't all these people considered going for a walk or something?) – was set up (in the 1950s) and edited by Norris McWhirter (with his brother Ross), who was not far off being a fascist. He was forever attacking CND, funding strike-breakers and defending sportspeople who went to South Africa during apartheid. A rabid anti-European, McWhirter was caught altering the 1975 edition book proofs just before they were sent to the printers, adding: 'World's Best Country: England' and 'World's Worst Country: the Boche'.

Also, more seriously, he was responsible for long-running children's programme *Record Breakers*. Which featured far, far too much tap-dancing.

H

Handball

People would take the Olympics a lot more seriously if they didn't include handball. They're just throwing a ball to each other like a bunch of kids. It's just stupid.

And if you win, how do you look, say, the marathon gold medallist in the eye? . . .

HANDBALL GOLD MEDALLIST: What did you get your gold for?

MARATHON GOLD MEDALLIST: I ran 26 miles in extreme heat.

HANDBALL GOLD MEDALLIST: Great. I threw a ball back and forth for a bit with someone about two feet away from me. Then I had a bath.

MARATHON GOLD MEDALLIST: Big twat.

'Hard-working families'

All through the 2005 election campaign, there was only one kind of family that mattered: one with its nose constantly rubbing against the grindstone.

At the 2004 Labour conference, Tony Blair set out his stall, envisaging 'a 21st-century Britain . . . where hard-working families who play by the rules are not going to see their opportunities blighted by those that don't'.

But, but . . . I didn't know there were rules about working hard. Why didn't you tell me earlier?

A better life awaits if you continue jumping through the hoops, ideally only popping home after work for 15 minutes before taking out your minicab all night. After that, feel the satisfaction of helping provide – to quote the other main conference slogan – 'A Better Future For All'. It's a poignant, beautiful idea.

No it's not! This never happens! Not ever! Not even one time! In reality, families who work so hard they barely see each other mainly provide better futures for divorce lawyers, builders of one-bed accommodation and breweries who do tinnies. Considering Blair's ideas about pushing the working age up to 70, it unfortunately looks like there's gold at the end of the rainbow like there's gold at the end of your arse.

Hare Krishnas

Hare, hare krishna
Hare hare
Hare bollocks
Bollocks
Bollocks krishna
Hare bollocks
Bollocks hare
(REPEAT)

'Having one of those days?' advertising

Having one of those days? Someone at the office giving you the hump? Got rained on at lunch? Hair? Him? And that? Don't worry, girls. Just relax on a big, snuggly sofa with a steaming mug of hot chocolate (lo-cal, natch!) and think about scrummy guys, etc., etc. With adverts for products aimed primarily at females aged 20–35, you can virtually hear the brains of lumpen creatives filling in the cliché boxes with a big lazy tick: okay . . . vulnerable, likes snuggling up, 'having one of those days?', shake it all off with . . . bubbles, thinking about scrummy guys, lo-cal hot chocolate . . . pamper pamper, more hot chocolate, mmmm, steamy and warm, mmmm, bubbles, luxuriant bubble bath absolutely everywhere . . . 'having one of those days?' . . . more bubbles. Candles! Bish bash bosh. Right! Lunchy?

Health-food entrepreneurs

Wholemeal breadheads.

Hedge-fund boys

In a get-rich-quick world, hedge-fund boys get rich the quickest. How they spend their cash influences whole lower stratospheres of vacuous consumption. Currently, 'hedge-fund boys prefer to splash their cash ordering cocktails for thousands of pounds a glass' at bars with names like Umbaba. 'Umbaba, Umbaba, that's how it goes,' they sing, à la Oliver Twist.

If professional watchers of the super-rich are to be believed, these 'lords of havoc' (the *New Statesman*) drive the tastiest motors, eat at the fastest restaurants, swim in the wettest pools and stalk London and New York like Knights of the Bastard Table. The *Sunday Telegraph* estimated that in 2005, around 200 to 300 UK hedge-fund managers carved up $4.2 billion of pure profit between them. In 2005, according to the US *Institutional Investor Magazine*, the top 25 hedge-fund managers earned an average of $251 million each. The amount of money the world's hedge-funders handle could be as much as $1.5 trillion.

So how do they do it? Well, it's tricky. Even people who understand economics do not understand hedge-funds.

These secretive, privately owned investment companies are massive – if they were a country, they would be the eighth-biggest on the planet. But it would be a country you could not visit or even see: hedge-funds, of which there are reckoned to be 8,000 in the world, mostly based in the US, 'fly under the radar' (CNN) and cannot be regulated – mainly because regulators don't understand what's going on; even though hedge-funds may be responsible for over half the daily turnover of shares on the London Stock Market alone. After looking into the matter, the Financial Services Authority, Britain's regulatory body, said: 'Chuff this for a game of soldiers.' It's very much like *Deal or No Deal*: people claim to know what's going on, and superficially there would appear to be some logic, but actually they're making it up as they go along.

I've looked into it and have to say it sounds a lot like internet gambling for the super-rich. Investors must place a minimum of a million dollars into a fund; at enormous risk, the fund managers take these tax-haven stashes and place stakes on anything and everything – FTSE100 companies, commodities, options, stocks in developing countries, anything that might shoot up in price or can be made to . . . Often they will take the tax-haven dosh and borrow against it – that is, borrowing money in order to gamble it; which is exactly the sort of responsible activity that should remain unregulated. When the hedge-funders lose their shirts (one Japanese fund lost $300 million in a week), it's okay because they've got more shirts. But often, other losers – like Colombia or Egypt (both of which saw their stock markets slump after the hedge-funders parked their mobile casinos in them) – don't have any more shirts. Which makes riding with hedge-funders quite a bareknuckle ride, with no shirt on.

In 2006, the 'hedgehogs' came into the light with Hedgestock, a festival at Knebworth that mixed bands and utterly incomprehensible business seminars ('Incubator Alligator? – sowing the seeds, but do they stay for a cigarette?'). It even had its own jingle, which sounded like the worst thing ever. To the tune of 'Sex Bomb', it went: 'Hedgestock, Hedgestock, groovy Hedgestock, a little bit of business and a whole lot of rock . . .' And you thought Glastonbury had gone 'a bit corporate'.

Contrary to initial feelings of disappointment, the fact that this event was headlined by The Who was actually quite fitting. In their pomp, The Who would enter town, take over a hotel, drive a Rolls-Royce into a swimming pool, stick bombs down the toilets, smash up the furniture and nail every piece of wood to the ceiling. Then, when things looked like getting sticky, they'd move on, leaving others to clean up their mess. For 'hotels', merely read 'emerging economies'. Perhaps replacing 'I'm a Boy' with 'I'm a Hedge-Fund Boy'.

Anyway, these festivals, which are also victory parades over the assimilation of the counter-culture, could really take off. You could have one specially for analysts, called

Analstock. And one for stockbrokers, called Stockstock. And, of course, the V Festival.

High-profile local businessmen

Every town has one: the local boy made good who always has his face in the local papers and plastered over buses. And it's always carpets, for some reason. He drives around like the king of the world, when he is in actuality the king of low-cost carpet retail in south Leeds, which isn't the same thing.

The nation's foremost high-profile local businessman is possibly Bruce Robertson of Trago Mills, the chain across Devon and Cornwall that resembles pound shops taking over an aircraft hangar. Bruce's father, Mike, who founded the Trago empire, had gargoyles made of local and national politicians he didn't like. Upholding this proud family tradition, Bruce supports imperial weights and measures by putting big boards up outside Trago stores saying 'Brussels be damned, We sell sprouts by the lb'. He has been, perhaps unsurprisingly, a major funder of UKIP.

Bruce has even paid for advertorials in the local paper putting forward his singular points of view. In 1988, one screed was censured by the Advertising Standards Authority for inciting homophobic violence: he advocated 'the castration of all homosexual perverts' – presumably with a pair of Trago-purchased shears. So, Trago is unlikely to be selling discount buttplugs anytime soon.

Reflecting the Robertsons' popularity among local people, when the Newton Abbot Trago Mills store went up in smoke in October 2004, e-mails flooded into the BBC Radio Devon website.

Nick from Brixham said: 'I'd heard the fire has caused £5 million of improvements. I suppose the charcoal barbecue bricks section will do a roaring trade in the next few weeks.' Peter from Exeter added: 'Poor old Trago. I was very familiar with the store. Shame it happened. On another note, if anyone has any interest in buying 500 fake Xmas trees – slightly blackened – then I'll be at Marsh Barton carboot this Sunday.'

James from Newton Abbot reckoned: 'I used to work there and it was rubbish.'

Ames, meanwhile, had clearly conducted some sort of survey: 'Everyone I have spoken to is really pleased the place has burnt down.'

And after everything Brucie had done for the local community, too. Presumably it's all a conspiracy by uncastrated gay Boche?

Hip holidays

'From the cliff tops of Mykonos,' the *Guardian* informs us, 'to the beaches of Mallorca, a quiet revolution is under way . . .' That's right. Revolution is in the air. But it isn't very loud. Can you hear it blowin' in the zephyr-like breeze? Was that it? Not sure. It's a whisper. But it's growing louder. Soon it will be a muffled roar.

'Today's savvy travellers demand cutting-edge design, lavish spas, infinity pools, sunrise yoga classes and sunset chill-out sessions with big-name DJs.'

So where to begin? According to a 2006 'Travel Trends' piece in *The Times*, Shanghai is now the 'ultimate hip urban hangout' for 'Gucci-loving City types'. Alaska is hot stuff with 'wannabe 007s with egos to flush, Armani snowsuits and

£170,000 a week to burn'. (007 wannabes?) The Indian state of Uttaranchal is 'set to take over from Nepal for moneyed, trend-conscious spiritual types taking a break from their busy-busy lives'. Hip holidaymakers are the leaders of the Gucci-loving, wannabe-007, trend-conscious spiritual pack.

This form of travel writing may seem new, but it's actually in the great tradition of Marco Polo, the legendary medieval Italian trader whose *Travels* detailed his literally ground-breaking exploration of Central Asia, passing through scalding deserts, desolate steppes and precipitous mountains to become the first Westerner to encounter China, then under the rule of the Mongol emperor Kublai Khan. On returning, his tales were so bizarre that many believed them to be fabrications: 'Chan-Ghain-Fu is a city of the province of Manji, the inhabitants of which are idolaters, subjects of the Great Khan, and use his paper money. They gain their living by trade and manufacture, and are wealthy. They weave tissues of silk and gold.' This playground for the well-connected was recently blessed by Philippe Starck's diva-defining new venture. Marble, gilt and deep-red velvet feature throughout, adding to the drama of it all and creating a very decadent space. 'The province of Tholoman lies towards the east, and its inhabitants . . . burn the bodies of their dead; and the bones that are not reduced to ashes, they put into wooden boxes, and . . . conceal them in caverns of the rocks, in order that no wild animal may disturb them. As the sun goes down, the big-name DJs speed things up – I particularly marvelled at Julesy – and exotic cocktails are served. Saucy sophistication to a tee!

'In a western direction from Painfu there is a large and handsome fortress named Thaigin, which is said to have been built, at a remote period, by a king who was called the Golden King. The sun-kissed terraces are great for power-lunching or just people-watching; plus there's the best lifestyle gym in the region. I've been there. And, unless I'm very much mistaken, you have not. Me. Not you.'

Hip hotels

Hip hotels might have boxy rooms, bad beds and shrill staff seemingly beamed in from another planet. But there's a great selection of Latin chill CDs.

- At Milan's über-trendy Hive Hotel, beekeeping is the theme. Visitors can join in the beekeeping themselves or just relax, put their feet up and let the staff take care of the bees.
- At Notting Hill's boutique hotel BOEulk, they've got an eight-year-old girl on a swing. Sometimes she sings 'Son Of A Preacherman'. Sometimes not.
- Every room in West Hollywood's Barker Ranch features a mural of a different member of the Manson family rendered in the blown-up-cartoon style of Roy Lichtenstein. Sheets are flecked with fake blood. To further resemble a cult of homicidal White Power hippies, all staff have tiny swastikas tattooed on to their foreheads (guests can get their own done too).
- Berlin's superb Hotel Hostel has knocked away the interior walls so guests effectively sleep in unisex dorms. Around the clock, the kitchen staff offer classic hostel fare like sausage 'n' beans and macaroni cheese.

Historical reconstructions

So you've devoted two years of your life to a prestige documentary series about Auschwitz. You've got hitherto unseen photographs, interviews with survivors, shedloads of CGI and a narrator with more authority than Charlton Heston. But there's still something missing. What if viewers think you're making it all up? It could happen. You've been reading all about this Irving guy.

So, obviously, you hire some actors to dress up in German uniforms and stand in a field (possibly in Poland) pointing meaningfully at a map. Ah, so *that's* what Nazis looked like. Cheers for that. Because I thought they just wore pinafores and cardies. That silly walk! It's mad!

The makers of the recent documentary *Munich: Mossad's Revenge* had the cunning wheeze of juxtaposing contemporary footage of Palestinian terrorist suspects assassinated by the Israeli secret service with reconstructions featuring actors who looked nothing like them. Unless you were pissed, squinting at them through tracing paper. Which is not something you do often. Any more.

During one revenge job, future Israeli prime minister Ehud Barak was obliged to dress as a woman to get close to his target. To illustrate that this *really happened*, the docudrama-makers recreated the event using the world's shittest transvestite, thus giving the impression that Mossad entrusted the biggest, riskiest operation in its obsessive mission to track down and eliminate its sworn enemies to Lily Savage.*

*We have been asked to make it absolutely clear that, to the best of our knowledge, Lily Savage has never worked for Mossad – neither as an agent nor as an agent of influence. Although they did try luring her away from ITV on at least one occasion.

Hollyoaks hunks

All that gel does at least make them more flammable.

Homophobic Christians

Casting around for the one true path in life, Christians often ask themselves: 'WWJD?' – 'What would Jesus do?' Apparently, he wouldn't 'make some stuff out of wood' or 'cure the sick', but would walk up and down the high street with a big placard reading 'GOD HATES FAGS'.

The 'Jesus as uptight, bigoted sociopath' reading of the Bible is proving incredibly popular with the world's rising band of evangelicals. Even the born-again movement's pre-eminent marketing arm The Alpha Course (which has seen over 1.5 million Brits pass through its doors) has raised hackles after Blairish founder Nicky Gumbel claimed the Bible 'makes it clear' that gays and lesbians need to be 'healed'. 'Although I strongly advise you not to say the word "healed" to them,' he once warned. 'They hate that word!' Sound advice.

Normal people flicking through The Good Book will find anti-gay sentiments quite tricky to unearth. The New Testament's supposed 'No To Homos' message basically boils down to Paul the Apostle's comments in Romans 1: 26–27 on the sins of the Gentiles – 'God gave them up unto shameful affections' – and depends on the translation of the mysterious Ancient Greek word '*arsenokoites*' (and I promise that's actually true) which might mean 'special gay friend' or possibly 'male temple prostitute' or even 'gigolo for rich women'. Now there's a solid bedrock for bigotry if ever we saw one.

For others, though, the Bible is just one big old book about hating queers; they're constantly finding startling new chapters like when Jesus, after healing the sick and helping the poor, draws together his disciples and tells them how God's vision embraces everyone – prostitutes, paupers, lepers, even tree-climbing tax inspectors . . . 'On hearing this, his disciples pauseth for a moment and said unto him, What about the gays, Lord? Jesus flincheth and spat, Oh no, not the gays. I don't like them, he ranteth. I don't like their white vests or their love of gaudy music. And I have it on the highest authority of a man down the tavern that there's a gay mafia running the Roman Empire. A man with another man? No way!

'Anyway, the lepers . . .'

In fact, the Big Bad Son Of God never mentions bum sex or any other gay-related issue even once, not even mutual masturbation. It's possible he planned on making his Big Speech Against The Gays right after Easter. We'll never know.

Horseracing tips

When it boils down to it, what you're being asked to do here is take financial advice off a gambler. Is that wise?

'Hot' collective cover shoots

Whenever magazines or colour supplements suffer crises of faith over whether they are still 'hot' or, in fact, 'not', they usually gather together a stellar array of undeniably hot, sometimes even hotter-than-hot, really actually quite burny-hot young things for a big old cover shoot that will jump off news-stands with an eye-grabbing headline like 'UK's Hippest Designers of Hip Stuff', '40 Hottest Writers Of Hot Books Under 40', 'The Hottest Human Rights Lawyers in Hotsville', 'The Britpack Take Off! Honestly! This Time It's True!',* or 'This Week's Hot Hollywood Hotties - In Their Hotpants!' Inside, the editor's letter will say: 'Can you feel the heat? Hot off the presses, here's the latest hot young things – they're hot like hot cats on a hot tin roof, like inappropriately hot soup on a hot summer's day, like hot cakes, hot tubs, hot potatoes and those hot flannels you get in Chinese restaurants. Hot! If things were any hotter around here ... oh, hang on ... I appear to be melting ... look at that, I'm actually melting! Aaaaargh!!!'

What everyone in these pictures should realise is that, as soon as the shutter clicks, they will start to cool. By the time they leave the studio, they will already only be 'warm'. In a year's time, nobody will remember even the slightest thing about them.

* Anyone partaking in a gathering referred to as a 'Britpack' might as well book an appointment with the DSS right away. Message to the world: the British aren't coming. Not now. Not ever.

Hotdesks

I can understand why you might want fewer desks than employees – to keep them 'motivated', that is, to create some kind of Hobbesian war of all against all, everyone doomed to insecurity and battling for scarce resources, never allowed to settle in one place and get the idea that they may have a job to come to tomorrow rather than being expelled at speed down a waste chute into a vacuum.

But do you have to make them hot as well? Is insecurity not enough that you have to fucking scald people? Jesus – actually burning your workers; it's positively barbaric.

'How I got my body back'

'I didn't eat anything.'

I

IKEA

When IKEA opened its new store in Edmonton, security guards were soon swamped by 6,000 shoppers grabbing at sofas and shouting 'Mine! Mine!' Many collapsed with heat exhaustion and 20 needed hospital treatment.

Of course, we're not suggesting the company was in any way responsible for the carnage. After all, a visit to IKEA is usually connected in my mind with inner calm, low blood pressure and a total absence of any thoughts of violence. No, hang on – I was thinking of the park.*

IKEA fucks with your head. All you want is some furniture: why do they want your sanity in return? The layout alone makes you feel like a lab rat. The stores are like psychoactive jigsaw puzzles with moving pieces, designed by a sick Swedish physicist with access to extra dimensions.

They have what look like short cuts between adjoining sections, allowing you to pop through a little walkway from one part of the store to another. But where you end up won't be where you were trying to get to, even if the store map said it would be. Worse, if you decide you were better off where you

*Incidentally, news reports on the Edmonton madness invariably noted a stabbing incident nearby – which was actually just a stabbing incident nearby. But for some it brought home the reality of what had just happened. One customer was quoted as saying: 'I turned around for one moment and someone stole my sofa. But at least I'm alive.' That's true, but what about the cheap sofa?

were, and pop back through the hole, you won't end up where you started, but in a different section again. Sometimes on a different floor altogether. In a different branch of IKEA.

There are some amazing statistics concerning IKEA. Apparently, 95% of all couples who move in together visit an IKEA within one month of moving in together. Of these, only 3% manage to buy the things they went there for, and 100% of them are related to the staff.

Young couples troop into IKEA with high hopes. They emerge as husks. And without having bought any furniture. IKEA still makes huge profits, however – all of which come from those funny Scandinavian hot dogs, meatballs and cakes they sell at the exit. And from light bulbs.

100% of people who visit IKEA buy light bulbs. IKEA do sell very cheap light bulbs. Everyone buys the light bulbs because a) they are so cheap, and b) they can't come away empty-handed having spent three hours of pain and panic in IKEA.

Everything in IKEA has funny names: you will find cupboards and beds called things like Dave and Philip, or Clare. Or Jurgen-Bergen-Heldenveldenstetser. If you try to buy any of them, you will be directed to a warehouse section where your item – a chair, say – is placed carefully on top of some 80-foot-high shelves. They will tell you that a man will come and get it down for you. The man will never come.

Improving the value of your property

Houses aren't for living in, they're for making cash out of. A good kitchen in a £100,000 property can add 10%. The introduction of a classic bathroom, that might cost just £4,000, can instantly add £1 million to the asking price.

But it's easy for beginners to make mistakes, so here we recommend our Twelve Quick Ways Not To Improve The Value Of Your Home – which is possibly going to be shown on the telly in the new year:

1. Ruthlessly cut out all natural light with ripped up rubbish sacks over the windows.
2. Scatter pigs' entrails around the landing.
3. Put a big sign on the door saying: 'Jesus loves this house.'
4. Shit on the floor.
5. Open up the hallway as a public bridleway.
6. Pretend it's built upon an ancient American Indian burial ground.
7. Disappear into the loft. And never come down.
8. In the middle of the living room, build a little wooden town for a 15-strong mouse troupe to scurry about in. Call this Mouse Town.
9. Redirect the sewers in any way whatsoever – they're probably connected in the right way anyway.
10. Take in waifs and strays.
11. Replace your cooker with a tiny plastic one made for children that doesn't even have any connections for the gas/electrics.
12. Burn the fucker to the ground.

Inconvenient truths

Al Gore's heart-warming global-warming documentary *An Inconvenient Truth* is a rotting bag of recycled compost. Okay, it's a film. We are told this talking-the-talk movie has been breaking US box-office records (although it's not clear which ones: possibly those for documentaries made by former vice-presidents). Of course, Gore's record on caring about the environment is second to none. It goes right back to the 80s. (He actually invented it, right before coming up with the internet and roller-blading.)

And since his failed presidential bid in 2000, Gore has been campaigning ceaselessly on behalf of the environment, urging everyone to reduce their carbon footprint before it's too late. In fact, there has only been one itsy-bitsy, blink-and-you'd-miss-it, tiny interregnum in Big Al's near-lifelong campaign for the environment: the years 1992 to 2000. During this short eight-year period, he was far quieter about the environment. So quiet that even those in the front row of the cinema auditorium, excellently positioned with regard to the surround-sound speakers, would be reduced to lip-reading lips that were not actually moving.

Oddly, this coincides almost exactly – no, completely exactly – with the time he was Vice-President of the God Bless the United States of A – in the Clinton administration that did slightly less than fuck all about reducing America's gargantuan carbon footprint.

Shame he took this particular period off from the environmentalism. Because he might have proved quite useful then.

Crikey! These inconvenient truths get everywhere, don't they?

Indian restaurants with irregular plates
Smaller portions yet larger prices than you get at Indian restaurants with round plates.

Square plates? Piss on them!

Actually, don't do that.

Innocent

It's like they're talking to babies. Innocent promise to never use 'weird stuff in our drinks. And we promise never to cheat at cards.' We're crazy guys, it says, but also we're crazy guys who don't fuck you over with chemicals when you fork out the best part of two quid for a small fruit drink; so we're pretty great people all round.' This whole tack is so twee it would make Heidi retch her berry smoothie all down her front, staining her one frock, which her grandad or whoever he is would then have to wash in a stream. And he's got logs to chop and all sorts. These are the sort of people who call food 'grub' and can't do anything without winking. Who winks? These bastards. No one else. They probably have 'Naughty person on board' stickers in their cars too. And these wacky, all-natural funsters are not even hippies. The crazy Innocent founders are ex-corporate types now turning over £75 million a year. So probably if you took them up on the offer to pop round to Fruit Towers ('Do pop by if you're ever in the area'), they might well not be there. They might be skiing.

You can even join the 'Innocent family' on their website – which has at least one thing going for it: come Christmas time, they're never going to be short of cranberries. Although they would get stupidly over-excited about the jokes out of the crackers. But do you really want to be in a family with people whose delivery vans are either made to look like cows or have fake grass all over them: 'When we're not busy making nice drinks, there's nothing we like better than doing up our vans and making them look sort of innocent. Naturally, this means that we now have a herd of cow vans and a couple of DGVs ("dancing grass vans" to the man on the street).'

Here's an idea: just deliver your drinks, quietly, in normal vans, then fuck off. If I want a fruit smoothie, I'll buy one. And that's it. I've got a family. I have friends. If I didn't, I'd even stoop to, say, joining a church before I'd organise my life around people who crush up fruit.

The Intel Inside tune

The four Intel Inside chimes (da-da da-ding!) are played somewhere in the world on average every five minutes.

Intel (da-da da-ding!) commissioned Austrian musician Walter Werzowa (the evil genius behind 1988 yodel-house hit 'Bring me Edelweiss') in 1994 to compose a three-second jingle that 'evoked innovation, troubleshooting skills and the inside of a computer, while also sounding corporate and inviting'.

More than a jingle, this is a 'sonic logo' that coincides with every mention of 'Intel' (da-da da-ding!). Which leads to some terrifying sonic pile-ups like a recent PC World advert in which the initial glowsticks-aloft trance jolted into the Intel logo (da-da da-ding!) before cutting back to the trance and ending with the traditional: 'Where in the world? PC World!' Wait till Intel gets outside. Then we'll be really fucked.

Interactive media

Seeing as the TV channels either get the licence fee or bombard us with a never-ending kaleidoscope of mind-numbing advertisements, and thus can by no means be considered skint, why aren't they paying professionals to make their programmes rather than asking me to fill in all the time? They are FOR-EVER canvassing my opinion on this, or getting me to speak out about that. E-mail us, they say, press the red button now, text, call in.

Why me? All I'm trying to do is watch the television, an activity I associate mostly with watching and listening and occasionally shouting and swearing and throwing crisps about, not sharing my opinions with an underwhelmed nation.

This is the very acme of modern democracy, though: don't bother going on a demonstration or writing to your MP, just text what's bothering you to *The Wright Stuff*. Same difference.

The programmes, by lazily reflecting back to us what we already know, can fill up time without having to go to the terrible trouble of getting people in who might, say, know what they're fucking talking about. Middle East road map irrevocably stalled? Just have a text poll; much easier than finding someone who could, say, identify Israel on a map. Don't worry about informing the viewers, they only want to see Z-list celebs wanking each other off anyway.

So, red buttons. Actually, no, while I think of it, 'shock-jock controversial radio phone-ins' – like John Gaunt on BBC London. That's public sector broadcasting, is it – an ill-informed fat bloke shouting at you?

And it doesn't matter how many times you and your mates press the red button during *Best Films Ever*, even if you run up a bill of £9,000: they will fiddle it and *Sex Lives of the Potato Men* will NEVER win.

Internet cafés

Particularly those with threadbare psychedelic carpets that do international calls in decrepit chipboard booths with no soundproofing, run by a money-grabbing misbegotten who probably owns half of Sandy Lane in Barbados purely from the profits he makes on printing charges, full of preppy Americans doing pretend higher-education courses sending long, banal e-mails home before realising that there are other preppy Americans in the room and sharing their inane platitudes loudly and at length while you are innocently trying to send abusive e-mails to cabinet ministers using fake Hotmail accounts and you only went in there because your shitty broadband has screwed up yet again and you have no alternative to coming back here even though the last time you went in they charged you 20 quid to send a fax and you told the usurer behind the counter that you'd never patronise their stinking digital shit-farm ever again.

Some of them are nicer than that, though.

iPod fashion

The iPod has been venerated in many extraordinary ways. iPods have inspired books, like *GQ* editor Dylan Jones's epic novel sequence *A Dance to the Music of My Lovely iPod of Time*. They have inspired songs, like the U2/Pavarotti collaboration 'Funky iPod (Funky iPod)'.

They have even inspired a panegyric from David Cameron, who recently declared: 'Unlike Gordon Brown, I actually understand all the complicated functions on my iPod. He doesn't even know how to use the party shuffle. The Jock twat.'*

Maybe slightly less extraordinary, but potentially more disturbing, in that it's actually real, is iPod fashion. That phrase exists. It is a phrase which exists. The mere phrase 'iPod fashion' – which exists – should make you shudder.

There's Karl Lagerfeld's rectangular gilded purse – roughly the size of 'a bread bin', oddly enough – which is lined with multicoloured cloth and incorporates a pocket for holding up to a dozen iPods. Or some crusty rolls, I suppose. (Incidentally, Karl Lagerfeld now owns 70 iPods . . . the newly thin German freak.)

Gucci recently introduced an iPod Sling, a 200-dollar carrying case with leather trim and silver clasps. Colours include Namba ('shines golden colour in direct sunlight'), Chocolate ('rich and dark, almost good enough to eat') and Deadly Nightshade Returns ('subtle and elegant').

There are even iPod pants – pants with a pocket for your iPod ('Party on with iPod pants').

There's also a swathe of new sleeves and hoods, with one internet reviewer deciding of the foofpod, that, 'Overall, it's a recommended sleeve for the iPod if you want to get away from the "skins" scene.'

Jesus Christ, there's a 'skins' *scene*? I need to lie down.

---

*The speech continued: 'And I was into the Arctic Monkeys way before he was. I told all my mates about them on MySpace when they brought out "Fake Tales of San Francisco".'

iPod popes

The Pope has got an iPod, hip hip hip hooray, the Pope has got an iPod and he's coming out to play.

Yes, the Pope has got an iPod. Of course he has.

A Vatican spokesperson said: 'He is very pleased with the iPod. The Holy Father likes to unwind listening to it and is of the opinion that this sort of technology is the future.'

He's up all night, you know, illegally downloading Gregorian chanting.

iPod wages

The iPod city of Longhua has 10 factories making iPod components for Apple.

Workers can sleep a hundred to a room and earn 27 dollars a month. It would cost them half a year's salary to buy an iPod Nano. Their wages are low even by Chinese standards.

At another iPod city outside Shanghai, 50,000 workers are enclosed in a barbed-wire compound the size of eight football pitches.

Yue, a worker in Longhua, said: 'We have to work overtime and can only go back to the dorm when our boss gives us permission. After working 15 hours, we are so tired. It's like being in the army. They make us stand still for hours – if we move we are made to stand still for longer. The boys have to do push-ups.

'And if we make the black ones, we have to listen to the preloaded U2 tunes. It is terrible.'

(She didn't say the last bit.)

Iraq War euphemisms

Having a great big war going on day after day requires a whole raft of new coinages to stop people from getting too hopelessly worked up about bodies falling apart and other things that really shouldn't concern them. The Iraq War has spawned a whole new range of such euphemisms to go alongside old favourites like 'friendly fire' and 'collateral damage'.

The whole affair was a 'preventive' or 'pre-emptive' war – a safety measure closer to fitting a smoke alarm to protect your home from the danger of fire rather than, say, protecting your home from the danger of fire by launching missiles at it. It was also a 'war of choice' – as in 'car of choice' or 'cereal of choice' – which makes the coalition sound like a happy consumer rather than, say, the kind of consumer who bombs shops.

'Pacifying Fallujah' became an almost comfortably familiar phrase (like 'Educating Rita' or 'Chasing Amy') – with its connotations of a dummy helping soothe a crying baby's distress. During the attack on Fallujah, the Foreign Office claimed displaced residents were 'visiting relatives' (presumably drinking too much tea with Derek Jacobs on in the background) and the Pentagon labelled the 10,000–15,000 universal soldiers helping interrogate/torture prisoners as 'private contractors'. Presumably, the word 'mercenary' sounded a bit, well, mercenary.

US news feeds would talk of another 'busy day in Baghdad' before going over to a correspondent who said, 'Yes, there's been some developments.' On one particular 'busy' day, 22 September 2004, the 'developments' included two US soldiers being accused of the cold-blooded murder of three Iraqi civilians, the discovery of the beheaded body of British hostage

Jack Hensley, multiple car bombings causing 11 civilian deaths, plus a further 22 people killed in helicopter raids on Sadr City. So yes, definitely a 'busy' day. If you were living in Baghdad, you'd certainly come home saying: 'Busy out there today. Busy busy busy! There's what looks very much like a big fucking war going on.'

Perhaps next time we could do away with the word 'war' altogether and replace it with the words 'birthday party'. This will reinforce how coalition troops are calling in by invitation. On entering this 'party', we will start dropping 'cakes' on the hosts. Unfortunately, this might lead to some 'crumbs' falling on to the floor. But don't worry, because we'll wipe up any subsequent mess with 'tissues'. Lucrative oil and rebuilding contracts will be the 'sweets' we take home in our 'goody bag'. Despite the invitations stating that the party ends at 4 p.m., we might stretch out the fun a little longer, possibly for some years.

It's a Royal Clearout!

Viscount Linley has always been the most intriguing minor royal. Firstly, he's called Linley, which no one is. Secondly, his first name appears to be Viscount, which is the name of a biscuit. But you do have to feel sorry for him. In June 2006 Viscount Linley was forced to sell off possessions left to him by his mother Princess Margaret in order to pay death duties. Oh, hang on. That's 'forced' as in he's broke because he only owns the two swanky furniture shops selling his own line of desks at six grand a pop and armchairs for a mere £2,885 each.

And that's 'his mother's possessions' as in most of them

were paid for by the state or were gifts from the Empire/ Commonwealth. So they weren't her possessions at all and in fact belonged to me (and all the other taxpayers). Linley got £13,200 for a George V gold menu-card holder carrying Margaret's initials (yep, that'd be mine); the same amount for George VI's personal set of playing cards; and £102,000 for his Cartier gem-set cigarette lighter, which he presumably used to light fags I paid for during stressful moments gambling my money over a game of those cards I seem to have bought him. My Fabergé clock netted Linley and his sister Lady Sarah Chatto £1.24 million. They even trousered £2,400 for a trio of 1960s disposable plastic umbrellas. The final tally was a whopping £13,658,728.

You could say he was trying to sell everything that wasn't nailed down. Except he did try and sell something that was nailed down. Linley was all set to auction a set of railings around his mother's (that is, my) garden at Kensington Palace. But the white iron balustrading was withdrawn from the auction, where they were expected to fetch between £8,000 and £15,000, when it became clear that, as part of Kensington Palace, which is a 'scheduled monument', dismantling the railings would have needed consent from English Heritage and the Department for Culture, Media and Sport. Linley decided instead – somewhat magnanimously – to 'donate the railings to the nation'. The nation could be forgiven for not getting overly excited about this, though, as they are in an area of the building not open to the public. So the nation will only be able to enjoy its magnificent bequest by craning out of an upstairs window of a palace they would have to pay to enter.

Personally, I blame daytime TV. If the Royals had proper jobs, they wouldn't be sat round at home all day watching

Cash in the Attic. Maybe they could do one called *Stealing My Cash*.

'It's what John would have wanted'

John Lennon appears to have spent the 1970s alternately baking bread; getting the English out of Ireland by putting tampons on his head; playing those mind games; not living with straights who told him he was king; getting shitted on drugs and wanking himself off practically all the time at every hour of the day and night (I read that in a book).

This sounds like a tremendous way to spend a decade, particularly if you could fairly have been described as 'very busy' during the preceding decade. But no. It seems that what he should have been doing was whoring his name out for any conceivable bit of tat. Handily, his death, while it had its obvious downside, liberated others to do this for him.

Real Lennon products include crockery for children, sunglasses, figurines, plates, watches, Nike Converse Peace trainers featuring lyrics from 'Imagine', innumerable piss demos ('Cold Turkey' sounding like a bad busker in an echoey Tube corridor in which it is somehow raining; revealing studio dialogue such as 'Can you turn my headphones up a bit? No, up. Not quite that much. Yeah, that's it') and an airport. The Liverpool John Lennon Airport slogan? 'Above us only sky'. Well, it's better than 'Help!'

Of course, John Lennon would have loved the reasonably priced transatlantic flight revolution (he loved revolutions). If only the flights had been cheaper when he was alive, he would have been nipping back to Liverpool all the time. Given these shimmering oceans of product, the scope for further diversifying the brand might be considered limited. But still, here follows a list of proposed Lennon merchandise which we humbly submit for Ms Ono's consideration . . .

- Bed-In bedding
- Bag-ism bags
- 'The Dream Is Over' alarm clock
- 'Mother' Mother's Day cards featuring the inner message: 'MOTHAAH DON'T GOOOOOOOOOO OOOOOO!!!!!'
- 'DADDY COME HOME!' get-well-soon cards for hospitalised fathers
- John's 'It Won't Be Long' longjohns
- A walrus

ITV News Channel, the

What could be worse than ITV News? Twenty-four-hour, rolling ITV News, of course.

Amusingly, in January 2005 the BBC had a big panic when an internal survey found that ITV had more prime-time current affairs coverage than them. Then someone realised that they'd included *Tonight with Trevor McDonald* as current affairs and they all had a big laugh and a huge lunch on expenses.

ITV Play

ITV Play's *The Mint* is on for up to four hours during the night, with viewers urged to call in, at 60p a pop, for a chance of winning a cash prize. All they need to do is answer a simple teaser such as 'Who was a smooth operator? Was it a) Sade or b) The Stone Roses?' or decipher a 'word snake' that looks to have been copied out of old editions of *Junior Puzzler* magazine. So far, so so. The innovation is to play each question for about one whole hour, with presenters Brian Dowling and Beverley French gabbling unscripted piss dotted with the phrases 'call in' and 'win' – filling the interminable spaces in which ITV rack up those 60ps.

French looks like the terrifying women who stand behind make-up counters in department stores – a bit like someone who has just had a *This Morning* makeover, then another *This Morning* makeover straight over the top of the first one. Even her name sounds like a makeover: 'Yeah, I'm having a Beverley French.' An alumni of Granada's Men & Motors channel, French is a professional Mancunian, but with a slightly strange, high-pitched accent. Imagine a glam Daphne from *Frasier* trying to skank you for 60p every two to three seconds – for four hours – and you'll just about get there.

Dowling can look a bit strained and shell-shocked. Like a usually bubbly individual with a hangover at a wedding, struggling to keep up the bonhomie because they feel they should and everyone's expecting it, even though their heart isn't really in it. He just repeats himself (and Beverley) in a hyperactive camp way. If anything happens – which it doesn't – he describes it in detail in a hyperactive camp way. He appears not to understand what is happening even when something happens.

You can see his point when someone gets through to fill in the blank in 'Water —————' (bear in mind that, if they made 10 attempts to get through, they have already spent six quid by now) and gives the answer 'mayonnaise'.

Water mayonnaise? Really – how is Brian supposed to understand this?

J

Michael Jackson fans

There was the lady who released doves into the air in response to the liberating verdict, while the man beside her shouted, 'Praise be!' to the skies.

And the lady who cooked raccoons over a log fire to pass around to her hungry comrades.

The fan who, as every 'not guilty' verdict was announced, sawed off one of his own toes to express his gratitude – sadly, but also joyously, running out of toes before the verdicts had ended.

The family from Arkansas who re-enacted crucial moments from Jackson's life – the *Motown 25* show, the baby-shaking incident, the Martin Bashir interview, the morphy video for 'Black and White'.

The SCID-suffering boy in the bubble whose mother was convinced that some tooth enamel from his hero would cure him of his strange, sad condition.

The South Dakotan death-cult who all sported white gloves and reinterpreted 'Man in the Mirror' in the style of Nine Inch Nails.

The Catholic priest who added a fifth gospel to the New Testament – 'The Gospel According to Michael' – featuring Jesus continually explaining to his disciples that he is 'bad, but bad meaning good'.

Whenever Michael Jackson fans gather in one place to give thanks and praise, you can guarantee some serious End of Days shit will be going down. Some appeared almost ecstatic that their idol was up for child molestation again. It's nice to have a reason to get dressed up, isn't it? 'Hi, sweetie, they're trying to kill Michael again by saying he's into kiddyfiddling, showing them porn and getting them drunk and all that kind of crap! Tell work I'm not coming in – it's the End of Days!'

Boris Johnson

Cheeky chappy Boris Johnson: is he quite amusing/a bit of a 'cove'/basically a 'good egg'? Or is he a Tory?

The case for Boris Johnson being a Tory:

- He's editor of the *Spectator*.
- He's a member of the Conservative Party.
- He's Conservative MP for Henley.

The case against Boris Johnson being a Tory:

- He's got floppy hair and he rides a bike.

Hmm. Tricky. But, oh, hang on: Tory MP – doesn't like asylum seekers – Brussels, blah blah – cut back welfare state and give money to the rich, blah blah . . .

Got it! He's a Tory! He's Nicholas Soames on a bike! Fooled us all! D'oh!

Juice drink

Juice: it is, almost by definition, a drink. Add the word 'drink' to the word 'juice' and you might imagine it becomes even more drinky, which is potentially delicious. But no.

If anything, it becomes less drinky. And it certainly becomes less juicy. In fact, your average 'juice drink' often contains a mere 10% juice; that's compared to the fulsome 100% juice that's always contained in 'juice'. Which should make people say things like: 'What happened there then? What did you do with all the juice?'

What if you needed to unwind after a hard day and fancied downing a bottle of tasty wine but the local off-licence only purveyed something called 'wine drink'; then, on returning home, you find the bottle contains just 10% of the wine of a normal bottle of wine (which is 100% wine) while the rest was just spit and rain?

You wouldn't be happy. You might not even get that pissed. And, when you start shouting about the whole matter outside your local off-licence, banging on the shuttered windows with your bloodied fists screaming 'Where is my fucking booze?' you'd definitely have justice on your side.

Justifying train/bus station concourse markups

Journey's *Friend*? If I got to the station and had neglected to pick up a bottle of water and a Twix on the way, I should have thought a friend – a *true* friend – would not look to profit by selling them to me – *selling* them! – at a handsome premium.

A friend – someone who really cared about me – would *give* me the Twix.

I know I can be difficult. Can't we all? There was that incident. Okay. But I'm loyal. I'll stand by you. But you? *YOU?* You're a user! I hate you!

K

Kabbalah

Back when people imagined The Future on programmes like *Tomorrow's World*, the 21st century was full of jet-packs and robots doing your ironing. None of the so-called 'experts' predicted that everyone would be getting into a weird sect vaguely related to an ancient Jewish tradition that sells bits of red string to its followers at £18.50 a pop. Dr Heinz Wolff? You're a fucking charlatan.

Apparently, the reason that Madonna, Posh, Melinda Messenger et al. wear the red string is to protect them against 'the evil eye'. Seems a strange length to go to to stop people giving you dirty looks, but hey ho. Oh, and it gives you 'total fulfilment'.

Spreading 'total fulfilment' has been the aim of Philip Berg since he gave up his job as an insurance salesman in 1970 to become a bit of a seer. Called the Rav by followers, the American rabbi set up his first Kabbalah Centre in Israel in 1971. Clever marketing – and the 'donated' labour of followers – has seen that mushroom into 40 centres worldwide and a turnover of millions. By setting up both not-for-profit and private Kabbalah enterprises – plus wheezes like the Rav 'blessing' businesses in return for a cut of the profits – Berg and his wife Karen have managed to build up an enormous property portfolio and although they take no salaries have lavish no-expense-spared lifestyles for themselves and their two sons. The Rav sold a ten-year copyright to his books to the KC for over $2.5 million. That's a lot of red string.

The reason the string is so powerful, says the Rav, is that it has been wrapped seven times around Rachel's tomb on the West Bank. The people who run the tomb claim to have no knowledge of the Kabbalah Centre doing this, however, and the Israeli Ministry of Tourism and also for Religious Affairs have stated that no special permits have been given to the Kabbalah Centre to enter the heavily militarised area at Rachel's Tomb with large quantities of red string. In fact, the tomb dispenses its own type of red string; although presumably this contains much less enlightenment, what with it being completely free.

The Kabbalah Centre is even trying to get a patent on the red string. Presumably this will involve answering the question 'How long is a piece of string?' – so at least it'll finally clear up that old chestnut.

Other money-spinners include a set of the key Kabbalah texts, the Zohar, at £289. To achieve enlightenment, you don't even need to read the books – you can pick up their 'energy' by just tracing your finger over them. Ah, now I see why it's so attractive to pop stars.

A 1.5-litre bottle of Kabbalah water – which the Kabbalah Centre claims is 'purest Artesian' water which can cure cancer – will set you back £3.95. A case is £45. In fact, the water comes from a bottling plant in Canada.

Never mind all that, though; what about Madonna?

According to a senior figure at the Kabbalah Centre in London quoted in the *Evening Standard*, Madonna joined to learn how to control her moods and 'how to be more tolerant with her husband'.

But I could have sorted that out for her, no $5 million dona-tion required. He's an arsehole. It's not actually intolerant to shout at him. I want to shout at him, and I've never met the bloke: you fucking live with him, you freak.

Kaiser Chiefs

The Kaiser Chiefs always act like they can't believe their luck. And they are right not to believe their luck. Their massive suc-cess is, frankly, unbelievable. Ricky Wilson, rock hero as balloon-animal party entertainer, famously said he would 'wank a tramp for fame'. This was meant as a typically affable, self-deprecating joke. Although, now that he has achieved his fame, we should maybe consider conducting an experiment into what he might do to hold on to that fame. I reckon it won't be pretty. The Kaiser Chiefs actually rolled up stinking of des-peration, like a junkie child actor trying to get a peas advert. So, now they've had a taste, God knows what they'd be capable of.

Of course, everyone's middle-of-the-road nowadays. Even New Wave guitar-tykes who sing 'state of the nation' songs about riots. From occupying the cutting-edge of Western social advancement (in terms of sex, class, race, peace, the big stuff), albeit often not that seriously, many bands now seem to find the cutting-edge a bit, well, sharp. And, unfortunately, quite edgy.

The Kaiser Chiefs were apparently mildly perturbed to hear that the local police played 'I Predict A Riot' before heading out on Friday nights. But this is hardly in the same league as Reagan appropriating Springsteen's 'Born In The USA'. There wasn't any message there to rewrite. Anyway, it's surely the Kaisers to a tee: *X-Factor* indie, ideal for helping psych up coppers for a night out belting bingers. It's only a bit of fun.

The Kooks sound quite kooky. They're bloody not, though. They're just called the Kooks. This doesn't mean that 'Britain's new favourite band' (the *NME*) have to be remotely 'kooky'. It's only words.

The Futureheads, meanwhile, sound all futuristic. They're not, though. Unless your idea of sounding like the future involves bands sounding exactly like they did in 1979. In full swing at least since 2001, this post-punk revival has lasted longer not just than the original post-punk, but longer than punk, post-punk and the bit that came after post-punk put together. Now *that's* entropy!

Any sexually frustrated tramps out there might want to form an orderly queue.

Vernon Kay

Occasionally I have real fears about Vernon Kay taking over the world. I find myself haunted by the thought of him presenting all current-affairs television programmes, breaking off from news stories to ask the viewers questions like: 'So, the McCartney sisters: seriously, which one would you go for? Sisters, eh? Eh? Wicked . . .'

I have visions of a future war with army-recruitment films being shown constantly on giant screens in every home and workplace and in public spaces across the town, featuring Vernon Kay in a thumbs-up pose intoning: 'Right, guys! This is serious, yeah?! Are you gonna do the right thing for your country or WHAT?'

These fears might seem misplaced, even slightly mad. But they are mine.

Keane

Keane need to be stopped, immediately, for these reasons:

- Singer Tom Chaplin's face has no edges, like runny cheese.
- The title of their debut album *Hopes And Fears* derives from the lyrics of 'O Little Town Of Bethlehem' which is their favourite when they go carol-singing around their hometown of Battle. Their next album is called *Little Donkey (Carry Mary) ('Long the Dusty Road)*.
- Look at them! Just look at them!
- Speaking after the 2005 Brits, pianist Tim Rice-Oxley said: 'We went to an after-show party given by our record company. I had a really good conservation with Jake from the Scissor Sisters, who I'd not met before. We did all get pretty pissed, I have to say.'
- Keane are not in any way related to Man Utd midfield hardman Roy Keane. Now that would be good: a piano-driven pop-rock outfit led by Roy Keane. Roy Keane repeatedly smashing his face against the piano keys and shouting: *that's* rock 'n' roll.
- Singer Tom Chaplin's face has no edges, like runny cheese.
- Understanding the importance of a 'consistent anchor', Keane got their own branding consultants – Moving Brands – before signing with their first label, together drawing up a list of buzz words including 'fascinating', 'innocent' and 'expansive'. When the band signed to Island, they absolutely insisted on retaining control over their branding. Forget about Roy Keane: *that's* rock n' roll.

- Singer Tom Chaplin's face has no edges, like runny cheese.
- Chaplin once claimed: 'There's always a strong, potent message to a Keane song. Whereas sometimes with Coldplay, you're not really sure what he's on about.' Which is only slightly less deluded than if he'd said: 'Hello, I'm Iggy Pop. Here's my big willy.'
- Just look at them! Again!

Keystone terror interrogators

Holed up in Guantanamo, one of the Tipton Three, Shafiq Rasul, was repeatedly asked: 'If I wanted to get hold of surface-to-air missiles in Tipton, where would I go?' Before being interned without trial for three years, Shafiq had worked at Currys, so maybe they saw a possible connection there. That's Currys, the high-street electrical store: 'Always cutting prices . . . on surface-to-air missiles!' (We're joking, of course – to our knowledge, Currys has never stocked surface-to-air missiles.)

Also in Guantanamo, Moazzem Begg was questioned about the US sniper John Mohammed (sentenced for shooting 11 people in Washington in 2002), because he was called Mohammed, which is Muslim. He was also shown pictures of the Pope taken from his computer's hard-drive and questioned about his apparent assassination plans. Begg was initially confused by these pictures, until he remembered that all computers' 'Temporary Internet Files' folders store all of the images from any visited website. So a visit to the BBC news website, say, might lead to your computer storing all sorts of pictures from the home page that you hadn't even paid any attention to at the time. (The interrogators also presented him with a picture of a camel spider and asked him for an explanation, although they did not accuse him of planning to kill it.) The Catholic major told him: 'If anything happens to the Pope, I swear I'll break every finger in your hands.'

Prior to being released, one of the Forest Gate brothers – arrested in June 2006 in a massive police raid after a tip-off regarding a non-appearing 'chemical jacket' – Mohammed Abdul Kahar was continually asked about his membership of a series of terrorist organisations, culminating with the question: 'Are you a member of the Ku Klux Klan?' He replied: 'Damn it! You've got me. I'm a white supremacist. I thought I had the perfect alibi – what with not being white and all.'

It was perhaps doubly rude of officers to question Mohammed Abdul Kahar in this way, what with having just shot him.

At the time of writing, none of these people has been charged with any terror-related crime. But even if they had been, it's hard to see how a viable comeback against extremism could ever involve asking really stupid questions.

Incidentally, according to Begg's account of his incarceration, the British MI5 officers reacted to their US allies' brutality with the patrician care of John Cleese's Robin Hood in *Time Bandits*: 'I say, are you absolutely sure that's all necessary?'

Which is at least a pertinent question.

Kitsch tat shops
Called things like Missy Kitty Mau Mau or Puss Puss or Funky Monkey Pants. Sometimes the innocent shopper

accidentally enters an emporium because they need to buy a present for someone and it claims to specialise in presents.

'Ooh,' they think. 'A present shop, maybe I can get a present in this shop for presents and thus satisfy my present-buying needs.' Then they go inside and remember that it's actually a festival of shit with price tags on. You can find:

- George Bush fridge magnets – you can dress him up as either Shirley Temple or Wonder Woman.
- A Monkey tape measure.
- Numerous cards featuring the picture of a 50s housewife and a rude slogan – something like, 'On Sundays, Doreen enjoyed nothing more than a good spit-roast'.
- A Wonder Woman cocktail shaker.
- A tiny little book about eating chocolate.
- Plastic action figures of a black Jesus arm-wrestling Che Guevara (see also **Che Guevara merchandise**).
- A monkey. With the head of Monkey.
- Something a bit Mexican.
- A baby's T-shirt bearing the slogan: 'I'm Such A Punky Baby – I've Only Gone And Cacked Meself'.
- Monkeys.

Of course, no one really wants this crap. But they get it anyway . . .

EMMA: Here you go, Gran – happy birthday. I got you a T-shirt with 'Porn Star' printed on it.
GRAN: Oh, cheers. By the way, I never liked you and your dad's not your real dad.

Knights of the realm

It's the 21st century and thus fairly safe to assume that we have reached the end of the Middle Ages – yet people are still being knighted. But most of them don't even have any armour and can't ride horses at all, let alone well enough to do jousting. They don't even get together round a round table. The only way this concept could mean anything is if, next time there's a war, Mick Jagger and David Frost led the charge. In fact, that would be really good for so very many reasons.

Jeremy Kyle

'Look at me. Look at me. Look at me!'

I don't want to look at you.

L

Lastminute.com

Not cheap, not even last minute. And what's the big deal about Martha Lane Fox becoming so rich? She was stinking rich anyway, so that's just easy.

Now there are lastminute shops – positioned in railway stations, exactly like normal travel and accommodation agents only, erm, more last minute. Not sure how exactly: maybe they talk quicker?

Meanwhile, back on the website, they're auctioning TVs and fridges. Handy for all those last-minute emergencies when you desperately need white goods in a goddam hurry and can only wait 28 days for delivery.

A lastminute online casino is also available – for all those last-minute needs to spazz all your wages staying up till three losing at poker. Next year, they're introducing last-minute penis enlargement.

Left/liberal apologists for Islamic fundamentalists

There are some ground rules that need establishing here: blowing oneself up in a shopping centre to forward a medieval theocracy involving the suppression of women and the stoning of gays is a bad thing, isn't it? I think we can all agree on that one.

Ah, apparently not. By some crazy twist of logic, reactionary bigots who seek to plunge the world into religious darkness can become freedom fighters – a 'deformed' liberation movement; the ANC by other means. If you don't like US imperialism (and, hey, even the Pentagon seems to be wavering on that one these days), you must be okay – even if what you do like is slaughtering people standing at bus stops because of their religion. So we end up with anti-war demonstrations where purportedly socialist paper-sellers mingle with thoroughly fundamentalist Hizb ut-Tahrir, chatting, their stalls standing next to each other.

There's George Galloway, of course (see also **George Galloway, unfair pillorying of**). Meanwhile, Ken Livingstone (yes, the 'Red' one) has warmly welcomed reactionary bigot Sheikh Yusuf al-Qaradawi to London. (Al-Qaradawi supports the execution of all males who engage in homosexual acts and 'personally supports' female circumcision. Of suicide bombers, he says, 'For us, Muslim martyrdom is not the end of things but the beginning of the most wonderful of things.')

Tariq Ali has set himself up as one of the world's premier cheerleaders for the bigots dominating the insurgency in Iraq, casting them as anti-imperialist warriors and saying: 'The resistance in Iraq is not, as Israeli and Western propagandists like to argue, a case of Islam gone mad. It is . . . a direct consequence of the occupation.'

It's a funny sort of business when you consider that, historically, the British left has failed even to develop a united campaign against racism. Recent decades have seen a profusion of mutually antagonistic, left-inspired anti-racist organisations – many, ironically, sporting the words 'Coalition', 'Unity' or 'United'. Yet the differences between these various battling groups are minuscule when compared with their differences to, say, the Muslim Association of Britain, who are major partners in the Stop the War campaign.

The MAB's leadership has sympathies for the Jamaat-i-Islami in Pakistan and Bangladesh, and the Muslim Brotherhood in Egypt – both of which firmly believe in the creation of an Islamic state and the establishment of Sharia law. A left that can ally with religious reactionaries but can't ally with itself might want to sit down for a bit of a think.

If ever the worldwide Caliphate is established, it seems like a few people will be in for a nasty shock:

THE MEDIEVALISTS: Ah, honoured gentlemen. If you'd be so kind as to file into this football stadium . . .

KEN LIVINGSTONE: Turned out nice again. I'm into buses, you know. In here, you say?

THE MEDIEVALISTS: Yes, please, and if you can hurry it up. We've got a load of stonings still to do – and we'd just like to slaughter you all.

KEN LIVINGSTONE: Lovely. I like buses, you know.

TARIQ ALI: What? You're going to what?

GEORGE GALLOWAY: They're going to slaughter us. It's nothing to worry about. It's customary among such peoples. Cigar?

TARIQ ALI: Don't they know who I am? You really should have mentioned this before.

THE MEDIEVALISTS: We did.

TARIQ ALI: Oh.

KEN LIVINGSTONE: Yes. Now I come to think about it, they

did give some signals in this direction. I like buses, you know.

TARIQ ALI: Well, I think it's rude. I'm going to write a big piece in the *Guardian* about it.

THE MEDIEVALISTS: We've burned it down.

TARIQ ALI: The *Independent*?

THE MEDIEVALISTS: Yeah, that too. We didn't like the new tabloid format. Only joking – it was for being infidel.

Lemsip

Of all the cold-and-flu-relief citrus-flavoured powdered drinks, only Lemsip would need spokesperson Reckitt Benckiser (who exists) to declare: 'It is fair to say that it doesn't cause poetry in most people.'

Lemsip is scientific, not versificatory. Science with a capital 'Science'. Even the blackcurrant ones. The heavyweight nature of the bestselling concoction is reflected in its various sub-brand names: Lemsip Fist, Agent Lemon and the all-new Lemsip Bird Flu Fuck You. I'm scared of it, and I'm not even the sniffles.

Oh, hang on, it's just some crushed-up paracetamol that tastes a bit lemony. It perks you up slightly, but then so do most things that contain caffeine.

What you need to make your own 'Lemsip':

- Paracetamol
- Hot water
- Packet of Refreshers

Nevertheless, Lemsip can be extremely dangerous, intoxicating and even addictive, as Poet Laureate Andrew Motion has found.

The poet told the *Daily Telegraph* he 'uses' the potent drug every day to help him write. It gives him the sensation of having 'a mild illness', which is good for the fine poetics, apparently. 'I've been doing it for years and it's become habitual,' he said. Every day, he chases the lemon.

Lists

1. *OK Computer*.
2. *The Bends*.
3. The Campari ads with Leonard Rossiter and Joan Collins.
4. Peter Cook.
5. Shepherd's pie.
6. Delboy . . .
7. . . . falling over.
8. The sax solo in 'Baker Street'.
9. *Kramer vs Kramer*.
10. *The Bends*.
11. 'Bohemian Rhapsody'.
12. *The Bends*.
13. The video for 'Bohemian Rhapsody'.
14. *Captain Corelli*.
15. *Star Wars*.
16. *Minder*.
17. Mrs Mills.
18. Moomin Mama.

19. The Cars.
20. The otter.
21. Jesus Christ.
22. This certainly is an
23. easy way to
24. fill up the pages
25. and schedules
26. and that.
27. Stanley Baldwin.
28. Lake Titicaca.
29. *The Bends*.
30. *OK Computer*.
31. *The Bends*.
32. *The Bends*.
33. *The Bends*!
34. *OK Computer*.
35. Martin Luther King.
36. The Shining Path.
37. Diderot.
38. *Angels*.
39. The Forth Bridge.
40. *The Bends*.
41. *Godfather 3*
42. was crap.
43. But the first two
44. were not crap.
45. Did you know that?
46. I didn't.
47. Jesus.
48. Jesus Christ.
49. Jesus H. Christ.
50. Might it just be possible

51. to start producing more culture
52. instead of lazily cataloguing
53. stuff that everyone already knows about?
54. Daley Thompson.
55. Brian Blessed in *Flash Gordon*.
56. Help
57. I want to get off
58. but I can't.
59. *Get Carter*.
60. Flea.
61. Timothy Dalton in *Flash Gordon*.
62. No, really.
63. *The Bends*.
64. I'm serious.
65. Nasty Nick.
66. This is killing me.
67. The otter.
68. Sankey's Soap.
69. *The Bends*.
70. *Gone With The Wind*.
71. Peter Cook.
72. Peter Cook watching *Gone With The Wind*.
73. Might it be possible
74. to just be quiet for a bit?
75. Okay then, let's see about that.
76. Here goes . . .
77. . . .
78. . . .
79. . . .
80. That's better.
81. . . .
82. . . .

83. Pure bliss, actually.
84. . . .
85. . . .
86. . . .
87. . . .
88. No longer . . .
89. hearing the worthless bleatings . . .
90. of a moribund civilisation . . .
91. turning everything of worth . . .
92. and integrity . . .
93. into another turdy fucking list . . .
94. . . .
95. . . .
96. *Revolver*.
97. NO!
98. *Pet Sounds*.
99. NOOO!
100. Delboy falling over.

Literary Heritage industry, the

In Kent, every house built before 1900 is required *by law* to claim that Charles Dickens once lived there. No business is considered off-limits for association with Mr D: consider Broadstairs' curry house The Dickens In India. Because Dickens is, after all, best known for his love of spiced meats fresh from the tandoor. Indeed, the adjective 'Dickensian' actually means 'having turmeric stains down one's front'.

And Hardy Country? What frigging Hardy Country? Note to Tourist Board sign-makers: THERE IS NO SUCH PLACE AS 'WESSEX'. It's an imaginative realm which, if it existed, would presumably be full of blokes who brood, treat their wives like shit for years, until they die, and then decide they loved her after all, then brood some more, on cliffs, while having visions of her. And who'd want to go there on their holidays?

Swan of Avon? Bollocks. The Literary Heritage industry is just a means of selling cream teas and notebooks with embossed plastic covers to people who don't read many books. If you do wish to appreciate some classic literature, your first port of call should rarely be someone from the Tourist Board who mainly specialises in giving out incorrect information about bed and breakfast accommodation.

Even worse than pretending imaginary places exist are places that obsess about writers who came from there even though they hated the place and did one out of there as soon as possible. Every visible square inch of Dublin contains tributes to James Joyce and Samuel Beckett. But Beckett hated Dublin so much that his rare visits back there made him physically ill.

Joyce left for good in 1904, aged 22, and in his lifetime was denounced by the Irish authorities as a seditious pornographer. Today, you can't move for statues of him or characters from his books. Strangely, though, no statues or plaques commemorate the bit in *Ulysses* where Leopold Bloom fantasises about eating a prostitute's poo.

Richard Littlejohn, gays constantly sharking after

Richard Littlejohn is quite hard done by. I don't just mean the way he looks – that face and so on. People can be really very rude about him. These people go around saying the million-pounds-a-year *Mail* columnist is 'just a greasy homophobic shithouse'. They say he's the sort of unmitigated nasty person who could suggest we should be pleased if refugees drown on their way to Britain. The sort of heartless fuck who could say of the Rwandan genocide and the terrorised people fleeing it: 'Does anyone really give a monkey's about what happens in Rwanda? If the Mbongo tribe wants to wipe out the Mbingo tribe then as far as I am concerned that is entirely a matter for them,' not caring about the gross associations of the word 'monkey's' or maybe even actively enjoying them. 'What a cunt.' That is what these people say.

But what is clear from Mr Littlejohn's articles (he often expounds on the matter), and what might go some way to explaining his advanced level of anxiety and social fear, is that he is under constant pressure from gay people – or, if you will, 'proselytising homosexuals and lesbians' who are often to be found 'recruiting outside schoolgates'. The country is being increasingly gripped by an all-pervasive, creeping, fully gay conspiracy, chock full of men whose only wish is to give Richard Littlejohn a good bumming.

It's 'poovery'. They want, quite literally, to touch his *little john*.

Maybe it's more than one gay man at a time – big chaps, with tattoos, perhaps five or six of them – perhaps even covered in sensual oils, caressing and massaging Littlejohn, fingers and tongues seeking out hitherto unknown pleasure spots, teasing his anus, rolling him over under a pulsating sea of supple male flesh. We just don't know.

Dick? He's having none if it. Maybe if all these 'homosexualists' gave him some space he'd calm down a bit and stop being such a fucker. We just don't know. But, please, for now, give the man a break and refrain from constantly trying to put his erect penis in your mouth.

Loft living

In the olden days, factories were for making stuff in. Poo! Smell-y! These days, factories have found their proper function: as places for executive tosspots to live in while feeling superior and self-regarding.

Welcome to the 'funky' world of 'loft living'. This is not, we must make emphatically clear, the same as living in the loft. Executive tosspots do not spend their leisure hours surrounded by Christmas decorations, broken train sets and fibreglass lagging that makes your arms itch. No, these lofts are 'funky artist spaces'. They're 'the ultimate in cool contemporary living'. Particularly if you have a 'cinema kitchen' (and who wouldn't want a 'cinema kitchen', if only they could work out what one was?) or a 'colourful shower pod'.

As the urbanspaces website explains: 'The loft offered not so much a style as an attitude. Something that would set you apart from the dull conformity of suburban living ... The disciplined order of conventional living in specific rooms for each task was about to be eschewed for the romantic notion of the bohemian decadence of open space.'

The disciplined order of conventional living in specific rooms for each task? Balls to it.

But that's just the start. With everyone wanting to live in factories, the artist Michael Landy has started moving all the houses into art galleries (starting with moving his dad's house into Tate Britain, which really, really pissed off his dad).

Meanwhile, all the art is being shunted into pubs and bars. Gradually, the drinks-serving aspect of pubs will be farmed out to the remaining houses. This will increase the demand for houses – because we all like a drink, however colourful our 'shower pod' – and the whole crazy cycle starts again. Factories will start making stuff again, with burly overseers driving the loft-dwellers out of their lofts and on to the looms. South-East Asian economies will nosedive in the face of sweatshop imports from the UK. Britain will occupy India again which, after initial resistance, the UK populace will support as it brings down the price of curry, plus, everyone's got pubs in their houses so they're pissed all the time and really confused.

And what's 'funky' about that, then? Eh?

George Lucas

Obsessively secretive movie mogul George Lucas spent years up in his Skywalker Ranch (crazy name, crazy ranch) plotting the second trilogy of *Star Wars* films. The renowned filmmaker, who last made a decent film during the final years of the Carter presidency, would spend hours explaining to his minions how the first *Star Wars* film was actually not the first film but, in fact, simply the fourth episode of a 12-part saga. There's a whole new back story concerning Anakin Skywalker that will show everything we already know in a new light. And there's a Rastafarian frog called Jar Jar Binks.

These new films, he would continue, would be far superior to those earlier works because they are 'digital'. George Lucas loves 'digital' – in the late 70s he was one of the first people ever to buy a digital watch (it could perform Beethoven's *Für Elise*, which used to drive everyone on *The Empire Strikes Back* set absolutely spare). In the 21st century, his prime mission has been to change worldwide cinema technology over from film to digital projection. The new *Star Wars* films, which history would see as his true masterworks, would display the first flowering of this innovation's awesome potential.

At some moments, after spending many hours in front of the blue screen, he would become distracted and cackle: 'They laughed at *Howard the Duck*. A film about a duck called Howard? Don't be stupid, they said. And . . . well, maybe they were right. But this time! This time I'll show them all. These three films will define the landscape of the blockbuster in the early years of the 21st century. At last, Spielberg will be my bitch!

'What's that, you say? Someone who actually knows about making half-decent movies is doing *Lord of the Rings*? Yeah, well . . . Those guys haven't reckoned on Jar Jar. Ha! *And* I've got Christopher Lee . . . What? They've got Christopher Lee too? Oh . . .'

Sadly, George was so distracted by the awesome potential of CGI technology that he turned the most loved film franchise of all time into arse sandwich. This was partly because the CGI-designed Rastafarian frog Jar Jar Binks was seemingly based Jim Davidson's hilarious West Indian character Chalkie. Not only that, he also based the story on a script so bad that the actors found themselves physically unable to act 'excited' or even 'remotely unembarrassed' in front of the camera.

Amazingly, Lucas was the only prominent New Hollywood director not on drugs.

Lunchtime boob jobs

All the fun of shopping. But shopping for tits! How fun is that?

The phrase 'lunchtime boob jobs' sounds particularly furtive and risqué – after all, lunchtimes can be boring, once you've paid in that cheque and flicked through the magazines in Smith's. So why not take the opportunity to undergo some major surgery?

The nifty lunchtime boob job op was first publicised in February 2006 by Cheshire's MediSpa Clinic because, said owner Carl Lewis: 'Professional women haven't got time to spend lying in hospital.' Lying around in hospital waiting to recover from operations? That's for losers. Tits to that.

The first wave undergoing this lightning incision included a Cheshire student who was afterwards trotted out for the media's delectation. Why did this perfectly attractive young woman feel the need to big-up her breasts? 'We live in a visual culture and my confidence was really affected,' she explained. 'My mum said they were saggy ... The surgeon told me it looked as though I had breast-fed two children.'

And it's not just women: men are having new pecs inserted as a kind of unsweaty workout. But as they are now also high on grooming products and mainlining Botox, maybe it's time the chaps went the whole hog. Certainly the idea that you can squeeze it into a lunch hour that would otherwise be spent browsing in Currys. Digital will be attractive.

So come on. Be a man! Get yourself some tits.

Lush, the soap shop

Here are some interesting facts about soap:

- The first soap-makers in England used tallow, made from cattle. (See, I told you this would be interesting.)
- Soap is believed to have been invented by the Gauls. They used it not on their bodies, but to keep their hair shiny and red (hence the popular children's book *Asterix the Ginger*). Soap-making began in this country in the 12th century.
- It's just fucking soap, so a soap shop, a whole shop just selling soap, is a fucking waste of everyone's time.
- King Louis XIV of France was said to have beheaded three soap-makers for making a bar which irritated his skin.
- Soap is mostly used in conjunction with other items, like shampoo and toothbrushes, which really you'd want to buy all in the one place, what with them being functional items; you really shouldn't spend too much time buying soap, what with there being more interesting things going on in the world like wars and the darts.
- Modern soaps are most likely to be detergents made from petroleum-based products.

- They don't even do soap on a rope! I checked!
- Soap is mentioned twice in the Bible, though it may be a generic term for all cleansing agents.
- According to an article in a copy of *Metro* I once found discarded on the London Underground, soap's not even the best thing for cleaning your skin anyway. It's cleansing milk or somesuch. Do you stock that, Lush? No, you fucking don't.

Luxury tat

On London's fashionable Bond Street you can buy all manner of expensive cack including Gucci dog bowls and solid silver bottle caps for HP Sauce and Heinz Ketchup bottles. Combine this with the statistic that Japan accounts for a quarter of the world's consumption of luxury goods and we get this disturbing conclusion: Japanese people are putting ketchup on sushi and HP on noodles. Luxury? It's madness.

This luxury mania is particularly amazing when you consider that luxury goods are not, according to Gucci CEO Robert Polet, real products: 'The goods are secondary,' he told *Time* magazine, 'because first of all you buy into a brand . . . [Luxury brands] give people the opportunity to live the dream.'

This doesn't just apply to handbags, mind. Asked by *Time* about moving from Unilever, where he was in charge of frozen food, to Gucci, which does not as yet offer frozen mixed veg or chicken Kievs, Polet said: 'I didn't sell ice cream. I sold concepts. I sold worlds in which people consume ice cream, but I didn't sell a piece of vanilla with a chocolate topping on a stick.'

He bloody did, though.

Apropos of nothing, by the way, the founder of Gucci was called Guccio Gucci. And that's true. Even better, his dad was called Gucci McGuccio Kajagoogoo Gucci. Okay, that's not true.

M

Mac junkies

'Oh, Macs are just so much better than PCs. The operating system is about 12 times faster and they're just so much more efficient in, ooh . . . so many ways.'

Are they? Are they really? And how the fuck would you know, when all you use it for is copying CDs and looking at porn? What you actually mean is: 'They look nice.'

The Mac junkie will also crap on without end about how Microsoft is a big nasty corporation. No shit? And Apple's what then – a workers' co-op? No, it's a smaller nasty corporation – which uses child labour and beats its workers, whom it pays in beans, with sticks (possibly).

Do you know what Apple employees call company chief Steve Jobs? I'll tell you: Big Jobs. Or Shitty Jobby Job-head. And that's true. Okay, it's not.

Managers' mind games

Football: it's a game of two minds. The managers' minds. Which is why every big game these days is prefaced with a fortnight to four months' worth of mind games, as opposing managers try to unnerve each other with a witty *bon mot* here or some *random nonsense* there.

Published examples include:

'It's Chelsea's turn to lose now!'

'Arsenal were a disgrace last time. The ref will keep an eye on them tomorrow I'm sure!'

'We're better than them and they're the world's worst bad losers.'

'Come on then, what are you going to do about it, you spawny shit?!?'

'His wife is a filthy slut and I have shagged her.'

The most oft-quoted mind game came in 1996, when Manchester United's Alex Ferguson supposedly outpsyched Kevin Keegan of Newcastle to gain the Premiership title. He did this by suggesting arch rivals Leeds, who Man Utd had just beaten, would not try very hard when they played Newcastle in a vital upcoming fixture. With just one 'outrageous' remark, Ferguson had broken Keegan in the head.

'He's gone down in my estimation and I will love it, just LOVE it, if we beat them,' chuntered little Kev infamously, a finger jabbing furiously, his decomposing brain bubbling out of every facial aperture.

Ferguson was instantly hailed a Machiavellian genius, whose mind game had been the deciding factor. However, this overlooks the fact that his gambit was facile and blatantly transparent; any sane person would simply have ignored it and calmly got on with his job: the pressured Keegan, though, had always been one step away from curling up in the foetal position. Plus, perhaps crucially, Man Utd were better at football.

Arsenal's appointment that same year of Arsène Wenger gave Ferguson a new debating partner. The Ferguson–Wenger dialectic has thrown up many fascinating theses and antitheses such as 'Ruud van Nistelrooy is a cheat' versus 'Arsenal are cheats,' and subtle put-downs such as 'Arsène – huh-huh, it's like "arse"; your name has got "arse" in it.'

The 2004–5 season, with the arrival of José Mourinho at Chelsea, saw this old rivalry become three-way.

Fergie said Mourinho had 'a shit coat'.

But Mourinho said it was Italian and 'really good'.

Comprehensively rebuffed, Fergie sulked for a bit and then went back to picking on Wenger, whom he called 'a shitter'.

However, the obsessive media coverage of Arsenal–Man U–Chelsea meant the season's real humdinger of a mind game got largely overlooked. In January, on the eve of a West Bromwich Albion–Manchester City showdown, West Brom manager Bryan Robson (and this is true) said that Kevin Keegan, now the Man City manager, had copied his trademark 80s shaggy bubble-perm hairdo off Robson. He, Robson, had pioneered the Dulux dog as England striker look, not Keegan.

This was quite a cuss: 'You had a shit haircut – and you didn't even invent it yourself!' With this sort of voodoo going down, how could Man City possibly score more goals than West Brom?

Weirder still: in cussing Keegan's bad hair, Robson laid claim to having invented the bad hair. He was cussing *his own hair*! What could this mean? Certainly, if I were Keegan, I would have been very much on the back foot – like a small, timid child lost in the woods, only more so. West Brom won 2–0.

Nelson Mandela, people comparing themselves to

In a major interview with the *Guardian* to coincide with the publication of his autobiography, Bill Clinton revealed that what got him through the Lewinsky scandal and Starr inquiry was the example of Nelson Mandela – who had been in pretty much the same situation.

Clinton said: '[Mandela] told me he forgave his oppressors because if he didn't they would have destroyed him. He said: "They took the best years of my life. They abused me physically and mentally. They could take everything except my mind and heart. Those things I would have to give away and I decided not to give them away." And then he said, "Neither should you."'

Mandela got into his spot of trouble by fighting one of the most powerful and effective systems of oppression ever conceived, apartheid. Clinton got into his spot of trouble spunking on a young woman's dress.

Mandela was jailed for 27 years. Clinton was told off a bit.

Martha Stewart, speaking about her impending incarceration for insider dealing in 2004, said: 'I could do it. I'm a really good camper. I can sleep on the ground. There's many other good people that have gone to prison. Look at Nelson Mandela.'

Stewart's situation would indeed have been identical to Mandela's – if only Mandela had owned a business empire worth $800 million and been jailed for lying to investigators regarding a suspicious stock sale.

Actor Johnny Depp, meanwhile, was so miserable working on TV detective show *21 Jump Street* between 1987 and 1992 that he tried to get himself fired by pulling stunts such as (and this is true) setting fire to his underwear. Speaking years later about his heroic struggle, Depp said: 'I was like Mandela, man.'

How true. And what if Depp had not managed to break those manacles of oppression? There would have been no *Finding Neverland*. Altogether now: 'Free-ee, Joh-hn-nny De-epp! Free-ee, Joh-hn-nny De-epp!'

In the world of international celebrity, you don't need to have been imprisoned to stand comparison with Robben Island's most famous inmate. Or have any discernible beliefs. After all, in his brave fight for what was right, what exactly did Bill Clinton stand for? La la la. Clinton Clinton Clinton – Old Billy Clinton: what did Big Bill C, 42nd President of the US of A, stand for? Nope, nothing coming. Ah yes, that's right: blowing his saxophone, staying in power for a while, having his saxophone blown.

There is, though, one major similarity between Mandela and Clinton: they are both black. The writer Toni Morrison called Clinton 'the first black President of the United States'. He wasn't though, he's white – I've seen him on the telly. And it's a funny sort of 'black President' who, during the 1992 primaries, would fly back to Arkansas, where he was governor, to oversee the execution of brain-damaged black man Rickey Ray Rector simply to look tough on crime.

Maybe Toni Morrison just meant that he was really into hip-hop. Or that he likes saying the words: 'You go, girl!'

Men's magazine pullquotes

The big, bold quotes extracted from interviews with young women to go alongside the pictures in men's magazines are 'cleverly formulated' too. The smuttier titles inevitably pick out lines like: 'I love my bum – it's great to hold on to' or 'Another woman? Sure, why not?!' or 'Yes, I definitely think the readers of your magazine would have a chance with me, I really do. I'm sure they're all fantastic lovers.'

In the more aspirational titles, when interviewing a bona fide respectable star like, say, Rachel Weisz, the interviewer will awkwardly throw in a quick question about doing nude scenes or having sex. The actress's world-weary, noncommittal answer – something like 'Well, okay . . . I guess you could say that I like sex . . .' or 'Hmm, my breasts . . . whatever' – will be printed in 40-point bold curlicues to hopefully bolster the impression that she is opening up her darkest desires rather than absent-mindedly wondering about lunch.

It will only be a matter of time before these pullquotes are artfully constructed by extracting phrases from throughout the interview to say: 'Kissing . . . another woman . . . in a big pool . . . of mud . . . is always something . . . I've wanted to try . . . preferably being . . . watched by . . . your readers . . . with their . . . co . . . cks out.'

Mini Coopers advertising estate agents

How far do you think your pseudo-graffitied, pseudo-retro cack wagons are from the already hackneyed ideal of the cheeky swinging *Italian Job*?

This far?
Or   this far?

Misery memoirs

There's not nearly enough misery in the world, is there? Every time you turn on the news, it's nothing but sunshine and everyone laughing and people dancing with puppies and attractive old people. Sickening. If only there were some way of escaping into a world where children are made to live in the washing machine and eat nothing but sanitary products and cigarettes. Thank jiminy, then, for misery memoirs. Which one do you fancy? Dave Pelzer's *A Child Called It* has someone being forced naked onto a hot stove. But then *Ugly* by Constance Briscoe has bleach-swallowing. You're spoiled for choice: *For Crying Out Loud: One Woman's Story of Hope and Courage*; *Friday's Child: What Has She Done That Is So Terrible?*; *The Little Prisoner: How a Childhood Was Stolen and a Trust Betrayed*. Excellent.

Some people really love their misery. Consider this Amazon customer review of Pelzer's *My Story* trilogy: 'these stories will leave you sickened shocked sad crying happy thankful every feeling you could feel you get when you are reading these stories they grip you from start to end'. Other misery fans are more demanding: 'in "a child called it" his mother did horrible things to him such as made him eat his own sick! but the others don't seem to be as interesting.' It's so easy to play the sick-eating card too early, isn't it?

In 2003, a reformed drug addict called James Frey wrote a memoir called *A Million Little Pieces*, full of can-you-handle-it-punk accounts of his junkie hell, rendered in short, punchy, macho paragraphs.

Just.

Like.

Fucking.

HEROIN!

This.

Oprah Winfrey, who really likes misery memoirs, loved *A Million Little Pieces* and had Frey on her show so she could tell him how moved she was. Naturally, it became a bestseller. But then the Smoking Gun website uncovered documents proving that Frey had made bits up, so it wasn't entirely real after all. There was misery in there, to feast on, but it wasn't the genuine misery suffered by another human being that people felt they were paying for when they bought into the whole thing.

Oprah invited Frey back onto the show and proceeded to tell him that he had let himself down, he had let the whole nation down and, most heinously, he had let Oprah down. He did, it must be said, look genuinely miserable.

Maybe he'll write a memoir about it. He could call it *My Oprah Sick-Eating HEROIN Pieces*.

Piers Morgan

Piers Morgan is the would-be Muhammad Ali of disgraced tabloid ex-editors, forever talking a good fight about being the greatest disgraced tabloid ex-editor of them all. Here he is on Jeremy Clarkson after their feud descended into actual fisticuffs at the *Press Gazette* awards: 'Clarkson is such a little squirt. If there is any repetition of that behaviour I shall make him go down like a sack of spuds.' (Clarkson had punched Morgan in the head several times.)

Following some long-running nastiness with Cherie Blair, during which she questioned his 'moral compass', he told her: 'We both know our feud was down to sexual tension.' Yes, that's right. I'm sure she's just like all the rest of us: on the sight of Morgan's face, we simply can't keep the sexual tension down. Sadly, relations were seemingly never cemented and Morgan is now feeling sour again. Indeed, according to David Cameron (interviewed in *GQ*), Morgan asked if he could climb aboard the C-Train to help savage Blair and New Labour, telling the Tory leader: 'Put me in a cage, and feed me on red meat, and I'll 'ave 'em. I hate 'em.'

Of course, Morgan's last flesh-fuelled efforts to bring down the government ended with his being sacked after failing adequately to check the authenticity of fake photographs of prisoner abuse in Iraq. So Number 10 is probably not shaking at the thought of him slavering to get at them. 'No, spare us the fake pictures, Piers! We can't take any more!' they might not say.

But, despite all, Piers Morgan is 'still the greatest!' I'm looking forward to him naming the round in which he's going to take down Ian Hislop, another rival whom he has previously dubbed a 'moon-faced little midget' and wanted to smear so much that he publicly offered money for dirt: 'Now you see me, now you don't. Ian thinks he will, but I know he won't! His *Private Eye* ain't gonna do no good when I start to dance! I'm gonna dance, Ian, I'm gonna dance! I'll be floating like a pig and snorting like a labrador. I'm so fast that last night I printed some pictures before checking whether they were real! It's hard to be humble, when you're as great as I am.'

Then he started a newspaper for kids.

Motorist, the, as oppressed group

There is one inalienable right of man – recognised as such from Ancient Greek philosophy through to the classic statements of liberal rights such as the US Constitution – that today is being repressed as never before, casting a shadow over all ye who believe in Liberty. I speak, of course, of the right to drive about in a car.

When the RAC call for 'a charter which safeguards motorists' rights' to protect the noble car-driver from Nazi measures like bus lanes and congestion charging, they are drawing on a rich tradition of political thought almost as old as man himself.

It was Aristotle who first invented the notion of 'pimping' one's 'ride'. 'These forks,' he wrote, in his *Politics*, 'are bitchin'.' George Washington, first President of the United States, famously said: 'As Mankind becomes more liberal, they will be more apt to allow that all those who conduct themselves as worthy members of the community are equally entitled to the protections of civil government. I hope ever to see America among the foremost nations of justice and liberality. And of course to be porky and drive round in SUVs. That goes without saying.'

Our modern-day Thomas Paine is, of course, Jeremy Clarkson, who said: 'The whole country has gone mad. If people want to sit in a traffic jam on the M25 for two hours in the morning on their way to work, why should anyone stop them?'

'Why,' he added, 'are all these German lesbians trying to get me out of my car and on to a bike. Bikes are gay. And I'm not gay. Jeremy Clarkson? Gay? Gay I am not. Just look at the size of my car. Is that gay? No.' Okay, I made that bit up.

Some people argue that Clarkson is 'just a tosser'. They point out his hair and his 70s rock jeans-with-shirt-tucked-into-them look, and they mock. Look at him, these people say, just look at the gangly great streak of cack – rocking out to AC/DC's 'You Shook Me All Night Long' and Bachman

Turner Overdrive. Can you imagine that great twat shaking you all night long? Fucking hell, no thanks. That is what these people say.

Chris Moyles

On 23 May 2005, BBC staff went on strike over four thousand planned job cuts inflicted without union negotiation. Among those spotted crossing the picket line was Radio 1 breakfast DJ Chris Moyles. According to that day's *Evening Standard*, this plain-speaking man of the people told union officials: 'I'm going to be sympathetic to your strike on my show.'

It's very strange, but on his show that day Chris mainly talked about the Radio 1 team losing to Iron Maiden at the music industry's soccer tournament, the Soccer Six, before adding that 'there's something to be said for good-looking women ... or even not so good-looking women, but tarty women, in a football kit'.

Later, he asked Rachel for her favourite Chelsea player and she replied it was 'a bit of a toss-up' between Terry and Lampard – which made Chris and Comedy Dave laugh in their trademark cheeky way. Then came the comedy version of Gwen Stefani's 'I Ain't No Holla Back Girl' called 'I Ain't Not Heaving That Girl' about having to move stuff round your girlfriend's flat which was ... well, quite hellish, actually.

Maybe, amidst all the craziness, there lay a deeply coded message saying: 'Stop the non-negotiated job cut madness!' Maybe he never promised anything of the kind to union officials and they just made it up to look like they knew famous people. Maybe, with so much hilarity going off all around him, Chris simply forgot.

To be fair, even though I had gone to the trouble of downloading the show from the Radio 1 website, I couldn't bear to listen to more than half of it – so maybe the second half was a radio rally that culminated in Chappers leading everyone in a lusty rendition of 'The Internationale' before they all occupied Mark Thompson's office and set fire to mocked-up redundancy notices out the window.

Or maybe he's just a monumental shit-bin.

Moylesy!

Museum tat

Surrealist pioneer Georges Bataille said 'a museum is like the lung of a great city: every Sunday the throng flows in, like blood, and leaves it fresh and purified . . . [a] torrent of people visibly animated with a desire to be at one with the celestial apparitions with which their eyes are still ravished'.

He forgot to mention how absolutely thrilled they are with their novelty apron and ruler.

German green-anarcho installation provocateur Joseph Beuys, subject of a recent Tate Modern show, was known for huge installations involving stuffed huskies or petrified trees, and vitrines containing everything swept up from the street after a vast workers' demonstration. Beuys would hold teach-ins where, standing in the middle of the crowd, he would frantically scribble all his and their thoughts onto a huge blackboard as they attempted to pack and unpack the world around them.

At its Beuys exhibition, Tate Modern sold . . . very small blackboards. About A6 size – a quarter the size of A4; the sort you might stick on the wall in your kitchen or next to the phone – maybe representing our ability to forget the things we really need. Still, at least you can get involved – although, of course, where Beuys's blackboards were full of inspired dialectical thought-storms, these will probably just say: 'milk, beans (2), lager, curry paste, glue, crisis, mother, mother, mother, mother, I'm dying'. (That's actually quite good; you should exhibit that.)

On sale at the 'Modernism' blockbuster at the Victoria and Albert Museum – as well as the pencils, the T-shirts, the canvas shopping bags, the mugs and Mussolini's bust – were, naturally, branded Utopia shampoo and soap. Presumably, the ravished-eyed throng coursing out onto the Brompton Road had conversations along the lines of: 'That really made me think about the social dimensions of design, and how it's possible to construct human environments in a human way rather than just slap up a load of shops and offices to turn a fast buck.'

'Yeah? I might have a shower later. With my new soap. That's my Utopia right there, so swivel . . .'

It's only a matter of time before art galleries and museums rearrange their space in line with their new priorities, using most of it for a giant shop with row after row – battalions – of fridge magnets. A small area near the exit displays a few bits and pieces of art they happen to have lying around. Actually, the Royal Academy of Art is virtually there, planning a shop in the City of London that's just that: all shop, no art. (Maybe they should call it the Royal Academy of Shop.)

Kit Grover is a leading designer of customised museum merchandise for Tate Modern and the National Gallery whose creations include the Gilbert and George Rubik's cube, art-themed fridge magnets aping *Hello!* magazine and, for Tate Modern's 'Surrealism' show, a huge crystal paperweight containing a photographic image of an eye. Which is sort of surreal, but not in a way that offers liberation from bourgeois mundanity.

'My crusade is to identify what someone would want to buy after they've had an intense experience,' said Grover. But surely buying is the most intense experience of all. Not buying is no experience whatsoever. The idea that a gallery is the sort of place where people might think more generally whether just going around buying stuff all the time is much cop is a patent absurdity; and people who have historically suggested otherwise – like artists – are, in essence, just twats. Incidentally, the Mussolini bust was modelled on Renato Bertelli's 1933 strange, revolving sculpture *Head of Mussolini: Continuous Profile*. It therefore has nothing to do with Il Duce's tits. Although, of course, he was very proud of his tits. You can tell that from the way he walked.

'Must have', the phrase

Being told how to be hip by media planks is a constant feature of modern life. For its June 2005 issue, *Red* magazine promised '235 Must Have summer fashion accessories'. Must we really have 235 summer fashion accessories? Why did they think summer would last that long?

Seeing certain films is 'utterly essential' – with TV pundits saying things like 'this is Christian Bale's year, without a doubt'. Imagine having no doubts that this year, or any other year, is Christian Bale's year. What certainty!

'The FeONIC soundbug is a must have' I was once told by a TV 'items' expert, because it turns otherwise useless flat surfaces like walls into speakers. 'Flat and rigid surfaces'? Balls to them.

Such figures are portrayed as modern oracles peering into the misty water to somehow divine the future of thinking, being, buying. In reality, they've been sifting through a pile of press releases. Or, sometimes, looking stuff up on the internet.

N

Nazi hate pop

Modern-day fascists have such poor taste in music. Anyone would think they have poor judgement generally. All that bad metal; all that *shouting*. You'd think they'd want to unwind after rupturing their rectums with all the Nazism: the marching, the bellowing ignorance, all those close-typed leaflets they hand out. But no: it's frenetic thumping and gruff slogans about white supremacy. Angry Aryans?

I ask you! One striking departure from fat, bald blokes screaming is Prussian Blue – a girl group who are a sort of Nazi version of the Olsen Twins. But where the Olsens appeal to fans of anodyne family fun, Prussian Blue appeal to fans of Aryan racial hegemony. Group members Lamb and Lynx Gaede are two blonde, blue-eyed 14-year-olds from Bakersfield, California, who wear mini-skirts and T-shirts with yellow smiley-faces on them (ah, cute), but the yellow smiley-faces are actually Hitler (oh, not so cute), complete with moustache and distinctive hair-do. (I'm not making this up!) It's like Girl Power, but it's White Girl Power.

'We are proud of being white,' says Lynx – unsurprising given that their shows incorporate *Sieg Heil* salutes and that one song, 'Sacrifice', is dedicated to Hitler's deputy Rudolf Hess (a 'man of peace who wouldn't give up').

Other top tracks are 'Road to Valhalla' and 'Aryan Man,

Awake'. Lyrics include: 'Strike force! White survival. Strike force! Yeah.' Gig itineraries sometimes feature Holocaust-denial festivals. (How would one of those 'festivals' pan out? 'I don't believe the Holocaust happened.' 'Neither do I.' 'Let's get a beer.' 'Okay.' 'Is David Irving coming this year?' 'No, he's in chokey.' 'Shame.')

Erich Gliebe, operator of notorious race-hate label Resistance Records, which releases Prussian Blue's efforts, believes young performers like Lynx and Lamb will expand the base of white nationalism. He said: 'Eleven and 12 years old, I think that's the perfect age to start grooming kids and instil in them a strong racial identity.'

Lamb and Lynx were 'groomed' by their mother April, who home-schools them using 1950s textbooks, and by their grand-father. He has a swastika on his belt buckle, on the side of his pick-up truck and registered as his cattle brand with the Bureau of Livestock Identification. (So he definitely likes swastikas. And presumably Nazi cattle.)

Lynx said: 'We want to keep being white. We want our people to stay white . . . We think our race is different to other races in positive ways and that we've done more for civilisa-tion.' We must wonder, though, exactly what benefit civilisation will garner from two barely pubescent girls gyrat-ing in front of mostly male white supremacists. The target market of this pop group would appear to be Nazi pae-dophiles. Which even a fascist must appreciate is, in PR terms, a double-edged sword.

Nazi paedophiles: what are they like, eh?

Nazi porn

When BNP leader on Barking and Dagenham Council Richard Barnbrook was outed as the maker of a gay porn movie, the former teacher maintained: 'It was an art film.'

Apparently *HMS Discovery: A Love Story*, which Barnbrook made as a student, contains scenes of 'flagellation, men undressing and frolicking in a river and a naked man . . . performing a sex act on another'. There is 'full frontal nudity', and also 'fondling'.

Despite co-writing and featuring in the film, Barnbrook has denied penning the erotic poetry recited in the gay bongo flick, which includes the lines: 'It bares you like a foreskin's folds' and 'Open-mouthed, I shall dream of altar boys.'

Not having seen *HMS Discovery: A Love Story*, I don't know the 'sex act' in question or the role played by Barnbrook, but it's easy to see how this could cause confusion within BNP ranks. I was definitely under the impression that the party was meant to be anti-gay. And if, in *HMS Discovery*, Barnbrook is the man involved in a 'sex act' with another man, well, that's not going to look very anti-gay.

If, for example, he's being pumped up the jacksy and loving it, that wouldn't scream 'anti-gay' to me. He might be screaming, but what he would be screaming are basically howls of ecstasy at the good seeing-to he's having. So the message could at best be described as 'mixed'.

Nazi wine

Marketed with the slogan 'Drink for Britain with the BNP', the party's own-brand wine – available at £8.29 a bottle from its website – features a fetching picture of leader Nick Griffin on the label. Well, it makes a change from an etching of grapevines on a hillside – albeit not a pleasant one.

But just when BNP supporters thought they had solved their gift-buying dilemmas for the undiscerning drinkers in their families, a problem occurred: because the British National Party's wine is not British.

It might be bottled by Cornish Moorland Wines, but the grapes come from Chile and Canada – both of which are very much Abroad.

Also, although I really don't want to get into advising the BNP on how to handle their PR, they really missed a trick here. The wine is red. Not white – like the super-race. Red – like communism. You want to do a white wine, you big sillies. You could call it White Supremacy.

Apparently, the BNP wine doesn't even taste very nice. So burgeoning fascists should, for now, stick to getting drunk on Aryan bloodlust.

Networking

The dark art of pretending to like people in order to advance one's own self – even though that self has precisely nothing to offer the world barring an extraordinary aptitude for self-advancement.

The so-called Queen of Networking is Carole Stone, who has a database of more than 20,000 'friends' among the 'great' and the 'good'. Each Christmas she invites a select bunch of them to an intimate soirée, generally keeping the number of guests down to around 1,500 to maintain that intimate, friendly vibe.

The author of books about crawling up the arses of the rich

and famous – sorry, making some really great mates – Stone says things like 'I felt I had been a failure so far that morning, as I hadn't yet exchanged one business card' and 'Will I ever accept that it is possible to say no to an invitation and live?' So, not at all insecure, then.

When her first book, *Networking: The Art of Making Friends*, was published, Carole wrote: 'I can't resist rushing in and buying a copy whenever I'm passing a bookshop. I have to stop myself shouting: "It's me, Carole Stone, I'm the author!" as I hand over my £7.99.' So, not at all insecure, then. She continued: 'And I'm doing all those naff things like ordering dozens of copies for myself and rereading the book in bed. Meanwhile I'm trying to fit in every promotional opportunity I'm offered. I have talked to any local radio station that will listen, agreed to speak at a literary lunch in North Yorkshire and I'm off to East Anglia at dawn for local television. Meanwhile, I've talked on the phone to *The Lady*, the Press Association and *Top Santé* magazine. I'm about to meet the London correspondent of the French daily *La Tribune* and I'm wildly clutching at straws to find an excuse that would make me eligible for a piece in *Cheshire Life*. I've had my hair done three times in as many days for photo shoots and now *Hello!* is on the phone – no money, but . . . I know I'll get withdrawal symptoms when I'm no longer in hourly contact with my publicist. I could get hooked on all this attention.' So, not at all insecure, then.

Who's weirdest, though – Carole for organising her bum-lick-fest parties, or the people who go to them? A couple of thousand of the great and good, and not one single one of them has got paralytic and started hurling abuse and food at the others.

Guests at the 2004 party included Peter York, Sir Peregrine

Worsthorne and Gillian Shepherd – and no one hit any of them. Not even York. What's the fucking matter with these people?

NHS computers

The disappearance of patient records, cancelled operations, delays in outpatient appointments: just some of the greater efficiencies wrought by the NHS's new £6.2bn IT system which are causing trusts across the country to withdraw from the scheme in horror.

At the time of writing, the government had revised the probable final cost of the network's installation to £20 billion – and it still didn't work properly. Computer specialists – who know more about computers than the government – said the figure would probably rise to £30 billion.

Just imagine what chaos might have ensued if the £30 billion project had been entrusted to the public sector? Thankfully, the £30 billion IT scheme was rushed through by the government, who are spending £30 billion on it, to showcase how dynamic private enterprise beats public every time.

It's about 'what works'. Even if it doesn't.

£30 billion? You could pay for an awful lot of inefficiency with that. Let nurses make paper aeroplanes out of those funny cardboard hats they wear. Maybe even just burn the money to provide heat for elderly patients? Why not? If we're just chucking it about anyway?

Of course, how the private sector tends to 'save' money is to reduce wages, lay people off and cut services to the bone. When you add in company profits and dividends to shareholders, and the fact that in PFI projects (where private consortiums borrow money to build facilities that the NHS then leases back from them) we taxpayers also chip in on the loans' interest payments, private provision actually costs more – for less actual healthcare.

PFI was, of course, a Tory invention. Its architect, Kenneth Clarke, later called it a 'terrible idea' (in part because the private sector has to borrow money at much higher rates than the public sector) before breezing off to market fags to kiddies. But, crucially, when Labour came to power in 1997, no PFI contracts had actually yet been signed. So they could have said, 'Knickers to that.' But they ploughed on so no one could question how pro-market they were. If anyone did question how pro-market they were, they could – in all good faith – answer: 'Very.' Former Health Secretary Alan Milburn liked to talk of PFI being the largest hospital-building programme in the NHS's history. He neglected to shout so loudly about the services being simultaneously cut or closed. As health expert Allyson Pollock says in her book *NHS plc*, PFI was paid for by 'major cuts in clinical budgets and the largest service closure programme in the NHS's history'. Which is a different way of looking at things.

So yes, it's about 'what works', particularly what works for private healthcare middlemen able to play golf in Dubai on our tax money. Because they're people too. The three founders of iSoft, the company behind the NHS computer, made £41 million, £30 million and £10 million respectively from selling shares in the company, which, at the time of writing, had just been made the subject of an investigation by the Financial Services Authority over irregularities in its accounts. Alan Milburn, of course, went on to take a 30-grand-a-year consultancy from private healthcare investors Bridgepoint. He might consider having the words 'NO' and 'SHAME' tattooed on his forehead.

According to *The Times*, NHS expenditure on management consultants increased by 23% to £3 billion in 2005. Presumably this army of shysters could work out exactly how much money is siphoned off from the public purse to private companies. If they had a computer that worked.

'Not like everybody else' advertising

We must not be like everybody else. We must be different. Original. And special. And we must always, *always* expect more. How do we know this? Because that's what the advertisers tell us.

'Try Something Different' suggest Sainsbury's and Jamie Oliver. 'Most of us are asleep most of the time,' he explains over footage of droney dozers. 'Even when we shop, we're sleep-shopping.' WAKE UP! Use your imagination. Stop being a droney consumer. Go to Sainsbury's and buy some supermarket produce! But slightly different supermarket produce!

It's an inspiring, almost Blakean, message: I will now go to Sainsbury's in a heightened, almost visionary state. That's right: I will take shitloads of drugs.

'Be Original' implore Levi's. We need to go 'moon-bathing', claim the ads, showing a buffed, shirtless, Levi's-wearing man balancing precariously on a moonlit rooftop. They make it look quite the thing. But if we do actually go 'moon-bathing', surely we are not being 'original'. We are being 'unoriginal'. It's like jumping in the fire because a bigger boy told you to, except it's climbing around on the roof at night because Levi's told you to. Which is potentially deranged. 'What, Officer? But the jeans people told me to do it!'

When IBM used the Kinks' proto-punk anthem 'I'm Not

Like Everybody Else', they subverted meaning with an audacity that would make a French philosopher gasp. The song fronted the computer giant's 'What Makes You Special?' campaign, which conveyed the idea that IBM was in fact an anarchist collective specifically there to cater for disaffected wildcards. Except that, in the ads, everyone was singing the anti-conformity song in perfect unison – like corporate Stepford androids. The levels of irony became so richly confusing that I started spinning out and needed talking to with patience and care – to be reassured that I am, at least in some senses, like everybody else.

'Expect More' say Matalan. And that's just taking the piss.

Novelists writing about current affairs

Reading newspapers these days, you need some basic ground rules if you want to avoid the sudden urge to throw yourself through a window. One of the most important rules (at least of those that don't involve *Sun* 'Youth Correspondents') involves first scanning right down to the very end of the article. If you see there a little copyright symbol followed by the writer's name, either turn over the page or in fact drop the paper and run off into another room.

This is because, whether you've heard of them or not, the writer will be a Very Important Author. They don't usually do this sort of thing but, on this occasion, they have chosen to lower themselves from Mount Literature and walk among us. They have been touched by current events, touched in ways we normal people just wouldn't understand. There are children dying, we've all seen the pictures. But have we seen the real picture? The big picture? The picture that tells us what we're all really feeling? Probably not. After all, we're not pompous novelists straining for pseudo-profundity.

How would any of us have made sense of the horrors of the World Trade Center attacks if it hadn't been for the likes of Salman Rushdie, Ian McEwan and Martin Amis telling us how horrible it all was? This was, without the slightest shadow of a doubt, exactly the right time for showboating prose.

Who could forget the opening lines in Amis's *Guardian* piece on 2003's Iraq War? 'We accept that there are legitimate *casus belli*: acts or situations "provoking or justifying war". The present debate feels off-centre, and faintly unreal, because the US or UK are going to war for a new set of reasons (which in this case do not cohere or even overlap). These new *casus belli* are a response to the accurate realisation that we have entered a distinct phase of history.'

So powerful! So readable! So succinct! So unclear whether he thought the war was a good or a bad thing! Imagine if his actual proper literary endeavours were as trite, jumped-up and egocentric and had such little connection with reality. Surely then we'd all stop buying them?

Oh, yes, that's right: they are. And we have.

Nu-snobbery

The poor are a right laugh: look, they don't have much money! Ha ha ha. But there's a downside, too: they sometimes have bad skin because they don't use the correct sea-salt based exfoliant scrubs, and they can be violent.

In Britain, of course, we have a long and proud tradition of despising the poor. Back in 1384, Chaucer was moved to write: 'Paupers? Ryghte bunche of queyntes.' In the 21st century, this tradition is looking almost absurdly healthy. In 2004, following the soaraway success of websites like ChavScum, ChavWorld and ChavTowns, virulent class hatred made it on to the bookshelves with titles like *Chav! A User's Guide to Britain's Ruling Class* and *The Little Book of Chavs*. The once-trendy website Popbitch started selling T-shirts emblazoned with 'Pramface', a slogan that righteously rips into girls who, er, push prams.

There was definitely some confusion, though: chavs are 'skinny and underfed', but also 'obese from always eating McDonald's'. They are 'inherently racist', but also 'spawn multi-coloured babies'.

'They all dress the same!' roared the ruggedly individualist middle-class professionals. 'They buy crappy jewellery at Argos!' Instead of, say, another chain store in the same shopping centre that's marketed at People Like Us instead. The sites attacking chavs for their aggression and mindless bad language were questioned by a journalist at the *Independent*. One respondent told him to 'fuck off and die'.

The word 'chav' actually derives from the gypsy word 'chavo', meaning 'little lad', and has long been familiar slang in Surrey and Kent (it's even on Sham 69's anthem 'Hersham Boys'). Now, however, it has started to denote a louty canker at the heart of our nation. Message boards were rammed with missives like: 'Chavs unfortunately don't yet fall into the category of rodent and in effect cannot be bludgeoned to death under the guise of pest control. Darn!' Or: 'Do not be fooled by there [sic] Humanoid looks, they are of another race, mainly scum.' Ha ha! What an hilarious parody of Nazi propaganda! Cool!

Of course, the *Daily Mail* couldn't wait to get in on this raw, virile fun and wrote of disgusting women who 'pull their shoddily dyed hair back in that ultra-tight bun known as a council-house facelift'. I'd have thought that, as a general rule of thumb, if your prejudices match those of the *Daily Mail*, you might want to shoot yourself. Amazingly, sometimes middle-class people in regular employment swear loudly and hit people too. And, get this: some, even those working for the *Daily Mail*, are more obnoxious than words can express.

Even so, it's clearly enormously liberating to rant on about single mothers and lazy workers like some gout-ridden Victorian bishop who's been at the laudanum again. Let's hope that soon there are just two words on everyone's lips: 'work' and 'house'. Put 'em together and what have you got? A sensible and modern benefits policy, that's what!

O

'Official sponsors' of sporting events

Mastercard, official sponsors of the World Cup 2006, received a lot of criticism for initially insisting that all ticket sales had to be done by extremely complicated bank transfers unless paid for by one, and only one, brand of credit card: Visa! Only joking – it was Mastercard.

Coke famously banned Pepsi products from events they sponsored. Now, you may ask what Coke are doing sponsoring sports anyway what with it making you really fat, but they've actually got quite a long tradition of sponsoring sporting events, having got behind the 1936 Olympics in Berlin – aka The Nazi Olympics, the one where Hitler wanted to show off Aryan superiority. Coke were pretty chummy with the Nazis generally. Indeed, Coke-staple Fanta was invented by improvising with local ingredients when the German Coke plants ran out of cola syrup during the war: they loved pop, the Nazis.

Anyway, at least Coke could argue it's an 'energy' drink. What about Canon – the 'official photocopier' of the England squad for Euro 2004? So, in the run-up to a big game, do the lads do a lot of photocopying, then?

Sainsbury's sponsorship as 'official supermarket' of England at Euro 2004 proved somewhat controversial, sparking the so-called Nectargate scandal. Wayne Rooney kept getting his Nectar card swiped during his team-mates' transactions and saving up the points to buy sweets. Steven Gerrard was particularly irritated, having done a big shop just before the fateful quarter final against Portugal – only to see Rooney dive in and hoover up the points!

Gerrard had specifically selected items he wouldn't normally buy, because they were part of an extra points offer. He'd been saving his points for a digital clock-radio and was really quite annoyed about it all.

England crashed out of the tournament only hours later. So, in what sense Sainsbury's were 'helping' really is beyond me.

Opening ceremonies

Great international sporting events like the Olympics and the World Cup are designed to bring people across the world together, to realise briefly our underlying commonality. And the opening ceremonies do indeed unite all the corners of the world with the same thought: 'Just fucking get on with it.' And also: 'Where did they get all that material?'

Wherever the host nation, these gammy displays of national pride always look like a school special assembly with serious money to burn. But there are moments to cherish: there's the grandeur in Barry Davies's voice as he reads from the script: 'And now . . . here come the grape-pickers . . . in their traditional costume . . . picking their grapes . . . from the grapevines . . . on the hillsides.' Or there's his mute disbelief at the sight of Björk dressed as an ocean singing about sweat.

The transcendent opening ceremony moment of recent years occurred at the opening of the 2002 Winter Olympics at Bonneville when each country was introduced with a short rhyming couplet – in French and English. One particularly memorable example went: 'They come from a land that's long and hilly / Welcome to the gallant athletes from Chile.'

Opportunistic vicars

The average vicar rarely gets the chance to shine. He is nominally at the centre of the community, but in reality no one in the community gives a holy toss. So it is understandable that, when he hears on the local news that there's been a terrible house fire nearby, quick as a flash he's got the dog collar on, he's into the Micra and he's round to the blaze to put his arm round a distraught parishioner who can't be seen to push it off in front of the local news even though their immediate thought is, 'Fucking vicar.'

Sadly, the vicar does not occupy a role in the centre of the community. In normal times, the community tends to keep the vicar firmly on the edge of the community. So surely, in times of distress, the community would be better served by rallying around a figure who is genuinely at the centre of the community. Like the chirpiest checkout cashier at Tesco. Or the man who peddles drugs.

Organic consumer scams

If you buy organic produce from abroad, and the organic produce has been transported by plane, then that organic produce, far from being an in-touch-with-nature, straight-from-the-soil bundle of environmental goodness, will have probably burnt its own weight in aviation fuel to get here (as part of a larger consignment; you don't get kiwi fruits individually flying themselves here from New Zealand).

The ethical farming group Sustain analysed a sample basket of 26 imported organic goodies: they found it had travelled a distance equivalent to six times round the equator (150,000 miles), a journey that will have released as much CO2 as a four-bedroom household cooking meals for eight months. But the supermarkets know that the little 'organic' sticker means more money for them, so they really could not care less about jetset comestibles.

It pains me to say it but, if you want to go organic, you might have to end up dealing with hippies. Farming is the only area of life where hippies are best. You never hear about hippy builders, say – oh, we got some hippies in to do the extension and they were really good.

For farming, though, I'm with the hippies: it's either them or you end up with subsidy-guzzling reactionaries who fuck foxes. That's the impression I get, anyway.

Oscars, the

Another year on and Hollywood's managed to turn out, what, maybe THREE decent films? That's right, give yourselves a big clap. Funny how you never seem to win awards in competitions not run by yourselves.

Over-sharing

'My husband thinks I'm sexy, which is great. He still loves me and fancies me. It's all about the boobies with him. Lots of booby-feeling goes on . . . He's a real booby man.'

So revealed Lorraine Kelly. And she didn't stop there. Here she is on her husband's penis: 'What a winkie it is. I'm very happy. I have no complaints in that department.'

From the amount of information the daytime goddess regularly divulges, you would think the showbiz interviewers shine torches in her face and show her pictures of her kidnapped firstborn. There is no evidence of that, yet she has also confessed to trying amyl nitrate, and to having outdoor sex in the wilds of Scotland with her 'winkie-boy' husband. I, for one, will now find it hard to visit the Highlands for fear of Lorraine Kelly, off her face on poppers, getting loose and jiggy in the heather. And I love the Highlands.

Or Trinny Woodall revealing the contents of her handbag on live telly and showing us the packet of baby wipes because, oh God, she can't stand having a 'dirty hole'. Bloody hell!

Then one episode of *The F-Word* had a whole feature about Giles Coren's sperm count. Sorry, this really shouldn't need spelling out, but Giles Coren's spunk is not a fitting subject for a food programme.

P
___

Paninis

Panini was once simply an Italian sticker company selling packets of footballers' dumpy faces from small boxes situated by the till in newsagents. Then they went into the cheese toastie market and really cleaned up.

They were so successful in fact that they overreached themselves and ran out of bread, so they started to make their cool, continental snacks out of cardboard instead. They also didn't have time to print the standard warning on the side of the packet: 'Do not under any circumstances heat this fucker to 200°C as that is hot enough to melt the inside of someone's head.'

In Milan, no one would serve you a Caesar salad panini straight from a lovingly sealed polythene bag that is now practically on fucking fire. Unless, for some reason, they hated your family. Hot leaves? Bubbling hot yellow sauce? This is not the Italian way. Breakfast paninis with scrambled egg? Balls to them.

Michael Parkinson

Here is a slice of classic Parky:

PARKINSON: You really are rather good, aren't you?

ASININE CELEBRITY: Yes, that's right! Ha ha!

PARKINSON: Marvellous. So, when did you realise you were so great?

ASININE CELEBRITY: Not really sure. Probably around the time of a tedious childhood anecdote.

PARKINSON: Marvellous. Would you like to come round my house and have some drinks?

ASININE CELEBRITY: Yes please. By the way, I just want to say that you're looking so good, Parky. It's Parky, everyone, look! Doesn't he look great? I can't believe I'm here! With Parky! On *Parky*!

PARKINSON: Marvellous. I'm from Yorkshire, you know.

Tony Parsons

'I do like many blokeish things – football, women, kung fu – but that doesn't stop me from being a loving dad, a sensitive partner, a considerate lover.'

Or a chemically pure example of a cockmonkey. What a guy!

Past Times

A shop about old stuff. But all the stuff's new and that means it's new old stuff, and that's just fucked up.

Past Times themes everything in a strange, pick 'n' mix historical way. Collections include Victorian, Art Deco, Medieval and even Post Modern (that's Beatles mugs and Mongolian wool pouffes, rather than Umberto Eco hipflasks). The

Medieval stuff includes things like the 'Depart for the Chase' wall hanging, depicting 'a richly dressed nobleman on a fine white horse out hunting with his falcons. Tabs for pole hanging (pole not supplied).' Bring back hanging? They're not saying that, but they are saying bring back medieval wall hanging.

So it's a mixed bag, with the main rule being: it must be new stuff that looks like old stuff, and as far as possible be made out of polyresin, a mysterious synthetic material that Past Times boffins may well have devised themselves. I don't actually know.

Recommended 'gifts for her' include the Lesley Anne Ivory musical waterglobe: 'This glass and polyresin waterglobe is based on a painting by the celebrated cat artist, Lesley Anne Ivory. It plays Beethoven's "Moonlight Sonata".' At last this piece's muted melancholia finds its rightful home: as the soundtrack to a plastic cat in a snowstorm.

One 'gift for him', meanwhile, is the Battle of Bannockburn hand-decorated chess set (yours for £149.95). The Scots are led by Robert the Bruce, who was 'famously heartened by the tenacious spider to persist in his struggle against the English'. The English are represented by Edward II, who ended up 'deposed, imprisoned and horrifically killed at the behest of his wife'. Murder by means of red-hot poker stuck where the sun never shines: now that's your authentic Past right there. In full, red-hot effect. And who wouldn't want to live somewhere like that? A major Past Times speciality is 18th-century stuff. Not stuff from the 18th century – which is pricey – but replicas of stuff from the period that really enjoyed replicating classical antiquity. So this stuff has been modified and refined *twice*, and must therefore have attained the kind of perfection unknown to those in ancient Greece/Rome/Etruria. In fact, when Plato spoke of another plane where everything existed only in its ideal form, he was probably thinking of somewhere like Past Times. The ancient Greeks hadn't even *heard* of polyresin.*

All told, you get the impression that this is the sort of con-servative-retro-items shop old people would run if old people were all on crack. A polyresin Mucha wall sconce in the shape of a woman with her hair and her light and airy robe billow-ing in the wind? That's old people tooting rock, that is. Past Times? High Times more like. Metaphorically, obviously. I am patently not stating that Past Times is run by old people on crack: they'd never open on time. Although it might be, for all I know. But I hope not: crack is a terrible addiction that would wreak havoc at any time of life.

*Polyresin wasn't even dreamt about until the Renaissance, when Leonardo da Vinci drew a picture of what it might look like, should he be able to make it, which he could not. Leonardo was always doing shit like that. He 'invented' the helicopter in the same sense that I 'invented' DVD-playing electric shoes – that is, he's got a jotting on a beermat somewhere, if only he could find it.

Pay off Your Mortgage in Two Years

With house prices now being set by absinthe-crazed madmen throwing dice at each other, people are taking out 35-, 40-, even 45-year mortgages. But you can do it in two.

Saving pennies makes pounds, so if you save a lot of pen-nies, well, there you go, you've paid off your mortgage. It's all about tightening your belt here and there. To the point where your waist measurement is the same as your shoe size.

Money-saving tips in the book of the programme by René Carayol include stopping smoking (they all add up, and are bad for you anyway), not buying coffee (instead, go to places where they give you free coffee) and, if you must buy things, getting them on the internet (it's slightly cheaper!). Be careful, though. One top tip warns: 'If foraging or looking for food in the wild, make sure you properly identify safe foodstuffs.' So try to avoid toadstools and deadly nightshade if you can. The road to early mortgage repayment is full of victims who, rather than shedding the dark cloak of mortgage, had their stomach pumped after munching the wrong kind of toadstool. But even this is amateur child's play to the King of the Saving of the Pennies, financial writer Cliff D'Arcy. If saving pennies were a sparky young lady with excellent conversation, he would be her Mr D'Arcy, Cliff D'Arcy. He's the sort of guy who thinks lying down in a darkened room is wasteful.

In July 2006 Mr D'Arcy announced in a promotional e-mail sent out by popular financial website the Motley Fool that he was about to embark on a period of 'Extreme Budgeting': 'In January of this year, my discretionary spending came to less than £15, which is a new personal best . . . [Now] I plan to steer clear of alcohol, cigarettes, drinks and snacks, fast food and takeaways, with my only treat being a weekend newspaper or two . . . I appreciate that extreme budgeting isn't everyone's cup of tea, because it is a tough test of willpower.' Speaking of tea, Mr D'Arcy signed off: 'I'm off to have a nice cup of tea, which is my only vice during my (financial) detox month!' Presumably reusing the bag for the twentieth time. Possibly a Value bag that came in a food parcel from the Red Cross.

Putting aside minor worries that money is just a chimerical, abstract way of exchanging goods, services and human effort, and that this might be an utter waste of miserable time which involves actively hegemonising yourself with the mores of Mammon, we have created our own 'Very Extreme Indeed and Certainly More Extreme Than the Motley Fool's, Which Isn't Extreme at All . . . In Fact They Are Just Pussies: I Could Pay off My Mortgage in Three Months, No Bother – What Do You Think of That Then, René? Budget'.

Take all of the measures we have listed here and you could be saving – quite literally – in the region of two or even three hundred pounds EVERY SINGLE YEAR:

1. Swap credit-card and utility companies to get the best deals. Switch companies anything up to four or even five times a day. By really staying alert you can save well over a whole entire pound each and every week. Some people might argue that if you expended the same amount of effort working, you would make considerably more, but screw them. They don't know.

2. Don't piss your money up against a wall. I get tired of endlessly telling people that if they keep going to pubs, buying beer and generally enjoying themselves, that they will inevitably have less money than they might otherwise have had. Why can't they just suck on the juicy beermats provided at the bar? Money's going in one end and getting pissed out the other. Unless you can find me someone who will pay for piss, I'm not interested. And you won't. Because that doesn't happen. A piss merchant, buying and selling piss – it's a fucking stupid idea. (If you do ever come across somewhere with a piss merchant, let me know.)

3. You should always – *always* – only use financial products you've never heard of. If you've heard of an ISA, you need a cash ISA. If you've heard of a

cash ISA, you need a mini-cash ISA. If you've heard of a mini-cash ISA, you need to call the Bank de Bank, Zurich, and ask for Juan. Say you need 'a dirty one'. The codeword is 'flaps'. You'll also be wanting a PEP, a PAP, the PUP and a PARP. Don't forget to claim your allowances for those either, like some sort of twat.

4. Boil up some grass to make grassy stew. Eat stuff out of bins.

5. Sell your toenails on eBay (what are they actually *for*, anyway?).

6. Never. Ever. Do. Anything. Ever. At all.

7. Help me.

8. Kill yourself. There's no surer way to spend less than being dead. As a bonus, any insurance policies you hold will be paying out like a fruit machine with three triple bars on hold – not that we'd know about that, not risking our precious pennies on such atrocious fripperies. Irony is free – so treat yourself to a highly poignant death by smashing your brains open against the window of your bank. (If you bank online – which I would advise; there are some great deals out there – just go to the nearest branch of the bank of which your online account supplier is a subsidiary.) Now, for insurance reasons, it needs to look like an accident. You'll need a big run-up to get enough force to kill yourself, so start from the other side of the road while looking down the street and

smiling and waving into the distance, as if you have just seen an old friend or acquaintance and have become distracted. Just keep running until you hit the bank and hopefully die. Remember to run very fast or you won't get enough force to kill yourself. No one wants to come round outside NatWest with blood from their own head smeared down the windows. Also remember, in the days leading up to killing yourself, that you can save money by not eating anything or turning on any lights.

Harold Pinter's anti-war poetry

Bombs.
Children.
Bombs on children.

Big bombs.
On small children.
With children's faces.
And children's arms.
And children's hair.
And that.

Shitty shitty shit shit.
Shit.

Up your arse.

Shocked? You fucking.
Should be.

Yanks: all scum!

Israelis: all scum!

Israeli Yanks? Don't get me.

Poledancing lessons

Sarah Davis, the managing director of PoleCats in Birmingham, was forced to abandon plans to run poledancing classes for youngsters of 12 years old and over after protests from child protection groups. Responding to these silly and oversensitive complaints, she said: 'Our aim was purely to provide a way to help kids keep fit and boost their confidence.'

Fucking killjoys. Poledancing's just a great way of working out – and it's fun! It's like Pilates for women who think: 'Let's play at being sex workers!'

Britain's top poledancing teachers Polestars assure us: 'Lessons are for fun, not professional training. All classes are a man-free zone!' This is a grave disappointment to many women who were actually hoping to spend their leisure hours swinging about for the delectation of drunken businessmen jiggling their hands around in their suit-trouser pockets.

Now, Polish dancing lessons – they get you really fit. And they're in the EU now.

Stephen Poliakoff's London

Said Robert Lindsay of working on *Gideon's Daughter* and *Friends and Crocodiles*: 'You think of Dennis Potter, Tom Stoppard, Alan Bleasdale and Stephen Poliakoff; he's one of a select band of writers who have elevated TV drama to an artform.'

'In an age of wall-to-wall popcorn drama, reality TV and soap opera,' declared *The Times* on the occasion of the eminent TV dramatist's BBC4 season, 'Poliakoff stands alone as the last genuine auteur in the medium of TV, given the room to express his vision.'

Poliakoff does often succeed in his stated aim of making 'something people remember'. Certain scenes from *Gideon's Daughter* are etched onto my brain like a recurring nightmare. A recurring nightmare that shouts, 'This – is – really – IMPORTANT!' Always there's this London, which is presumably meant to be a stylised version of the London that actually exists. But it's really a stylised version of the London that exists in a book called *London for Deluded Shit-at-Writing Beardy Dickheads*. There's a spin-doctor moneyman property developer who lives in a castle made of steel and glass: he eats canapés, swaps bons mots with an American capitalist and secretly plans to turn a cherished playground into a nuclear dumping ground (or it might have just been toxic waste – can't remember). These portrayals are so cack-handed that even people who despise yuppies and all their works will start to rethink their position: hey, if this utter numpty hates yuppies, maybe they're not so bad . . .

It's forever an 80s where super-yuppie parties in large English gardens are invaded by cartoon lefties who grab the mike and yell: 'Four million unemployed! Four million unemployed!' The better to convey the fact that, while super-yuppies were having parties, four million people were, in fact, unemployed. *Never* forget that.

Then come the kooks. Oh God, the kooks . . . in particular, the kooky ladies. With some grindingly awful outsider figures – like a cult which lives in a big house surrounded by the feral children of south London. Or the brother and sister who shag each other because they hate Thatcher.

In *Gideon's Daughter*, kooky Miranda Richardson – her son had died (can't remember how, but it was probably thanks to a decision by the moneymen) – showed spin-doctor-in-chief Bill Nighy another side to London: the subterranean pleasures far away from the canapés and poncey dinners. It was a secret place. Somewhere only she knew. It opened his eyes to another sort of life. He had not known that down-to-earth, albeit kooky, people could find such pleasure in their simple lives. Perhaps, after all, the future lies with the proles and not with the assorted celebs, spinners, spoiled brats and media barons with whom he thought rested the complete world. That's right: she took him to a curry house.

Yes! Curry! It can taste amazing, apparently. It can even make canapés seem unappealing. I know! Who'd have thought it? And can he go back to his old life after this discovery? He cannot. Eat canapés, like some sort of spin-doctor-moneyman-twat? Now he's had pakora with yogurty sauce? Of course not!

He even missed his important meeting with a Berlusconi-like-Italian bigwig. *But he didn't care*!

So he arranged for this beautiful curry house to host one of his renowned bashes, to show the capital's assorted advertising-moneymen-spin-doctor-celebs how shallow their lives were. He really stuck it to 'em.

Spread now among the moneymen and the usurers and the warmongers the revelation that is cumin, turmeric, chilli and oil. Let's show the fuckers what life is all about. Take them to a curry house. Order some poppadoms. Maybe some prawn puree. I like those.

Thus revealed Poliakoff. Curry: it's fucking real.

Policemen cutting up dead people on the telly

Incessant.

Politicians called David

David Blunkett, David Davis, David Lammy, David Cameron, David Owen . . . Need I go on?

True, David out of David and Goliath was good – he helped the Israelites, who had latterly been sore-oppressed, to defeat the Philistines, who were ignorant. (Although he did later commit adultery with Bathsheba, wife of Uriah the Hittite, which would have given the tabloids a field day.)

Thirty-one sitting MPs are called David. Of these, only one refers to himself officially as 'Dave'. Dave Watts, Labour MP for St Helen's North, has presumably adopted the matey sobriquet to avoid people bellowing Kinks lyrics at him in the street: 'I wish I could be like Dave Watts/Lords Commissioner of the HM Treasury . . .'

While we're on the subject of politicians' names, and very much in the interests of holding our leaders to account, here are some non-David MPs with quite funny names: Mr Bob Blizzard, Mr Andy Love, Mr Peter Bone and Dr Howard Stoate.

Now *that's* satire.

Politicians' 'sexual aura'

In 2003, Gordon Brown topped the *Erotic Review*'s top 25 list of male sexual icons: 'Gordon Brown represents the scheming anti-hero women find so attractive. They don't want bland hero figures like Blair – Brown's brooding malcontent is much sexier.'

Okay. And how much sexier exactly? Would you, for instance, want to see him wrestling in the nude? Light glistening off his oiled flesh? Is the Chancellor really the kind of man you're drawn to in the street? Sort of pallid and hefty like he sits eating white bread all day with the curtains drawn? If so, you're just mental.

And is he really sexier than Blair? Don't write the PM off as a repressed freak who probably only does it with the lights off. Interviewing him for *Saga* magazine, Valerie Grove wrote: 'He is every woman's favourite shape, six foot tall, good shoulders, lean hips, weighing just under 13 stone, less than he did 10 years ago.' Sorry, how desperate do you have to be to find Tony Blair sexy? Have you ever *seen* other men?

'Shagger' Norris? John Major!! John bloody-fucking Major!?!?! Are you even technically alive if you look at John Major and think, 'Hey, stud-muffin, let's get it on!'???? Ah, but in the flesh, he's got that undeniable something. Biographer Penny Junor famously mooned about his 'knack of making you feel that, for that moment, you are the only person he is interested in talking to'. Sorry, but the idea of John Major zeroing in towards you and telling you he'll treat you like a laydee is simply revolting.

Something has really gone wrong with your attitudes to sex if you want to whisper sweet nothings to Oliver Letwin or suck off Peter Hain. What next? Pieces eulogising the blubbery intensity of John Prescott? Ah, but when you meet him . . .

Porn, misleading use of the word

Porn gets everywhere these days. Even where it patently is not.

We are now dangled 'gardening porn' (porn involving hostas), 'car porn' (porn involving Jeremy Clarkson), 'gadget porn' (porn with Inspector Gadget) and 'gastro porn' (belly porn).

One episode of celeb-foodie show *Eating with* ... was trailed by announcers as featuring 'Nigel Slater, the king of gastro-porn'. They repeated this three times, presumably in the hope that on at least one occasion we might mishear and think, 'Wow, porn's coming up.' You half expected to see a big flashing sign saying: 'Something quite porny! This way comes! Oo-er! We said "comes"!'

Anyone thinking the next programme would feature something of a stimulating bent might have been disappointed to see a speccy man talking about his dark, painful childhood being brought up by a cold, distant father. That's not porn. Or, if it is, only a tiny minority will get their rocks off over it.

It's surprising they don't trail the news as 'topico-porn'.

And the weather could be called 'Hot 'n' Wet'.

Maybe it could be introduced: 'Now here's Peter with some hot fucking.'

PowerPoint

The Microsoft tool that encourages people to think and talk like fuckheads.

Prawnies

Prawnies, available fresh-fried in big paella pans from stands at markets, events put on by councils, festivals – all that sort of behaviour – are reconstituted prawn and fish meat, coloured and flavoured to give the taste and impression of prawns, then moulded into the shape of large prawns. They are, according to the blurb, 'a revolutionary new product', related to seafood sticks (the rubbery things with the pink coating). But if you want a foodstuff that looks and tastes like prawns, why not try prawns? It's almost as if they are designed to look and taste like prawns.

Presenters speaking to the camera while driving their cars

There are enough dangers in the world already, without current affairs presenters trying to present pieces to camera while negotiating heavy traffic.

Has no one learned from the tragic maiming of Fergal Keane: 'I'm driving down to Kinshasa now, to . . . *Cows!* Aaaaarrgggghhhhhh!'

Prince Andrew

In 2003, the fourth in line to the throne decided to travel from London to a lunch engagement in Oxford by chartered helicopter at a cost to the taxpayer of £2,939. When faced with complaints about squandering the public purse, a Palace spokeswoman explained that reliability was paramount as the Oxford date was a state banquet in honour of Vladimir Putin. Sadly, 'setting out earlier' was, she continued, simply not possible as there was 'something he'd forgotten to do' and also 'something on the telly'.

Prince Andrew loves helicopters so much that, when no helicopter can be found for him, he scampers up and down the Palace corridors shouting: 'Mummy! Copter! Mummy! Copter!'

Private members' clubs

Private members' clubs are the places for 'like-minded' leaders of the 'urban-hip revolution' to 'mix business with pleasure in a relaxing environment'. These burgeoning boltholes are places where media-savvy movers display their 'cool, don't-mess-with-me, *GQ*-reading suavity' (the *Independent*). They are for the guys at 'the forefront of a lifestyle revolution that has since become established hip-urban style' (the *Sunday Times*). Essentially: to get into a private members' club, you need to be a member.

There is very little parallel with the posh gentlemen's clubs of yore. Yes, the new private members' clubs are expensive and exclusive; but they have much cheaper furniture. Basically, it's lots of chaps with Johnny Vaughan accents who relish 'stylish fun with a strong whiff of naughtiness'. People who know the best way to enjoy a drink is to look up every time someone walks in the room and then look down in disgust because it's not Sienna Miller or someone from Oasis. It's a bit like Bertie Wooster's Drones Club, but with more cocaine meltdowns: 'I say, will you take a look at that, Jeeves. Adrian from Web Your Own Hole's got his trousers round his ankles and is rubbing his old feller on all the leather sofas. What a rummy rotter!'

Product, the word

'What products do you use?'

'Oh, you know . . . pens, ball bearings, all sorts.'

'No, I mean beauty products.'

'Oh, sorry. You needed to be more specific. And less of a fucking twat.'

Property ladder, the

A marvellous system that separates society into two camps: the smug and the damned.

Public conveniences, lack of

Thank God for McDonald's. As a pleasing bonus, when you relieve yourself in McDonald's without purchasing one of their special patties of death, you are quite literally taking the piss out of them. Actually, no – you're quite literally giving piss to them. Anyway, they don't like it.

Bookies are also very handy for a cheeky wiz. And pubs. Except the one I popped into in Manchester in 2001 where the burly landlord made me buy a lemonade on reappearance from the lav on pain of a punch in the face. The fat bastard.

Pubs selling shit art

If someone produced good art which they planned to sell at a reasonable price, would they need to display it in a place where people habitually become drunk?

Q

'Quality' Hollywood movies

People often stereotype Hollywood as a machine always prey-
ing on our basest needs for violence, sex and glamour. It's not,
though, sadly. It also tries being deep too, which, when it
comes to making films, is something that is best left to the
Europeans. Except the British.

These films can generally be spotted by any sign of the following: Sam Mendes; Jude Law doing an American accent;
Kevin 'I love the theater best' Spacey; Spielberg and Hanks!
Together again!; a 'normal' middle-American suburb where
everything is not as it seems; Gwyneth Paltrow playing a
famous poet; Nicole Kidman playing a famous author (with a
big nose); lives being changed forever by a car accident;
Anthony Minghella; and Sam Mendes and Anthony
Minghella! Together again!

Having directed *Truly, Madly, Deeply*, *The English Patient*
and *Cold Mountain*, Minghella should be crowned king of
ersatz profundity/portentous schmaltz. So it was almost
inevitable he was chosen to direct the 2005 New Labour election broadcast designed to show the deep love and
understanding between Tony Blair and Gordon Brown. The
script, as far as I recall, went as follows:

TB: I think we can agree, Gordon, that it's all about the little ones. Don't you think?

GB: Oh yes. Hur, hur . . .

TB: I mean, we can talk about all this other stuff, but really, it's the precious little children that we love, isn't it?

GB: Sure.

TB: You do love them too, don't you, Gordon?

GB: 'Course . . .

TB: Oh, I love the babies, Gordon, I bloody do . . . save the babies!

GB: . . . righto . . .

TB: All the special little ones, I mean.

GB: . . .

Queen musicals

Writer Ben Elton blamed *We Will Rock You*'s terrible reviews on Britain's pervasive 'tall poppy syndrome'. Yes, it could be that. Or it could be Britain's pervasive 'thinking Ben Elton is a premier fuckwit syndrome'.

The posters of *We Will Rock You* show the back of a cast member punching the air in mimicry of the sainted Mercury. This image prompts the question: how did Freddie manage to perform like that – punching the air, skipping around the whole stage and thrusting his crotch everywhere while also carrying on singing his opera-flavoured rock? Hey . . . maybe, just maybe, it was at least partly thanks to all the massive pre-show lines of cocaine?

'I don't know where he gets all that energy from,' said Mum. It's from the cocaine, Mum. Mainly the cocaine.

Questioning the whole basis of fashion

At the Autumn 2005 Paris Fashion Week, designer John Galliano claimed to be 'questioning the whole basis of fashion'. This meant having his collection modelled by giants, dwarves, identical twins, fat women and body-builders (but mostly dwarves).

This really socked it to the notion of the fashion industry serving only the rich and the beautiful. Either that or he'd just seen *Time Bandits* on DVD and thought it might be a laugh. Certainly, it questioned the whole basis of fashion, but possibly not in the way he had intended.

As a target for satire, the fashion industry is not a difficult one to hit – a little like hitting a very big barn door with a large herd of cows. Taking potshots at its money worship and body fascism (and borderline actual fascism) could not be simpler. (Cathy Horyn in the *New York Times* reported that someone came up to her after Galliano's dwarves show and asked, 'So what did you think of the monsters?') Except you cannot convincingly satirise things which you in fact are. You cannot credibly live for bon ton in the pay of one of the four global behemoths that own all the fashion houses and simultaneously say, 'It's all bollocks.' That's like pointing at yourself in a mirror and going: 'Look at that twat! Just *look* at him!'

By the way, interestingly – and not a lot of people know this – when Gucci bought out Alexander McQueen, they didn't just buy his company; they bought *him* – his actual self. Say they wanted him to run down to Gregg's for some pasties, or ring up Isabella Blow and call her a stupid tart, or just to give him a slap, they could, quite legally. Not a lot of people know this because it is not true. But still . . .

Quick recipes

By strange coincidence, the British craze for cooking fancy food has coincidentally coincided with the craze for working into the evening and then feeling the need to pass out from drink. This has led to a craze for quick recipes.

So all food magazines advertise the 'Quick and Easy' aspect of their 'Tried & Tested Recipes'. (What, you've actually tried out the recipes? With this trying and testing, you are really spoiling us.)

In his book *Jamie's Dinners*, Jamie Oliver claims that, in the past fifteen years, the average time spent making a meal for the family has slipped from an hour to thirteen minutes. He then describes some extremely quick 'Five Minute Wonders', a section which should more accurately be called: 'Five Minutes, My Giddy Sweet Back Bottom'. He even adds a challenge: 'Each recipe has the time it took for me to make it – you never know, you might be able to beat me on some of them!'

Well, you try making beef with pak choi, mushrooms and noodles, for instance – which can apparently be done and dusted with coriander in five minutes 12 seconds – including slicing the red onion, slicing the ginger, finely slicing the chilli and brushing and tearing up the mushrooms and quartering the pak choi – without slicing the tops of your fingers clean off and leaving the kitchen a blood-spurting mess. Particularly when you've been drinking.

Really, your partner might as well have the car running for

that mercy-dash to Casualty. Is this what he wants? A&E wards full of wannabe quick chefs! Is this part of his bold vision for public sector renewal? And your partner's in no fit state to drive a car – they've been drinking. Look at the fucking state of them!

Honestly, he comes across as such a saint. But really he's still a bastard.

R

R&B ballads

That is not an album. That is somewhere in the region of one decent fast song followed by 30 tonnes of Disney-does-gospel-with-satin-sheets-in-hell mush with no discernible words except, 'Woh-oh-oh-oh-aaaaaahhh! Ooooooh! Oooaoaoaoaoaoaoa! Aaargh! Aaargh! Aargh! Yooo-hooo!'

And those aren't even real words. Rubbish, really.

Railway menu cards

The idea is to make you feel less like a big mug and more like a valued guest. Okay, it says, you've waited an hour for this train, and you only got a seat because it's the middle of the day – but, look, we'll give you crisps: here is a picture of a packet of crisps, to illustrate this amazing good fortune.

The glossily produced menu cards left on your table offer an intriguing array of cuisines including said Walker's Crisps, costing '£0.60', Twiglets also costing '£0.60', and Mars Bars – today, a mere '£0.50'. Freshly caught, too, I'll be bound. Mmm. More obscurely, there's also 'Gourmet Bread Products' – currently retailing 'from £3.00'. How chi-chi is that? Oh, it's just really bad sandwiches.

The whole clinking-trolley-full-of-snacks-as-restaurant

motif has not yet reached its fullest potential. In future, perhaps they should consider employing a *maître d'* figure to bring round a leather-bound list of delicacies with the words: 'As madam will see, the specials are sandwiche cheddar au pickle and an amazingly tiny tin of juice. The chef handpicked the dry roasted peanuts himself this morning at a service station on the M6, and I can tell you the Mini Cheddars have that perfect balance between MSG cheesy flavouring and flour. Aperitif, anyone?'

Razor blades that can shave even closer than the hitherto closest-shaving blade, which was already really quite close (also: washing powder)

Shaving has certainly come on in leaps and bounds since men dragged flinty bits of flint down their hirsute faces, pulling out clumps of hair matted with animal fat and their own fetid blood. 'Aaaarrrgggghhhhh!' they would say. 'For fucking fuck's sake. That really hurt and now it's all stingy and raw and throbbing and raw.'

Then there were the so-called 'cut-throat' razors, but these took a dive in popularity after barbers started cutting people up and putting them in pies. That's when the safety razor was invented by King Camp Gillette, in 1895. (Hur hur, King Camp. He's called King Camp.)

And bang! The race was on – to make the safety razor bigger, better, closer and, crucially, more expensive. Along came lubricant strips and 'spring loading', 'open cartridge architecture' and handles with 'knurled elastomeric crescents'. First there was one blade, then there were two. Then there were three, then – you can see where this is going. Now there are five – yes, five. Count 'em. And weep.

The new Gillette innovation has five razor blades in it. *Five*. Not four – like the Wilkinson Sword Quattro – but five. Five. Can't you count? I said five. It's very exciting.

Now, some people might suggest it's probably impossible to get closer than existing razors in a way perceptible to the naked eye. They might say it's a colossal waste of a billion dollars and the full-time efforts of a hundred people to go round developing new five-blade razors like the old ones were going out of fashion, which they are. Perhaps these people would agree with Roger Hamby, of the Cutlery Allied Trades Research Association, who said: 'The Holy Grail of closeness was reached 30 years ago with the first twin-blade razors.' But what do 'some people' know?

The names of these babies alone should be enough to re-assure us of their scientific veracity and general goodness.

Sensor – you know what it's all about. Mach 3 – the blade that is so manly it has a name vaguely reminiscent of strafing Afghan villages. Mach 3 Turbo – it vibrates! Mach 3 Turbo Gforce! (Don't know what that one does.) The five-blader, which has 75 patents on it and is made in a Class 5000 clean room in Berlin, an environment purer than an operating theatre, is called Fusion. Yes, it has capacities so mind-boggling it can only be described by conjuring up the spirit of jazz rock. Dark magus! Also: washing powder.

Ready meals

Should you stray off the modern food-Nazi holy-eating track for a sneaky fix of bubbling additive-paste, you might need to develop the appetite of a particularly picky three-year-old. Because these things really ought to be called ready-for-another-meal-in-an-incredibly-short-space-of-time meals. Or 'snacks', as I believe such meagre portions were termed in the olden days.

'Serves 2'! Serves two *what*, exactly? Cockatiels?

I HAVE GIVEN YOU FOUR POUNDS AND FORTY-NINE PENCE – AND I *DEMAND* SUSTENANCE!!

Real Football Factories, The

In the feral, vicious world of cobbled-together 'Real' documentaries riding in the slipstream of anything remotely popular (*The Real Desperate Housewives/Footballers' Wives/ Brokeback Mountain*), *The Real Football Factories* is The General – a fat-necked psycho going toe-to-toe with your telly who NEVER runs. You NEVER RUN. 'Ave it! Pie-eaters! Etc.

This clip show's claim to be a serious study of football hooliganism was undermined somewhat by its sole sociological analysis being a professor claiming: 'The Midlands is a strange area; it sort of falls between London and the North.' Presenter Danny Dyer spends most of the 'ARD-'ITTIN' DOC- UMENTARY ABAHT RIGHT NAUGHTY FIRMS 'AVIN' PROPAH FACKIN' TEAR-UPS dressed in a rudeboy trench- coat, 'snout' dangling from his yap, strutting through underpasses on council estates, randomly stringing together words like 'PROPAH', 'FIRMS', 'FACK' and 'ABAHT'.

'Dunno whevva you've seen a movie called *The Warriors*,' the Britpop actor gorblimeys while loitering outside Upton Park tube station in his trenchcoat looking TASTY. 'S'about a New York gang travelling through the city by subway, bumping into rival mobs along the way. PROPAH FILM! Now that's pretty much what it was like here in the 80s, as rival firms fought battles at train stations like King's Cross and Euston.'

Sat in a pub with some PROPAH hooligan nutcases, though, his mask slips. The studied sneer quivers, his top lip giving off micro-actions that silently scream: 'Don't cut me! Not the face! It's my livelihood! Not the face! Not the face!' PROPAH DOCUMENTARY!

Dyer, of course, also starred in the real *The Football Factory* – the 2004 film of the book of the fight. It, too, is straightforwardly about fighting at or near football grounds. It opens with a fucking great big fight scene. It continues with some more fight scenes. It culminates in a big fight scene.

The film was advertised as being about fighting, with a DVD extra called 'Fight Scene': arty stills of burly blokes knocking shit out of each other under a thumping soundtrack with snatches of dialogue from the film dotted through it like 'Don't fuck abaht – just ping 'im.' To sum up: *The Football Factory* is about fighting.

Except, according to director Nick Love, it's not: 'The thing I love, and will never get away from, is men bonding. They're not gay or anything. It's deep male friendship. I'm obsessed with male friendship. It doesn't mean it's a gay film. You just do it nice and gently and subtly and everything.'

The Football Factory's portrayal of male relationships is indeed subtle – the relationships being expressed wholly by them hitting each other.

Love's next film was *The Business* (also starring Dyer), a lads' own voyeurism flick about 80s villains living it up on the Costa del Geezah – the money, the drugs, the manly man-on-man fisticuffs, the clobber, the casual glassing of waiters, the improbable plot and terrible dialogue, the sub-Ritchie pop-video direction, the wooden performances, the male bonding with fists . . .

Forthcoming is *Outlaw*, due in 2007, about 'what happens when crime victims take the law into their own hands'. Its website describes it as a 'challenging and thought-provoking . . . exploration of social complexities in contemporary Britain'. But don't worry, it also pledges 'anarchy and off the wall naughtiness', which isn't nearly so complex.

But we probably shouldn't hold out much hope for a challenging take on Asbo Britain, given that the film's logo involves a hoodie-wearing youth hanging from a gibbet and balaclavas with blood dripping off them.

And the website features an online game called Nonce Hunter: 'Use your pistol, assault rifle and sniper rifle to kill those evil nonces and get to have a shot at Fred West and Ian Huntley.'

PROPAH FILM!

Restaurant service charges

Different from a tip in several key ways: it's not voluntary and it doesn't often get to the staff. Many establishments either split the service charge with the staff or just keep it all for themselves. So it's not even a 'service' charge, a charge in appreciation of the staff, who might reasonably expect to get paid properly anyway. It's just a charge: someone asking you for extra money for no reason whatsoever which they will then simply keep. You can see why they don't call it that on the menu.

Restaurant service charges that only apply to parties of more than 10 people

More service, certainly, but only because there is more stuff *being served*. You thieving shits.

Restaurants with unfeasibly small toilets

As you squeeze between the door and sink into a cubicle that was last cleaned – that is, given a cursory wipe with a damp toilet roll – some time in the latter half of the 20th century, note how the extra table space in this Indian/greasy spoon/Chinese restaurant created by making the unfeasibly small toilet into which you are now trying to prise yourself so unfeasibly small is NEVER occupied by a diner. It will ALWAYS either be empty or occupied by restaurant staff smoking fags.

Sometimes these restaurants exude an air of genuine tragedy and thwarted ambition. This expresses itself in the need to walk a very long way to reach the unfeasibly small toilet. You must travel either upstairs or downstairs, through the never-used overflow room, full of piled-up tables once upon a time destined for stag do's and office Christmas parties that never came. These rooms often manage simultaneously to smell musty but also smell of paint, even though nothing that could rationally be described as 'decorating' has ever taken place there.

And there you are, in the semi-darkness, a bit pissed, whizzing your tits off on MSG, wading through this shrine to the Unknown Diner, this culinary purgatory, Godot's own bistro – just to piss in a cupboard.

Condoleezza Rice

Oil giant Chevron loves its former executive Condi Rice so much they named an oil tanker after her. How truly awful must you be for the oil industry to like you that much?

When news of this homage caused controversy, the company quietly renamed the ship. The name they chose instead was *Condoleezza Rice? Oil-Loving Secretary Of State Who Oversees The Invasion Of Middle-Eastern Countries To Privatise Their Oil Infrastructure For Use By US Oil Giants? Never Heard Of Her! We Did Once Know Somebody Called Condoleezza Rice, But Not That One.*

Or it might have been the *Altair Voyager* – I can't remember now.

Everyone always goes on about Condoleezza Rice's supposed 'cleverness'. But she herself rates George W. Bush as 'someone of tremendous intellect' – so the bar has been set quite low here. Let's hope she never gets a job as, say, a GCSE examiner, because that could blow her mind.

Rice did attend the University of Denver at the age of 15 – but it was only to study the piano. And that is not, let's face it, a proper subject. Neither does it prepare you for high office: no one's going to look to Jools Holland in a crisis, are they?

Not unless it somehow involved boogie-woogie.

Rich, the

The sumptuous invitation cards read:

'From the château steeped in history,
We enter a world of maharajahs and mystery,

A gilded palace from Bikaner brings,
A lavish feast fit for a king.'

The 'king' was steel magnate Lakshmi Mittal, the richest man in Britain and the third richest in the world. The 'château' was the finest in France, Vaux le Vicomte, on the banks of the Seine. The 'lavish feast' was the June 2004 wedding of Mittal's daughter Vanisha, which lasted for six days. India's finest chefs were flown in, and Kylie Minogue performed; there was a live Bollywood extravaganza about the happy couple. Fireworks exploded in every direction, lighting up the whole of Paris.

The feast certainly was 'lavish'. Thirty million quids' worth of 'lavish'. I think the point they were trying to make was: 'We – let's not beat around the bush here – are the dog's very rich bollocks.' Mittal couldn't flaunt his wealth more if he flew over the poorer quarters of Mumbai in a helicopter shouting through a megaphone: 'You, yes you there – I am rich and you are poor. Look at me, up here, the rich bloke in the helicopter. Yes, me – Mr Moneybags here. Do not look at you, who is poor, look at me, who is rich.'

Fans of the rich, the kind of people who want to press their nose against the Mittals' glass and marvel at the shiny objects – people such as the author of the recent book *Rich Is Beautiful* – often invoke the so-called 'trickle-down effect', whereby the great wealth of a tiny minority, despite them apparently spending it on gilded palaces and lavish feasts, is quietly and invisibly percolating down to the rest of us. I'm not sure how: maybe they hide pound coins down the back of single mothers' sofas?

The rich are supposed to be useful and great and good. But, according to the 2005 *Sunday Times* Rich List, the five richest people in the country are:

5. Phillip Green (£4.85 billion). Owns a load of shops that are a lot like a load of other shops. So that's good. (See also **Philip Green**.)

4. Hans Rausing (£4.95 billion). Invented the Tetra Pak milk carton. Then fucked off from Sweden to the UK to (why, of course) pay less tax. Tossing milk cartons. Tremendous.

3. Duke of Westminster, the (£5.6 billion). Go-getting enough to be born absolutely stinking-filthy-rich. Puts the 'lord' into landlord. And also, come to think of it, the 'land'. To be fair, does let poor people live in his Mayfair properties for free. Not really.

2. Roman Abramovich (£7.5 billion). Russian oligarch. Pocketed Siberia's oil wealth. Got a shit haircut. (See also **Football buyouts**.)

1. Lakshmi Mittal. Best known in Britain for slipping Tony Blair a few quid.* Worth a staggering £14.8 billion, having started with just the one humble steel plant. (Which was bought for him by his parents.)

Even the most cursory flick through the rest of the Rich List will see they're all fat, boring, self-serving bastards who no one's ever heard of – podgy old blokes from the City who are 'in finance'. And when you have heard of someone it's fucking Sting.

Either that, or it's aristocrats. There are 125 aristocrats in a list of 1,000 – or 12.5%. Of course, this just reflects the percentage of aristos in the population generally. Oh no, hang on.

Whether their blood is blue or red, the one thing that unites everyone in the Rich List is, of course, really, really, really hating tax. You'd think that as all the super-rich's super-riches are generated by the whole of society (and with the trickle-down effect turning out to be a little, well, 'inefficient') governments might risk slightly offending the delicate sensibilities of the rich by enquiring if, after all, they might like to, you know, pay some fucking tax?

Even a tiny increase would raise sums so large the Inland Revenue would run out of carrier bags to put it in. That way, the wealth could go directly into things like education, culture, healthcare, that sort of thing; steering it ever so slightly away from bank accounts in tax havens and sweetmeats for a clique of rapacious, parasitical, reductive, generally unpleasant shits. If only it were that simple. Both Tony Blair and George Bush have found that, although clearly they'd love to tax the rich, it is a physical impossibility. Even if the rich didn't 'move abroad', there still wouldn't be any surplus billions heading towards society's coffers. Bush explained: 'The really rich people figure out how to dodge taxes.' Blair claimed that if top-rate tax were raised: 'Large numbers of those taxpayers – probably the wealthiest – would simply hire a whole lot of new accountants to do this and that.'

Compared to, say, using military might to recast entire societies in parts of the globe where everyone hates them, these two eminent men consider that closing a few tax loopholes would be 'too difficult'. Suicidal Jihadists? Bring 'em on.

Accountants? Accountants doing 'this and that'? To the boats! To the boats!

---

*Before the 2001 election, Mittal donated £125,000 to the Labour Party. Blair then wrote to the Romanian government persuading them to let Mittal buy a steel factory. Blair claimed it was a coincidence. But that was bollocks, wasn't it? Also, £125,000? With all that cash he's got? If I were a Labour fundraiser, I'd have said: 'Come on, you've missed a nought off that, you stingy cunt.' This is just one of the many reasons why I am not a Labour fundraiser.

Keith Richards

Keef is the original punk. The everlasting renegade pirate outlaw riffmeister. In a world of fakes, the Stones' legendary guitarist is the real deal, the keeper of the flame. Except, erm, he's a pampered old jetsetter and a very silly man.

The road of excess is meant to lead to the palace of wisdom. In Keef's case, it has led to the palace of tottering about playing the same riff for 30 years with a scarf tied round your head. Is that wisdom? Shouldn't have thought so.

But millions believe Keith has lived the rock 'n' roll dream so they don't have to. For them, personal nirvana would be to party with Keef back in the day. Even though partying with Keef back in the day would generally have involved watching someone fall asleep and drool and then wondering if he's started turning blue or if that's just the light.

The rock 'n' roll thing to say is that the Stones are 'his band', that Mick is just his singer. In which case, why does this renowned renegade let 'his band' tour the world sponsored by T-Mobile? Or cancel a string of UK dates because they were worried about paying more tax? That certainly doesn't sound very rock.

Keef is the fearless spirit who said: 'If you're going to kick authority in the teeth, you might as well use two feet.' But, in living memory, the only 'authority' Keith has kicked with two feet is The Ramblers' Association. In 2002, he won his long-running battle to move a footpath further away from his West Sussex mansion – even though it was already separated by a thick hedge and a moat.

Thankfully, Keith's lawyers took on the ramblers on his behalf. Nevertheless, Keith prides himself on being A Bit Tasty – and, to be fair, he is fairly dangerous. But only in that he's an addled old soak who insists on carrying concealed knives. While pissed.

During sessions for cobblers 1983 Stones album *Undercover Of The Night*, the guitarist would emphasise any point by swishing a swordstick. People said this was 'cool' when what they should have said was: 'Come on, Keith. Don't be such a twat all the time.'

Roadtanks – SUVs, 4x4s, etc.

Market researchers are good. The ones employed by the US car industry found that people who buy SUVs are insecure, antisocial fucks who couldn't give a beggar's testicle about their fellow man: and who'd have worked that out on their own?

Here's what Keith Bradsher of the *New York Times* reports the US auto industry says about 4x4 drivers: 'They tend to be people who are insecure and vain. They are frequently insecure about their marriages and uncomfortable about parenthood. They often lack confidence in their driving skills. Above all, they are apt to be self-centered and self-absorbed, with little interest in their neighbors and communities.' No way!?

If pushed, the head of General Motors would say they are 'right twats'. Probably. He'd certainly think it. Probably. And Humvees? Where I come from a Hummer is a really smelly fart – and I'm not driving round in one of those, not for all the tea in Tesco. Poo! No way!

4x4s are just a way of saying: 'My family's got a big cock.' They are a marvel of science and technology, though: when we were kids they only had 2x4s, and they were just pieces of wood. You couldn't off-road on them, not even in Chelsea. So things have certainly come on in leaps and bounds since then.

Amazing, science and technology, isn't it? Last Bonfire Night my girlfriend gave me toe warmers – they're little sticky gel packs you stick to the outside of your socks and – get this! – even though they are cold when you take them out of the packet, stick them to your socks and they go all hot and keep your feet toasty. Now, how does that work if not by sorcery? By science and technology, that's how. Or it could be sorcery. I don't actually know.

Romantic comedies

'I really loved *Maid in Manhattan*' is a phrase one never hears. Or 'I really loved that film *Wimbledon*.' This is because romantic comedies are commissioned on the basis of a six- or eight-word premise, which then everyone who is involved neglects to expand into an actual script. Com does not ensue. Nor does rom.

The king of such films is Matthew McConaughey, a man who can smirk quizzically in posters next to Jennifer Lopez or smirk quizzically in posters next to Sandra Bullock. He was recently seen smirking quizzically in posters next to Sarah Jessica Parker for *Failure to Launch*: she's falling in love, but he still lives with his parents! Oh, and he's a boat broker, hence the title – it's applicable both to his familial situation and to the boats that, as a boat broker, he brokes. It's almost like literature.

Coming soon: *Staying away from the Herd*. Wealthy socialite Sandra Bullock is smitten after meeting Matthew

McConaughey at a high-class masquerade, but then she discovers he's not a Wall Street banker but herds cattle. Can this relationship ever be a dung deal? You'll be laughing till the . . . well, you know.

Coming soon: *She's So My Dad's Date*. Matthew McConaughey plays the son of ageing womaniser Sean Connery. There's trouble in the family when son falls for father's new girlfriend, played by Lindsay Lohan. Age-gap comedy extreme!

Coming soon: *That's No Lady*. Matthew McConaughey is smitten with new girlfriend Cameron Diaz . . . but is she really all she seems?

Coming soon: *Secure Unit*. Starring Matthew McConaughey and Kirsten Dunst. He's a prison visitor – she's a real nut!

Coming soon: *My Big Fat Racist Wedding*. Starring Matthew McConaughey as a black lawyer betrothed to white girl Mandy Moore. When is he gonna find out that Daddy's in the Klan?

Royals, the

All shit.

Well, except for Prince William who even I – a heterosexual male with strong anti-monarchist beliefs – have to admit to finding so unbelievably beautiful that I almost want to cry. Lord knows, I didn't want this to happen. But just look at him!

Sometimes, I actually find myself wondering whether it's love and start spinning involved romantic fantasies in which we both write each other poems and laugh and giggle and laugh some more.

Then, in my darker moments, I can't stop thinking about being taken roughly from behind by Prince Harry dressed as a Nazi.

Rude films

Reviled actor-director Vincent Gallo's 2004 flop *Brown Bunny* famously featured a scene in which the actor-director is explicitly fellated by a character played by his ex-girlfriend Chloë Sevigny.

So how exactly did this happen? Maybe he phoned her up and said: 'Hi, this is your ex-boyfriend. The one with the cast-iron reputation for asshole-ism. Look, I'm not gonna mess you round, I'm gonna come straight out with it: basically, it's like this, baby . . . I want you to suck it on camera for this new thing I'm doing. Whaddya mean, is it justified? Woah, yeah! Course . . . I can't even believe you even asked me that. I'm outraged! I'm Vincent Gallo, important film director! What do you think? That I'd just ask you to suck it for cheap kicks or something? Man, that would be sick! So, anyway . . . that okay with you?'

In which incredibly strange world of strange fucking strange would the answer be 'yes'?

Donald Rumsfeld

When the Abu Ghraib pictures surfaced, US Defense Secretary Donald Rumsfeld told Congress that he and his staff were 'offended and outraged'. But it's kind of hard to see how he was even mildly surprised.

Certainly, I wouldn't have been very surprised if I was Donald Rumsfeld. Not if I knew the US intelligence community had long been intrigued by the possibility of sexually humiliating Arab males to extract information. Not if I'd helped set up a highly secretive Pentagon operation, sometimes called Copper Green, which, according to a CIA source speaking to *New Yorker* correspondent Seymour Hersh, responded only to the rules 'Grab whom you must. Do what you want.'

Not if I'd sanctioned General Miller to 'Gitmoize' the prison system in Iraq and extended the programme so far that army reservists, including what one official called 'recycled hillbillies from Cumberland, Maryland', were being used as prison guards. Certainly not if I knew that even the CIA (those drippy liberals) were finally holding up their hands and saying: 'No way. We signed up for the core program in Afghanistan – pre-approved for operations against high-value terrorist targets – and now you want to use it for cab-drivers, brothers-in-law, and people pulled off the streets.'

Personally, all things considered, I think that if I was Donald Rumsfeld and I'd heard that no one was being stripped naked and made to climb into human pyramids, I would have been absolutely fucking amazed.

But then, Donald Rumsfeld has highly refined powers of compartmentalisation. In fact, this skill has now become so advanced that sometimes his right leg can be kicking an Arab's head in while he himself is completely unaware of any violence taking place anywhere in the vicinity.

Then someone nearby points out: 'Hey man, look! You're kicking that Arab's head in!'

And when he looks down, he can't believe what he's seeing. 'Oh my God!' he says. 'That's terrible! Look at my leg kicking the Arab's head in! Jeez Louise!'

At this point, Donald Rumsfeld starts repeatedly shouting: 'You're going home in a fucking ambulance!'

To which he immediately responds: 'Oh my God! I'm so offended! My mouth just shouted the words, "You're going home in a fucking ambulance!" Can you believe this shit? It's outrageous! And offensive! I'm sickened to the very pit of my being by what I've just heard! Have you seen this Rumsfeld guy? Man alive!'

S

Salt lobbyists

The salt lobby is working tirelessly, heroically, day and night. On behalf of salt. The rights of salt. To be sprinkled on potatoes. To be utilised in the boiling of vegetables. Or used as a major ingredient in salty snacks.

'I'm lobbying – for salt!' This is what they say.

The Salt Manufacturers Association are keen to teach us Salt Sense. It's a beautiful thing, and sensible.

Cut salt at your peril: this is the salt lobby's prime message. Cut salt and you could be cutting your life – '37% increased risk of death from heart disease' says new study. Here's a picture of a running woman with the caption 'salt if you exercise'. She eats up her salt . . . and so should you. Here's an elderly lady eating a salty meal with salt on, captioned 'salt and the elderly'. Don't take away her salt. It's all she's got.

And here's a salt gritter (caption: 'salt for gritting icy roads') which would, let's face it, be nothing without salt. Isn't it obvious? Stop using salt and icy, skiddy, mangled carnage will result. Do you see now?

'Sassy' songs about body parts

You're playing with your bits,
I'm playing with my bits,
Ooh baby, I betcha wish you were playing with my bits,
Instead of your bits . . .
My bits, my bits, my bits, my bits, my bits, my bits.

That sort of thing.

Arnold Schwarzenegger

- 3 July 2003, pre-campaign appearance in LA: 'I told you . . . I'll be baaack!'
- Summer 2003, campaign trail: 'By the time I'm through with this whole thing, I will not be known as The Terminator . . . I will be known as The Collectinator!'
- 14 September 2003: 'Davis and Bustamante . . . have terminated jobs. They have terminated growth. They have terminated dreams. It is time to terminate them!'
- 17 September 2003: 'I know that on 7 October, we will recall Gray Davis and say, "*Hasta la vista*, baby!"'
- 24 September 2003, during televised campaign debate to opponent Arianna Huffington: 'I just realised that I have a perfect part for you in *Terminator Four*!'
- 2 October 2003: 'When I get to Sacramento, I will immediately destroy the car tax. *Hasta la vista*, baby! To the car tax!'

- 31 August 2004, Republican National Convention: 'One of my movies was called *True Lies*! It's what the Democrats should have called their convention!'
- 31 August 2004, Republican National Convention: 'In one of the military hospitals I visited, I met a young guy who was in bad shape! He'd lost a leg, had a hole in his stomach – his shoulder had been shot through ... Do you know what he said to me? ... He grinned at me and said, "Arnold ... I'll be back!!"'

Did you see what he did there?

Self-examination columns

'Hmmm ... have you noticed that no one eats avocados any more? Wow, think about it a second – it's true. That's amazing – no one eats avocados any more! We all decided at exactly the same time. Isn't that weird? Or maybe some people do eat them ... they are still on sale in most places, after all. Anyway! Do you ever get a funny feeling in your left leg? Do you get that? ...'

The essential skills of the modern columnist rarely overlap with old-style journalism. No more going outside and meeting people, checking facts or any of that passé nonsense – just make a big sandwich and start examining your own self. Go deep, because when exploring the self, you simply can't be too self-centred. There's no code of conduct to abuse when it's your own privacy you're invading. That would just be like abusing yourself.

But writers can't just write down whatever flickers across

their consciousness. Okay, they can. But they also need a gimmick. One successful figure currently produces a weekly treatise focusing solely on their fingers. Going under the title Can You Digit?, a recent missive went: 'Hmmm. That nail needs cutting. Look, this one's growing faster than the one on the other hand. Unless I nibbled that one some time after I last cut them all . . .'

Another writer stepped up to the challenge with Fenced In, every week detailing the progress of the creosote they covered their garden fence with: 'I thought the bottom of the third panel needed recoating, but when I got closer I realised it was just the light. The fourth panel used to be the brownest one, but it's not any more. It still smells the way creosote usually smells. I quite like it. I know a lot of people don't, but I do.'

Then there was Everyone I've Ever Wanked About. This was followed up with Everyone I've Never Wanked About, which was bits of the phone book typed out. That column immediately boosted news-stand sales by an estimated 20,000 a week.

A competing title, inspired by such successes, employed another writer to explore the random sounds they could make with their mouths. Called Sounding Off, it started: 'Clickclickclick. That's nice. Babbety-babbety-babbety-bab. Not so sure about that. We're not getting anywhere here. I know – ratatatatat! ratatatatat! ratatatatatat! Yes, I likes it!'

To bolster the now slightly passé fingers column, the original title decided to employ a writer who had no thoughts of any description whatsoever. Under the title Dry Brain In A Dry Season, its most recent entry went as follows . . .

'...................................what?.....................wait................there was something...
no......................it was nothing........'

Serving suggestions

Have the makers of hummus, say, *ever* received a letter complaining that there was no parsley included inside? 'The label clearly depicts a parsley garnish atop the tasty chickpea-based Greek dip. So where the shitting blazes is it, you robbing pack of thieving bastards? Is it customary for supermarkets wilfully to cheat their customers in this way?'

It seems extremely unlikely. Yet there are always two words found on every scrap of food packaging to guard against such an eventuality: serving suggestion. They may be small, but they're always there. Like people expect a jug of ice-cold milk to be included in their cereal packet. Even though that would represent a major spillage hazard – which nobody wants. Or a single cherry tomato in their pot of sour cream and onion dip.

The serving suggestions are not only dumb, they're woefully unoriginal. Readybrek is always – always! – served in a clean blue bowl. Why not, just once, show an illustration of the oaty cereal having been dished up into a bowl of another colour, or into another kind of receptacle altogether: like lots of tiny walnut shells or a pair of child's Wellington boots? Now *that's* a serving suggestion.

Sex tips

Some people are so expert at sex that they become 'sexperts'. Very much leaders in the field of how to use one's bits, these people inhabit a world of non-stop sensual erotica. They really know about genitals.

For any willing recipient of the awesome wisdom of a 'sexpert', 'sex tips' will inject your sex life with such unbridled naughtiness that any passing Bangkok whore would be moved to widen her overpainted eyelids with fearful fascination. Some of the most common 'sex tips' include the following:

- Breathe on each other. As one of you breathes out, the other breathes in, so you inhale each other's breath. Breathing – it rocks!
- Cover each other's legs in sealing wax. Hey, it's not for everyone but don't knock it till you've tried it. Waxy, isn't it?
- Don't underestimate the erotic potential of the elbow. Find out what you can do with yours and before long your love buddy will be dragging you upstairs as soon as you walk in the door.
- Lather up each other's pubic regions with shampoo and make amusing shapes. Laughter is a great way of creating a sexy atmosphere!?!?
- Stuff each other's mouths full of cheesy biscuits – then lick each other all over. You'll be amazed at the new sensations that you both experience.
- You'd be amazed how talking can get your partner feeling horny. Try reading aloud favourite passages from *The Aeneid*. Trust me . . . phew!
- During penetration, why don't you both imagine

you are both soaring through the clouds on the wings of a giant swan? If either one of you can perform a convincing swan's call, so much the better!

- Oh . . . just, you know, new positions and that. Put your legs in funny places, that sort of thing.

Shops that play shit music at ear-splitting volume

That's quite a nice shirt, I think I'll pop in there and try – oh, fuck, no I won't, they're playing Jamiroquai at 12 trillion decibels. Jesus, one of them's even dancing.

Nigel Slater

As a frontispiece in his book *Real Food*, Britain's Greatest Ever Cookery Writer (Says Everyone) Nigel Slater declared: 'When I say butter, I mean unsalted; when I say salt, I mean Maldon sea salt; and, when I say sugar, I mean the golden unrefined stuff from Mauritius. Pepper is ground from a mill as I need it and not, absolutely not, bought ready-ground . . .'

What is it about New Britain's aspirational icons that they impart advice with this weird sense of barely concealed menace? As though not completely devoting yourself to Getting It Right – and possibly even just preferring sport and ciggies – might bring down more shame upon you than if you had shat the bed.

I was only wondering what to have for dinner. I wasn't planning on invoking the kind of wrath more usually found in the officer class of the 19th-century Royal Navy.

'Salted butter? Salted with salt that is not Maldon sea salt?! You, sir, are a *shit*! LASH HIM!! Lash him well . . .'

Snack-a-Jacks, the name but not necessarily the product

The product I am not prepared to take a line on, for I am confused. My brain says it's wrong. Salt 'n' vinegar rice-cakes, it says. Screw that. Stupid idea. But my hands disagree with my brain and put them in my mouth, and I enjoy them. Is that good? I don't know.

The nutrition Nazis would crap on about salt and preservatives and what-not interfering with the basic rice and corn goodness – but who wants to eat plain rice cakes? Except babies, and they don't know anything about food. And, for me, it's nothing to do with health anyway: it's the taste and texture (I know!); I'm like a moth to cloth; I bakes for them rice cakes. You can see why this is an issue for me.

Anyway, they are not really helping me out with the name. To be purchasing something called Snack-a-Jacks feels somehow foolish and undignified. Snack-a-Jacks? It's a name, frankly, that only a prick could love. Luckily, Snack-a-Jacks are usually in boxes or on shelves and thus liable to self-service, and not, say, behind a counter, like Rennies and fags. If I had to ask for them, they certainly wouldn't be selling any Snack-a-Jacks to this snacker, Jack.

As for the new Snack-a-Jack chocolate orange flavour? *I'm trying to be on your side here, Quaker, but you just keep taking the piss out of me.*

Soap characters loosely based on Osama bin Laden

Nothing says daytime TV like a medievalist mass-murderer who wants to establish a worldwide Caliphate.

So full marks to long-running NBC soap opera *Days of Our Lives* (the one that supposedly starred Joey from *Friends*) for finally developing a character based on Osama bin Laden.

Clearly, it would have been better if *EastEnders* had got there first, but you can't have everything. (Phil Daniels: 'I brought them kids up on me oah-n.' Osama: 'We love death. The US loves life. That is the difference between us.')

The character was created by Kola Boof, author of the forthcoming novel *The Sexy Part of the Bible* (please note: don't look for the sexy part of the Bible; you'll be sorely disappointed) and, she claims, a former mistress of bin Laden.

Really stripping away the layers and getting to the heart of her creation, the writer said: 'This character wants to take over the world.' Fortunately, it appears she never personally met Osama's late bad lieutenant in Iraq, Abu Musab al-Zarqawi. But still, maybe she could be tempted to introduce a Zarqawiesque character into *Days of Our Lives* too. Perhaps the skanky younger brother, like De Niro's Johnny Boy from *Mean Streets*, only always getting into beheading-related scrapes. She could sum up his motivation thus: 'This character wants to behead everybody.'

Incidentally, according to al-Qaeda expert Jason Burke, when bin Laden heard of his wildcard follower's death he might have felt 'sneaking relief'. How truly awful must someone be for bin Laden to find them irresponsible? 'He was a bit of a handful, really,' says Osama. 'Just trouble from the word go. That kind of guy we just don't need . . .'

'Sold' signs

The property is no longer 'For Sale'. This is surely the point at which to take down all those big, fuck-off, multicoloured signs outside it. Not put up a new one.

Want to buy this house? Tough shit, you can't. It's not for sale. You should have been here last week. Go and buy another house. Cos you ain't buying this one. Want it? I bet you do. But you can't.

Soundtrack albums from shit films with shit soundtracks

Who – *who?* – emerges blinking into the foyer, dusting off a confetti of fumbled Revels and Butterkist, after sitting through, say, 'Can Pierce Brosnan's master thief resist one last big score with tough cop Woody Harrelson on his tail?' crappy adventure flick *After the Sunset* and thinks: 'Hey – great film, must get the soundtrack.'

'Music from and inspired by . . .' That's 'inspired' in the financial sense rather than in the actually-having-seen-the-film sense.

Toon-based, FIFA-sponsored footie-fest *Goal!* seems to have spent more time totting up potential soundtrack sales than writing the script. Mexican ball wizard Santiago Munez (he's poor, but he's moral) goes for a very, very, very, very long run along the Northumberland coastline, the waves crashing in and the music thumping away as he runs on and on and on and on and on. Plot-wise, a few seconds would have done – but how then could one crowbar in all of a pumped-up remix of Oasis's 'Cast No Shadow'? What's the story? I can't remember – there's just this bloke running all the time.

Even good films generally have no necessity for a sound-track release. Who cheers themselves up by popping on the available-at-all-good-record-stores soundtrack to *The Elephant Man*?

Are there really flatmates and couples, staring down the end of another evening's TV braindeath, saying to each other: 'Let's make a night of it. I'll nip out and get a box of two-for-one Cava and some tabs – you slap on the sound-track to *Jean de Florette*.'

Or: 'Which track from mentalist-insomniac-psycho-factory-worker thriller *The Machinist* do you like best? I really like "Miserable Life", but I *love* "Trevor in Jail".'

'They're both great, but on balance I definitely prefer "Where is My Waitress"?'

'Yes! The posing of the question, the lack of resolution – it's quite, quite beautiful. Do any of us know the where-abouts of our waitress, really? That's what he's saying. Where is *your* waitress? Where is *my* waitress?'

TV's at it too, with CD spin-offs from *Cold Feet*, *The Forsyte Saga*, *Ideal* and *The Virgin Queen*. 'That quite good drama of Elizabethan power-plays certainly enlivened our Sunday evening viewing – let's get the background music from the bits when they were walking down corridors.' 'Cool. We could walk down our hall.'

Even computer games have soundtrack albums now – the various volumes of *Grand Theft Auto* have their own section in music stores. 'Do you know, later, I think I might pimp some women for a bit and then crash my car.' 'Ace. You'll be wanting to put this on then.' 'Cheers. You motherfucker.'

As a general rule, if it's not a musical, it probably doesn't need a soundtrack album. Actually, that holds for most musi-cals, too. Particularly *Chicago*.

South Bank Show Little Britain Special

The crying shame of this programme is that many of the best bits couldn't be jimmied into a mere hour and were anyway either too interesting or too worthwhile to warrant inclusion. Until the suits at ITV get their blummen silly act together, here is a transcript of some of the prime offcuts:

EXT. LOCATION SET IN THE BACKGROUND. MATT AND DAVID IN LEOTARDS, SITTING ON PLASTIC CHAIRS. WALLIAMS IS WEARING BLACKFACE (NOT FOR THE SKETCH THEY'RE ABOUT TO SHOOT, HE JUST IS).

BRAGG: Tell me about the new characters you're working on.

WALLIAMS: Well, we're very excited about a West Indian character we've been developing.

LUCAS: Yes, she's a fat black witch who lives on an estate – she's called Mama Shakalakaboo.

WALLIAMS: (*loudly*) Aaaahm gon' put a spell on you!

LUCAS: Ha! She's always putting spells on people.

WALLIAMS: And chanting. Mama Shakalakaboo! Mama Shakalakaboo!

BOTH: Mama Shakalakaboo! Mama Shakalakaboo!

LUCAS: Then there's Ray. He's got a club foot. *Fade.*

INT. KITCHEN AREA OF WRITING OFFICE. MATT AND DAVID SIT AT A TABLE ON WHICH ARE VARIOUS POTS OF YOGURT.

LUCAS: Strawberry yogurt.

WALLIAMS: (*smiling affirmatively at Lucas and nodding his head*) Yes, we've certainly had one of those.

LUCAS: Or raspberry?

WALLIAMS: Hmm.

LUCAS: Fudge even? (*Pause. Glances at Walliams.*) Or sometimes we don't even have yogurt. (*Both shake their heads.*)

Long pause. Lucas and Walliams smile awkwardly at the camera.

BRAGG: Do that anecdote you always do about how you met at the National Youth Theatre.

WALLIAMS: What? Christ, even I'm sick to death of that one. (*Long pause.*) Do you want to see my cock?

BRAGG: What?

WALLIAMS: Do you want to see my cock? I'll show it to you.

BRAGG: What, no, I really don't think that's –

WALLIAMS: Go on, I'll just pop it out.

BRAGG: No, really, definitely –

WALLIAMS: I'll just get it out *a bit.* (*Fumbles with himself.*) There he is!

BRAGG: What? Jesus!

Cut.

INT. DRESSING ROOM OF *LITTLE BRITAIN* THEATRE TOUR. LUCAS'S DRESSING ROOM. HE IS HOLDING A CARD THAT SAYS 'GOOD LUCK' ON IT. WE FAINTLY HEAR PRE-SHOW SHOWBIZ HUBBUB FROM THE CORRIDOR.

BRAGG: So here you are, playing to packed houses of schoolchildren right across the nation. How does it feel?

LUCAS: It's very interesting and pertinent you should ask that, as we're actually doing a book about precisely that.

WALLIAMS: Yes, I just think everyone out there just really wants to know how we're feeling right now, doing a tour, being on the telly, being in the papers, being so very, very popular. Matt and David. What are they feeling? What are they thinking?

BRAGG: Well, not to try to scoop your book too much, but what *are* you thinking?

WALLIAMS: Eh?

BRAGG: This thinking. What is it you think about?

Long pause.

WALLIAMS: There's, ah . . .
Long pause. Walliams and Lucas exchange looks.
LUCAS: Well, you spend quite a lot of time thinking about pretty ladies, don't you?

WALLIAMS: Not 'arf! (*mugging*).

Long pause.

LUCAS: The model for the book is *Feel* – by Robert Williams. Are you familiar with it?

BRAGG: No.

LUCAS: It's a chance to answer our critics. The ones who say we're just socialites doing jazz hands.

WALLIAMS: We don't do that. Not even a bit.

LUCAS: And anyway, where are the so-called victims? We haven't had a single letter of complaint from an incontinent old woman. I'm sure they're quite capable, if they're offended, of saying: 'Come on now, I'm an incontinent old woman, and I say no, that is wrong.' But they don't.

WALLIAMS: Exactly. Or take fat black women – please do! Eh? Not 'arf! (*Pause.*) But, anyway, they're quite capable of speaking up for themselves. All the fat black women I've met – well, seen, I've seen some on the telly – they've all been pretty teisty. (*Pause.*) Rusty Lee.

LUCAS: Rusty Lee. She had a right gob on her.

WALLIAMS: Ooh, Rusty Lee. Do you remember Rusty Lee?

LUCAS: We love Rusty Lee.

Pause.

LUCAS: A million plastic-figurine-buying children can't be wrong. So nay to the nay-sayers, that's what I say.

WALLIAMS: And if not, well . . . aaaahm gon' put a spell on you! (*Widens his eyes and glares at the camera in triumph.*)

LUCAS: (*chanting*) Mama Shakalakaboo! Mama Shakalakaboo!

BOTH: (chanting) Mama Shakalakaboo! Mama Shakalakaboo! MAMA SHAKALAKABOO! MAMA SHAKALAKABOO! MAMA SHAKALAKABOO!

Fade.

Spam porn
'TODAY IS JIZZ DAY!' . . . Is it? Is it really?

Specimen cheques
'A personal loan from our highly reputable credit card arm could give you a helping hand for those moments in life when you need a little extra: remember last winter when the kids all demanded jet packs and you'd jizzed it all on elephant tusks and cockfights? As an existing customer, you're pre-approved to borrow up to £12,000. So we could soon be paying a cheque like the one enclosed into your account.'

And there it is – a cheque for 12,000 big ones. Okay, the word 'SPECIMEN' is stamped across it, but it's still a thrilling sight. And it's certainly a good job the company included this amazing document; if not for this fake cheque – featuring my own name! – I might not have fully appreciated the reality of the situation. Without that, I might simply have binned the fucker thinking it was more junk artfully designed to drag me up to my titties in debt.

Of course, the reverse includes a disclaimer: 'It is important that you make sure you do not take on more than you can afford . . . Banko Bastardos is a responsible lender . . .' But surely the inclusion of the specimen cheque implies that they're chasing the kind of person who not only has trouble managing their finances, but also has difficulty lifting a soup spoon to their mouth without scalding their ears. The sort of person who might shout: 'Hey honey, come look at this! All those zeros . . . this is an amazing thing that's happened to us here. These guys have chosen *us*!'

They're certainly not chasing people like Barclays chief

executive Matt Barrett who, in November 2003, told the Commons Treasury Select Committee that he didn't use credit cards and advised his kids not to either, as they're a rip-off. As recorded in *Hansard*, Barrett said: 'Borrow on a credit card? What do you think I am – some sort of twat?'

Spotted!

Someone. Somewhere. Out. Doing stuff. Thanks for that.

Stag weeks

Not just stuck with people from the office. But stuck with people from someone else's office. For a week. And they're off the leash and up for Fun with a capital 'Fun'.

Mere stag 'nights' now have the same quaint associations as powdered egg. 'I'm getting married in the morning . . .'? Not when you can sing: 'I'm getting married in about six months – just after I've shagged my way round half of the New Europe.' Let's face it, there's no more fitting way to see off your single status than by furthering a Baltic state's slide towards sex industry gangsterism.

Companies like Prague Piss-Up are finding much of Eastern Europe now ripe for exploitation. They've just launched the offshoot Tallinn Piss-Up – combining the two is a 'double-header'. In Tallinn now, any non-sex-related businesses are losing trade and being eaten up by criminal enterprises; to meet the demand, women are shipped in from Estonia's poor, depressed north-east to service Marcus from the office who is up for trying out some stuff he's seen on the internet.

This, increasingly, is the New European way: hordes of Elvises, hunting alcopops in packs, all hoping to service their Little Elvises. Love me tender? Thanks to the fantastic exchange rate, love me for not much tender at all. But what the staggie boys should bear in mind is that unbridled sensual delight does not necessarily lead to a life of total fulfilment. If it did, John Leslie would be king of the world. (And he's not.)

'Stress-busting', the phrase

It's interesting that, in this day and age, you are even obliged to try to reduce your stress in an aggressive way.

Bust that stress! Get it down on the floor and really stick one on it! Faster! Really fuck it over! You're not good enough! You're not good enough! There isn't time! There isn't time!

Stupid arguments for being paid too much for being on the telly

Gabby Logan once justified being paid in excess of a million pounds a day for what basically amounts to 'watching the football' by saying she sometimes has to react to the unexpected. What, like air traffic controllers and firefighters react to the unexpected? How unexpected does football get? Are the players going to spontaneously combust, or be beamed up into a passing Martian spacecraft? Shouldn't have thought so. Or is she going to be waiting for Chelsea to come on and 'Oh, hang on, orange strip? It's Dunfermline fecking Athletic! And they're – they're playing themselves!'

Newsreaders argue that wheelbarrows are required to pay them because reading the news is 'very difficult'. Now, I seem to manage it fairly well when I read the paper. I'd go as far as to call it 'easy'.

The worst shoddy excuses for minting it for doing nix are from people on breakfast radio/telly, who always use the argument 'We get up really early.' This is the reason that they are the third-highest-paid occupational group, just behind milkmen and paper boys.

Summer bodies

'Beach panic! Beach panic! Beach panic!'

You've got to get your body ready for summer. Don't, for fuck's sake, leave it to its own devices. That way lies ruin and derision. Which means, according to the women's magazines, getting in training in the middle of winter. Of course, tans tend to be at their best in autumn, when people start covering up. It's a fundamental flaw in this whole 'seasons' thing which we are now thankfully doing our level best to eradicate. By introducing artificial tans that make people look like they have covered themselves in toffee.

It's all-important if you are not going to end the summer sad and lonely, with nothing to look forward to but winter.

Superloos on trains

Don't work/not super.

Supermarket flowers

It's a hopeless and forlorn sort of concept, even before you consider their pre-supermarket life cycle: farmed in Colombia by sweated labour, backs to the sun and faces to the earth, wages – topped up with all the free toxic chemicals you can inhale – as pitiful as the blooms; all those wasted, wasted air miles to get them here. That's an oppressive enough litany for coal or iron ore, but for a flower?

Simply of itself, it's quite melancholic: supermarket flowers. In fact, I'm surprised somebody hasn't written a sad song incorporating the gift of supermarket flowers as the potent signifier of an empty, artificial relationship. It could be called 'Supermarket Flowers'.

If anyone now writes one, there'll be no legal comeback from me. It's the sadness I can't bear. That's all.

Television on mobile phones

Far too small.

Tennis parents

Human foetuses can't play tennis (not even if it's twins: where would they get the racquets from?). So a parent who decides their unborn child is going to be a tennis star has to be some kind of freaky freaking freak-nutter freaking freak.

Richard Williams, father of Venus and Serena, consulted psychiatrists about the best way to bring up children destined for sporting stardom. Possibly quite sensible, given their early promise on the tennis court. Except he did it before they were born. Freaky freaking freak-nutter freaking freak.

Melanie Molitor, mother of Martina Hingis, was so determined her unborn child would be a tennis star that she named her after Martina Navratilova. Still, that's better than calling her Boris. Or Goran. Or Pat Cash (Pat Cash Hingis – that's a shit name). Anyway, aged four, Martina was playing in tennis tournaments – as opposed to, say, with Stickle-bricks.

So keen was Damir Dokic – father of Jelena – on dominating his daughter that he has found it very hard to let go. The

right-wing nationalist Serbian ex-boxer made a name for himself by getting expelled from matches for hurling Serbian
abuse at officials (which puts your dad's 'embarrassing' cardie
in perspective). Perhaps wisely, his daughter expressed her
gratitude by dumping him as manager and moving to a different country. He responded: 'She left us. We don't need
her . . . She did things that she was not supposed to.'

And why tennis, anyway, which is shit? Why not mould
your children to do something useful – like perfecting nuclear
fusion, or playing the drums like Animal out of the Muppets?
And those freaks who 'hothouse' their kids into genius math-
ematicians are no better. Hothouses are for growing tomatoes
in. Is that what you want your child to be: a tomato? Freaky
freaking freak-nutter freaking freaks.

Me, I believe the children are the future. Teach them well
and let them lead the way; show them all the beauty they pos-
sess inside. Let the children's laughter remind us how we used
to be. Actually, come to think of it, that's not me – that's
Whitney Houston. Same difference.

Tesco

Is Tesco a state within a state waiting to take over Britain and
run it as a quasi-fascist enterprise regulating every aspect of
our lives?

The case for this proposition:

1. Tesco employs over twice as many people as the
    army – 237,000 to 110,000.
2. Not content with already pocketing £1 of every £8
    spent in UK shops, Tesco is expanding its tentacles

into every area of our lives – including insurance, online DVD rental and banking.
3. Tesco's colours are red, white and blue.

The case against:

1. It's a supermarket.

You decide.

Testing children to make them clever

Tests used to be a way of seeing whether children were learning stuff rather than, say, just picking their noses and flicking it. Nowadays, children learn stuff so they can pass tests, so everyone can see that they are good at passing tests. If the first is the horse pulling the cart, the second is more like the cart pulling the horse and then making it sit a test.

Ticketing hotlines

'The bill for your £12.50 ticket comes to £26.99.' 'Great.'

Toast, overpriced

There's a lot of overpriced toast out there. Watch out.

Toy cars

Are aspirational these days. They're all big Mercs and Audi TTs. Visit any toy shop looking to gift-up a little person, and you'll find all the household names in the die-cast mini-motor universe – Matchbox, Siku, Hot Wheels – wholly obsessed with premium motors.

There's seemingly a ban on ordinary cars – the sort most people drive, the sort most children might ever see. No Mondeos or Yarises or Focuses or Kias – or even any Golfses or Lexi (that's the plural of Lexus, by the way). Xsara Picasso? Not on your giddy arse. The message: 'Hey, I know you think he's good, but sorry, kid, your dad's a loser.'

You'll be falling over huge delivery lorries branded with DHL or UPS logos, but searching high and low for an ambulance. You can still get fire engines – except they have to be either 40-foot long with 18 retractable ladders and called Flame Tamer, or have 'TURBO' written down the side.

Matchbox? You might as well call yourselves Hegemonising The Kids.

Trade union leaders pretending to be hard

New Labour's rise to power left Old Skool trade union leaders with a case of the Emperor's new clothes (WARNING: do not dwell on this image – I just did and now can't get a nudey John Edmonds out of my head). After years spent telling their members (fuck it, now he's dancing) to wait for a Labour government to make everything peachy, here in Downing Street were (now he's having a shower – Jesus, why must this be happening to *me*?) a bunch of Thatcherite shitters taking their orders directly from The Man (ah, that's better – Bill Morris has just put a towel round him): 'Workers? What workers? You mean those people who clean my house? They look okay to me. What's the fucking problem?'

Union leaders were reduced to saying things like: 'Colleagues, when I said things could only get better, I meant, erm, a bit later on. I wouldn't exactly say there will be jam tomorrow. But certainly, one day, at an unspecified point in the future, there will be, in some unspecified quantity, some jam . . . or fruit preserve of some description, or an equivalent – it could even be honey – for some people, the identity of whom will become known later. Possibly. Of that, Brothers and Sisters, there can be no doubt.'

Amazingly, their members weren't overly impressed and started wondering what their glorious leaders did all day. Bungate – when MSF leader Roger Lyons was caught charging a 25p bun to his union credit card – gave them the answer: they sat around eating buns. Buns paid for by the members – quite literally, the fruit buns of their labours.

So some union memberships voted out the bun-eaters and turned instead to the so-called Awkward Squad – a bunch of Molotov-hurling desperadoes like Dave 'Knuckles' Prentis of UNISON, Billy 'Haymaker' Hayes of the CWU, Bob Crow-'bar' of the RMT, 'Handy' Andy Gilchrist of the FBU and Mad 'Frankie' Fraser.

The Awkward Squad immediately issued terrible threats to fight for workers' rights and to save the welfare state. Then they put some ambiguously worded motions into the Labour Party conference. Then they withdrew them. Grr! I'm telling you, these boys are fucking animals. They will stop at nothing. And they frequently do.

The Awkward Squad have variously done such dangerous

and frankly awkward things as stopping the Iraq War being debated at the 2002 party conference – you know, the one just before the war. Or buried motions on PFI in return for vague and shady backroom commitments by Labour bigwigs to 'you know, generally be a bit nicer'. Strangely, though, this hardball strategy of occasionally mouthing off and then running away hasn't delivered the goods.

So, what now? Maybe train drivers' union ASLEF has inadvertently shown the way forward: during a disagreement over the direction of the union after Awkward Squad member Mick Rix* was replaced as General Secretary by union right-winger Shaun Brady, they took the time-honoured route favoured by the labour movement for generations: they held a barbecue. Then they all got pissed and had a big fight. None of that compositing motions then withdrawing them at the last minute or making gnomic remarks at conference fringe meetings. Just a good old-fashioned, bare-knuckle punch-up.

So maybe this is how the labour movement should deal with the government – invite them to a barbecue then leather the bastards. It'll be like *West Side Story* (in fact, I suggest you play the soundtrack from *West Side Story* to create a bit of atmos). Except this 'rumble' isn't over a girl, it's over the link between pensions and earnings.

Prescott, we know, has got a serious right hook so watch out for him. And Brown's a big fella, if out of shape. I suggest you first distract them with a table full of pies – then Bob Crow jumps on them from a wall.

Follow up with a swift jab to John Reid's goolies and setting fire to Peter Hain. Then give Blair the pasting of his life. But look out for Hoon – he's the sort of dirty bastard who might pack a blade.

This might seem a harsh and primitive way of dealing with

the situation – but what's the alternative? Say you organised a big demonstration to kick-start a mass movement to save the welfare state. It might rain. And then what would happen? You might get wet. That's what. And who wants that?

*Mick Rix sometimes went under the name Dave (I'm not making this up). Certainly a man's name is his own private business, but it's unlikely to instil confidence in your members:
    'What was the meeting like?'
    'Pretty good: he said he'd start a cross-union campaign to get the railways renationalised.'
    'Great.'
    'Yeah, but on the down side, he didn't seem to know his own name.'

Trends in interior design

Interiors magazines tell you that September is the month to:

- Decorate the walls with bird motifs.
- Discover the beauty of stained glass.
- Use summer's harvest produce to make jellies and chutneys.

No, it's not. It's the month to go to work/school/college, eat toast, drink too much, not get round to stuff and watch some telly. Rather like October. And November.

What do you mean you haven't repainted the whole house yet this week? Didn't you know that 'warm, vibrant and lively, orange is set to become next season's hottest colour'? Meaning that having a stylish house actually means having an orange house.

Until, that is, six months down the line when – with your house barely free of the smell of orange paint – the same homes mag wags its shitty little finger at you and says 'sophisticated, mellow and organic, sage green is set to become next season's hottest colour'.

What shall I do with my orange carpet? Burn the bastard in the street as punishment for it not being sage? My house looks like a fucking Tango commercial.

'New looks for table linen'? Shove them up your arse.

Trailers for programmes that are on the telly now

A blipvert trailer of a programme advertising the fact that said programme is on 'Next' or even 'Now' – that is, as soon as this trailer and the announcer announcing that the programme is starting get out of the way, the programme will start.

Surely trailers should trail programmes that will be on in the future, rather than those which are on in the present. I don't think of that as a complicated point.

Donald Trump

US *Apprentice* supremo Donald Trump – and this is true – claims he grows those amazing trademark eyebrows *on purpose*. They are alpha-male stag antlers designed to intimidate opponents in negotiations. Okay, but what about the stupid hair?

Big Don has a holiday website called – and this is equally true – www.gotrump.com.

He also has a property website called www.parp.org. Okay, he hasn't. But gotrump is real. In fact, I'd highly recommend listening to Trump's welcome speech on the homepage, where he shouts at you like an evangelical car salesman pumped up on sales after a sales seminar at a power-selling away-day: 'There's nobody better – there's nobody even close.'

Advanced megalomania – that definitely puts me in the holiday mood. Although I would be even more enthusiastic if they had animated the eyebrows.

T-shirts, insanely expensive

The turnover for T-shirts in the UK economy is now greater than for all other commodities combined – including food and oil. This is due to the strategy of charging cackloads of money for them, even though, at the end of the day, they're only T-shirts that cost approximately jack fanny-adams to produce.

Not long ago, one could reasonably be expected to be an outcast from society for wearing a Donnington Monsters of Rock T-shirt. Not any more, though – not now they cost 70 quid. What about a fake-aged AC/DC T-shirt – a brand new T-shirt that looks like a faded eighties' tour T-shirt? A mere £69 (Selfridges, summer 2004). Or maybe a fake-aged Electric by The Cult T-shirt – a tad more expensive at £75 (because it's about 8.7% more ironic).

This desirable item is produced by a company called, ahem, Buddhist Punk. An iron law of insanely expensive T-shirts-making states that your company must have a silly name – a bit, you know, funky. (See also **'Funky', the word, as applied to anything except a musical genre**.) Top marks here must go to the company Maharishi. Christ, if you're chump enough to give them 70 quid, you can't say they weren't advertising the fact they could see you coming. You couldn't give a much bigger clue short of calling your company Fakir. Or Snake-Oil. Or Skank.

Oh, but they've probably been also 'customised' (someone has added a bad print of Hong Kong Phooey or Michael Caine as Carter). Or even 'deconstructed' – that is, with seams on the outside, or bits of material added to, you know, consider the workings of your T-shirt and unpack its very, erm, T-shirtness. 'Deconstructed' T-shirts are the very apex of T-shirt design and are always – always – the work of major designers. M-A-J-O-R. People who don't just design T-shirts but also do, you know, trousers, and maybe even coats.

Please understand that these T-shirts are very expensive – anywhere up to 200 quid – because it takes a major talent to do this and only a major talent. Or a monkey. For fuck's sake.

U

United Nations

See **Vox, Bono.**

Understanding business

Everyone thinks we should 'understand business'. We have no business not understanding business. We should very much make it our business. To understand business. Personally, I make it my business scrupulously to avoid business. But that's my business.

Gordon Brown wants 14- to 16-year-olds to understand business by attending Enterprise Summer Schools, where they forgo any summer-job cash opportunities to attend a kind of business boot camp. (Gordon Brown has never met any 14- to 16-year-olds. Not even when he was fourteen to sixteen.) Here, they will look at pie charts. All summer.

Sir Alan 'Sir Alan' Sugar wants business to be taught in schools from an early age. Talking to one interviewer, he read from an imaginary Janet-and-John-style book that he keeps in his head: 'Mummy gets £100 a week from Daddy because Daddy goes to work.' (Mummy eventually ends up bashing Daddy about the head because he's 'never there'. Daddy, it transpires, has been spending those evenings when he claimed he was Auditing Entertaining Clients at Strip Clubs. Then Daddy robs the Pension Fund. Actually, now I think of it, I don't think Sir Alan 'Sir Alan' Sugar's story continued quite like that.)

It seems that nobody these days considers business to be a very boring thing that other people do. In olden days, at least business types marketed themselves as dull but necessary. Now they have to be fun and sexy, too. All those boardroom pay rises must be going to their heads. If the opening credits of *Dragons' Den* are to be believed, it's got quite a lot to do with waterskiing.

In *The Apprentice*, according to the *Sunday Times*, Sir Alan 'Sir Alan' Sugar 'made business look sexy' (I'm having difficulty again!). Certainly, *The Apprentice* contestants appear to think Sugar is not a prat but some kind of elemental warlord – like the hero in a Kurosawa epic.

But other businesspeople say this is wrong, that Sugar is a prat after all and that he might lead people to misunderstand business. 'Young people will be turned off because they think they will be shouted at by a horrible, fat, old, rich bloke,' said former CBI overlord Digby Jones (a fat, horrible, old, (quite) rich bloke).

One thing I have learned from *The Apprentice* is that even people who are really into business don't understand it. Most of the contestants haven't got a fucking clue. About anything. Set them a simple task like 'go and buy these items in London for the cheapest price' and they will flap around like an elderly person suddenly commanded to drive Formula One. Unless I'm missing something and one key business skill involves being fairly average but shouting loudly that you are, in fact, not average. 'Average? Me?! Get out of here! I'm the best. I know I'm fucking everything up and no one likes me, but I'm the kind of guy who gets things done and can get on with anybody. Buy stuff, people! Buy stuff!'

Aspiring businesspeople being numpties brings us neatly to *Dragons' Den*. Or, as we like to call it in our house, 'Please God no, please don't tell me she's mortgaged her house and ploughed it all into the Solar Travel Juicer. She's got kids.'

Dragons' Den unintentionally completely destroys the Thatcherite dream. On the one hand, we have the poor, deluded hopefuls who really believe that by giving it a go, they will enter the bright, goodies-strewn world of entrepreneurialism, rather than just get eaten alive. And then we have the Dragons – and a more charmless bunch of bastards you'd struggle to assemble.

Ah, but no. They are heroes. A bit like, er, rock stars. Duncan Bannatyne is so keen to propagate business, he has founded a magazine, *The Sharp Edge*. One editorial summed up the key things to remember about being in business. There were only three points. And two of them were 'remember to have fun'.

That would be where the waterskiing comes in, then. Bannatyne says business involves 'tough challenges (as tough as the notorious ridge in the Lake District which shares my magazine's name). And to cut it on your own takes a sharp edge too: quick thinking needs hard decisions.' In a few lines, he drops four heroic adjectives – 'tough', 'sharp', 'quick' and 'hard' – which rather suggests sex as imagined by a 13-year-old boy who still plays war.

The Sharp Edge magazine also featured a glossy spread on the potential rewards of flogging your guts out for years at a stretch (bigger watches, basically).

Peter Jones, meanwhile, refers to himself as an 'ultrapreneur'. The hideous yellow mansion featured in the credits with the stone lions on the gates? That's his ultrahouse. Architecture and social critic Jonathan Glancey called it 'Kentucky fried Georgian'.

So let's get all the young people down to Uncle Gordon's boot camp. They can practise foreclosing and workplace bullying for a bit, then Duncan Bannatyne can come and give a lecture. He would glare at them with those big eyes of his, before declaring: 'I bet you want a watch as big as mine. Oh look, time for waterskiing.'

Unnecessary digitisation

Virgin's new Pendolino trains have special tiny screens set into the carriage walls just above the windows, telling you whether seats 045 and 046, say, are AVAILABLE or, conversely, NOT AVAILABLE.

The screens are tiny. The carriage lights are set into the wall just above them – and thus shine directly over the faint LED lettering, which sits on/merges into a light grey-green background. Even with 20/20 vision, you have to squint to read them, leaning in right over the top of the double seat.

So maybe a more efficient, faster, easier method of discerning whether a seat is AVAILABLE or NOT AVAILABLE would be to look at the seat and decide whether there is someone sitting in it. (Or, conversely, NOT SITTING IN IT.) Old-fashioned, perhaps, but less likely to require the utilisation of binoculars.

Digital scales, meanwhile: the only people who need those are Heston Blumenthal and drug dealers. By which, we don't mean to imply that Heston Blumenthal has anything to do with drugs. It's just his food that's on drugs.

He pricks each chip individually to let the steam out. But he's not on drugs.

Unofficial 'sponsors' of sporting events

It is one of the finest memories of 2006: settling down to watch a World Cup match with a newly opened tin of World Cup SPAM. What do you mean you didn't eat World Cup SPAM? It was the World Cup, for Christ's sake – when else are you going to eat World Cup SPAM? Wimbledon? During the Open? That's golf!

World Cup SPAM was, of course, just regular SPAM with the words 'World Cup' added to the label. It wasn't individually tailored for different countries: no 'Come on England/Croatia/Ghana/Deutschland über Alles' SPAM; just generic, all-inclusive World Cup SPAM. 'Now you can enjoy SPAM® in match-time sandwiches, on pizzas and in salads or straight from the barbecue as a SPAMBURGER® Hamburger!' If you didn't wish to spend your half-time devouring SPAM salad, there were many other unofficial 'sponsors' of the event, alongside the official FIFA-endorsed tat-hawking industry which raked in over a billion dollars.

Then there was 'in-urinal entertainment', as the promotional material for Wee Goals had it – Wee Goals being small plastic goalmouths with a ball dangling off them that sit in pub urinals so men can wee on them.

It was an international festival of cashing-in in slightly odd ways. Manchester's Piccadilly Station boasted of being a venue in which to watch the match. It is certainly easy to get to – by train.

One Japanese restaurant in Camden, London, filled its

window with a sign exhorting us to: 'CELEBRATE THE WORLD CUP WITH A TAKEAWAY!' This was audacious: beyond simply pointing out that, if you are watching the football, you will be less inclined to cook, so why not enjoy some of their prawn tempura. It was more than that: it was positing a direct causal connection between buying a takeaway and vicariously participating in a sporting event that was taking place hundreds of miles away. As John Motson put it during his commentary on the Germany–Argentina game: 'What a festival of sport. I expect they'll all be eating udon soup noodles in north London tonight, Mark . . .'

On the same busy road as the Japanese restaurant was a sauna/massage parlour displaying the handwritten sign: 'Come and watch the World Cup in our climate-controlled premises.' Don't know if they offered 'extras'. Maybe when it went to extra time? Or, as Motson put it: ' . . . and then I expect they'll continue the celebrations by being wanked off by a stranger for money, Mark.'

But the best, and also the darkest, unofficial tie-in was the German undertaker who offered a discount for the duration of the tournament. Which full-blooded Englishman facing bereavement wouldn't want to capitalise on that? 'All I'm saying is – and I know everyone's upset and all that, but if you look at it rationally, if you just look at the facts for a minute, what I'm saying is – if we took Grandad out there to be buried, we could spend the considerable saving on, you know, tickets for a game.'

'Hello? How much? Is that all? Great. Of course, he was almost buried out there before, during the, erm . . . See you on Thursday. Come on England!'

The Times said the World Cup is not even about football but about 'the expression of a wondrous web of personal, national and geo-political plotlines that weave into an intoxicating drama'. How true, and nothing evokes this heady global spirit like processed meat, piss and death.

US versions of UK reality shows

Dancing on Ice becomes *Skating with Celebrities*, what with the original being too hard to understand.

Utilities competing for your custom

In 2004, watchdog body Energywatch received 40,000 complaints from baffled customers. Companies often stopped customers switching to competitors; salespeople regularly made false claims (I know!); bills didn't come for months, then all arrived at once; customers would find themselves circled by rustlers on steeds, whooping loudly. That kind of thing.

Oh, and my particular favourite: people signed up to new suppliers thinking they were signing campaign petitions about the French.

Thankfully, the DTI and Ofgen have identified the culprit: it's not deregulation, which has caused prices everywhere to skyrocket, but us. We should shop around more. This, however, presupposes being able to read the small print on my bills without wanting to kill myself.

Signing up to a new supplier thinking you're signing a campaign petition about the French, though? That's quite stupid.

V

'Various Things To Do Before You Die' lists

Whole series of listy travel books convey the message: 'Don't die before seeing Borneo. For then, you will not have lived.' Or even the Menai Straits. The Menai Straits! Look, I've seen the Menai Straits, and I can honestly say I could have easily lived without seeing them. They were okay but, well, I haven't been back – which kind of says it all. I could see Anglesey on the other side. It was okay.

'Unforgettable Things To Do Before You Die'? Although there is not much point doing something 'unforgettable' just 'before you die' because you won't actually have too much opportunity to forget it. Maybe a subtitle should point out that: 'You might want to do them a while before you die, otherwise their unforgettable nature might be somewhat wasted on you.'

I don't want to die.

Virgin Galactic

Virgin are already great. But they are about to get better: now they're going into space.

Richard Branson, who is like a cross between Nietzsche's Superman and Noel Edmonds, has promised space tourism to ordinary, everyday, stinking-rich citizens off the street within a few short years. He even envisages a string of hotels all orbiting the planet. Thanks to Virgin, humanity can finally embrace the cosmos. It's a glorious vision. They'll probably balls it all up, though.

Certainly, the omens aren't good. On 27 September 2004, the very day that Branson announced the deal with Mojave Aerospace Adventures – the firm behind SpaceShipOne, which left the atmosphere the previous June – the inaugural journey of Virgin's revolutionary tilting Pendolino train suffered a mechanical fault 25 miles after leaving Glasgow Central. After tottering along at 55 mph, the 85 passengers eventually had to change at Carlisle. Virgin called the glitch 'highly unusual'.

Clearly, Virgin like a challenge. So do I. But I also like not being torn into a million pieces in the upper atmosphere, and Virgin's experience of not letting that happen to anyone is, so far, not massive. There are loads of 'highly unusual' things that can happen in space, and the fact that there isn't any such thing as a replacement bus service 60 miles above the ground does, at the very least, give one a certain amount of pause for thought. If it all goes wrong and you end up drifting off into the void, listening to the freezing silence as the oxygen runs out, you'll find scant consolation in an amazingly small cup of complimentary tea or coffee.

And even if everything does go to plan, there are other worries. For one thing, you could never be sure that, at some point during the excursion, when you peer out into the infinite void you wouldn't be blessed with the sight of Branson himself in a spacesuit tapping on the glass.

He would then point at himself and pull a grin that says: 'Yes! That's right! It's me! In *space*!'

And no one will hear you scream.

Volume of TV ads

Too loud.

Vox, Bono

In the run-up to Live8, Bono explained to the *Evening Standard* the full burden of his responsibilities: 'I represent a lot of people [in Africa] who have no voice at all . . . They haven't asked me to represent them. It's cheeky but I hope they're glad I do.' Cheeky? Not a bit of it!

Previously, during the 50th anniversary celebrations of the United Nations, he explained exactly why the institution was so important: '[I] live off some of the statistics provided by [the UN] – it gives [me] the facts so that when I rant I have something to go on. Without Kofi Annan saying, "You have an open door at any time, Bono," I wouldn't have the same intelligence. You need to know what's happening on the ground.'

People often wonder what the UN is for. It is, we now discover, essentially a fact-finding service for Bono, the world's most important man, who has come here to save us, each and every one of us.

Bono is all around.

Tonight: thank God it's him, instead of you.

W

Water

If you are still drinking ordinary water, you must be some kind of freaking loser. I wouldn't drink ordinary water – bottled or tap – if you paid me, which, apart from anything else, would be quite a weird thing to do on your part. I only drink 'ultra-purified', 'restructured' Penta – 'the Choice of Champions'. Too fucking right it is.

This shit is scientific. Consider this blurb from the side of the bottle: 'Top athletes use Penta for ultimate performance.' Drinking this stuff makes you run faster: FACT.

'Busy mums and high-flyers use Penta to rise above the daily grind.' Anything endorsed by both athletes and mums – well, that's got to be some serious shit. Which it is.

High-flyers are usually right shitheads but, hey, they need water too. And it's reassuring to know that when some tosspot in the City is bankrupting Guatemala, they're very, very hydrated and are therefore much more likely to piss their pants.

So, what's in it? Water! Yes, just freaking water – but more water than in old-fashioned water. That's right, there's more water per centilitre of my water than your Earthling water, you shit-water drinking fool. If you had 500 millilitres of your shitty water, and I had 500 millilitres of Penta, I'd have more water than you. Having trouble getting your brain round that?

Try getting 'Bio-hydrated': it makes you alert, more intelligent and (oh yes!) more likely to cop off with fit people.

Not only is Penta 'easy to drink' (how difficult can water get – unless it's just been boiled in a kettle? But still, cool), it's also 'fast acting'. Because old water, while perfectly adequate for the Steam Age, is now just so frigging slow. If you've got broadband but still use taps, you're clearly some kind of chumpy monkey. So get with it, monkey chump.

In fact, the next time your local water authority comes knocking, demanding to know why you haven't paid the bill, tell them to shove their water up their arse, it's shit.

Westminster Village, the

'So, Ms/Mr Important Political Journalist, have you been out researching stories about how power is affecting the populace?'

'No, but I've been to lunch with a figure whose name I can't mention! And, well, you wouldn't believe what they said about, er . . . thingy. Sorry, can't say. As you know, I'm quite an important figure in the Westminster Village.'

Weirdly, given that exam results keep on rising, the past decade has seen the number of 18–35-year-olds watching news fall by 9%. True, this is partly because some 18–35-year-olds can't be arsed. But it's also because the news is just full of phrases like 'the Westminster Village', which – as in 'the word in the Westminster Village tonight is' – actually translates directly into English as: 'This is some serious bollocks I'm talking right here.'

Other implied meanings include:

- The fact that journalists don't need to visit any places where people's lives are happening – unless, of course, Westminster Village politicians are going there too ('No, not a fucking HOSPITAL?!? There'd better be some fucking sandwiches . . .').
- How the reporter who gets told certain things over lunchy actually gets given a little badge saying: 'ME SO IMPORTANT, YOU NOT SO IMPORTANT'.
- The way any genuinely important issues are only relayed through a series of self-referential winks, tics and raised eyebrows – like the Jane Austen mating ritual only with more backstabbing shitters.

Web 2.0

Haven't finished reading the first one yet.

Wembley

Far be it from me to have concerns about national pride, but when Jon Bon Jovi is righteously laying into the competence of our construction projects, lo, we may have pause for shamed thought. If the permed warbler, a cowboy, on a steel horse he rides, denounces the failure to complete the new Wembley Stadium on time as 'a shambles', surely even the most liberal and internationalist among us must momentarily reflect upon Stephenson's *Rocket* and Monty?

The Jovi, having played the last gig at the old Wembley, were due to open the new one in high style – that is, by playing 'Bad Medicine'. But the gig had to be cancelled as the almost-a-billion-pounds stadium languished unfinished. Blaze of Glory it was not.

Jon Bon Jovi lamented: 'I'm broken-hearted – it's a shambles.' Not to take his pain in vain, one amusing side-effect of the Wembley farrago was that the bookies managed to mug themselves completely over the issue.

When Multiplex announced there was only a 70% chance of the stadium hosting the 2006 FA Cup final on 13 May, Irish firm Paddy Power opened a book on whether the new stadium would be ready in time. More than 60 workers from the Wembley site placed bets that it wouldn't – with nearby Paddy Power branches taking wagers totalling around £10,000 in just two days before betting was suspended.

A Paddy Power spokesperson said: 'I suppose we should have reacted quicker when we saw men in hard hats placing big bets in the Wembley area.'

Bon Jovi, who were not implicated in the betting scandal, played in Milton Keynes instead.

Here's that FA mismanagement timeline in full:

1994: FA bigwigs convene to discuss crumbling national stadium. Should they rebuild Wembley, which nobody can get to, not even if they live in Kilburn? Or should they whack up a new stadium near Birmingham that everyone in the country could reach quickly? After two and a half hours of heated debate, talks stall. It's time for lunch.

1995: Lunch.

1996: Lunch.

1997: Action! Ah, no, lunch.

1998: Coffee, petits fours.

1999: FA bigwigs finally announce decision. Wembley

will be demolished, then rebuilt at a cost of £475 million. Internationally renowned architect Sir Norman Foster is asked to knock up one of his fancy building doodles. He's told the plans should also feature an athletics track, accommodation just like Chelsea FC's successful hotel venture Vacancies, and a fountain spouting free beer.

2000. An independent assessor has a quick look at internationally renowned architect Sir Norman Foster's plans. He spots that many of the 90,000 seats would have restricted views, while the roof would cover only three of the proposed athletic track's eight lanes, rendering any race ever run in the rain a total farce. Foster is told to bugger off and come back with a better plan, one which doesn't bother with the hotel or the running track, and includes seats that face the pitch.

2001: Plans in. They'll do. Multiplex contracted to do the job on the basis of a two-page letter which reads, 'We will build big building.' Demolishing work begins. Building work signally does not. Cost of project now £660 million.

2002: Builders begin construction . . . of nine-skin spliffs as they sit around doing sod all. Well, the ones who aren't queuing up outside the bookies to take the 9/1 on Wembley not being completed by 2005 are, anyway. Cost of project now £900 million.

2003: Builders decide to 'make good' by putting down some hard hats for goal posts and making 'stands' out of three old sofas and an armchair that they found in a nearby skip. 'Will this do?' they ask.

2004: FA bigwigs discuss whether it will do.

2005: Lunch.

2006: Germans host World Cup, utilising five brand-new stadiums, including the tastefully refurbished Olympiastadion in Berlin. Munich's showpiece Allianz Arena, which cost £190 million, is made from 2,874 hi-tech panels which change colour to reflect who is playing at the time, and took about a fortnight to construct. Meanwhile, at Wembley, some bricks have been placed on top of one another, making quite a high pile of bricks, actually.

Football Association? You Give Great British Construction Projects a Bad Name.

William, King, Court of

What do we really know about our future king? Well, we know that, as the eldest son of the eldest son of the sovereign, his arms are differenced by a label of three points unlike the arms of other grandchildren of the sovereign (if granted) which are differenced by a label of five points. That much is certain. But what do we know of William, the man. Is he a prince among men? Well, yes, he's a prince. But what else? We know he's in the army, but isn't mad keen on the colour scheme: 'Everything is khaki this and khaki that,' he told a pal, who then told a newspaper. 'It's all completely army.'*

We know that when things get a bit army in the army, he passes the time by dressing up as a 'chav', tipping up to a Sandhurst party wearing a tracksuit and hilarious 'bling jewellery', which is popular among his less wealthy future subjects. As a 'source' told the *Sun*: 'It's not often you see the heir to the British throne trying to put on a silly accent while dressed as a chav.'

We know – because he told Ant and Dec, which is the closest thing we have to a constitution – that the geography graduate (no sniggering) likes *The X-Factor*, *I'm a Celebrity . . .*, *Pop Idol* and, particularly, *American Pop Idol*. Well, to be fair, it's the only way he'll ever get to vote for anyone.

We know that the future King Bill is a 'die-hard traditionalist' (royal biographer Brian Hoey) in thrall to his grandmother ('what the Queen says, William does'). So the prospects of any self-imposed scaling down into a European-style bicycling monarchy look thin – unless you mean accidentally on purpose cycling over some foxes.

But what of William's future court? Through the ages, princes have used their boundless power and riches to suck the greatest talents of their generation, the science-and-arts movers and shakers, into their orbit. William hasn't done that. One of his best mates, Guy Pelly, eschews all arts, with the exception of the art of getting his bits out. This serial exposer (hobbies: 'impersonating the Queen and mooning') has the nickname 'The Naughty Waiter'. Yes, It's a Right Royal Cockout whenever Guy's about. The twat.

Another close mate is James Murray Wells.

Murray Wells, 'a joker' often found 'frolicking' with The Naughty Waiter, broke his leg on Christmas Eve 2005 when trying to climb into a girls' boarding school in Westonbirt with Pelly – 'on the hunt for skirt'. There wasn't any skirt, though, with it being the school holidays. The twat. And, if there had been any skirt, it would have been the skirt of a schoolgirl, presumably fairly perturbed at being woken by a couple of pissed arseholes, one of whom was probably naked. The twats.

Other great mates include polo-playing, 'chiselled' Luke

Tomlinson, one of Otis Ferry's comrades in storming Parliament to defend fox hunting. Undermining democracy in the name of bloodlust? It's what the great British monarchy is all about!

William's girlfriend Kate Middleton – 'a "boys" girl' – is apparently 'one of the few women who find William's boorish sense of humour amusing'. This raises the slightly terrifying possibility that, of the brothers, Harry is not the boorish one. And what's with all these women not finding the future king's shit jokes funny? Are they stuck up or what?

And there we have it, the Court of William: a load of hoorays sitting around bullying women, watching *The X-Factor*. Casting thousands of votes with *our money* while one of them keeps getting his cock out 'for a laugh'.

God Save the King!

*The British monarchy has a long and noble tradition of going all 'army'. Henry V, obviously, and Richard the Lionheart, who was so 'army' that he kept going to war against his father in league with his brothers, then going to war against his brothers with his father. If things ever looked like going a bit 'not army', he'd fuck off to the Middle East to slaughter Muslims. He was a bit like Wayne Rooney in the World Cup: if you didn't let him have a war, he would only start injuring himself in training. Sometimes, the monarchy goes a bit 'navy'. George V went so 'navy' that he got loads of tattoos and a parrot. In more recent times, Prince Philip served on battleships in the Second World War, and was present at the Japanese surrender in 1945. 'Come on, you slitty-eyed nippos, sign!' is *not* what he found himself shouting uncontrollably at the ceremony.

Willyoujoinus.com

Willyoujoinus.com wants to get everyone together under one umbrella, in a friendly environment inside the same environmentally friendly tent – academics, eco-warriors, Lenny Henry. A counter on the home page shows the number of barrels of oil and gas consumed globally during your visit. And let me tell you, it's loads. That counter's whizzing away. There are loads of scary stats on there, and a moderated discussion board on which you can get really quite worried. Oh, and it's been put up by Chevron. The oil company. The one that sells oil.

At first, I wasn't sure whether they wanted us to join them in donating hundreds of thousands of dollars to Arnold Schwarzenegger and the California Republicans who in turn coincidentally forgot their promises to regulate the oil company's activities more tightly. Or whether they needed help, after buying Texaco, in maintaining their massive legal/PR offensive against a class action from the people of the Ecuadorian Amazon, where, after destroying vast areas of pristine rainforest, Texaco left behind 600 open toxic-waste pits that continue to leak into the water table, producing what Amazon Watch has christened the 'Rainforest Chernobyl'. Or even whether they wanted us to join them in being implicated in the murder of protesters in Nigeria. But no, apparently they've got all that covered.

It really is all about joining them to save the planet. And who could do more in the global struggle against rapacious cash-hungry behemoths plundering the Earth than the very rapacious cash-hungry behemoths that are doing all the plundering? They're ideally placed. All they need to do is have a quiet word with themselves and bish, bash, bosh – teepees! We're all pushing in the same direction here, and that can only be a good thing. The coming century is undoubtedly going to be a stretch – in terms of energy, water, etc; there's a lot of shit to sort out here. Who can we rely on to sort things out equitably and without major bloodshed? Well, how about the oil industry? When have they let us down before?

These people have money to burn, too – always a boon in times of need. Shell and BP both recently notched up £10-billion-plus profits (all of which would be wiped out if the social and environmental costs of their emissions were taken into account). And BP cares so much it has even changed its name – from British Petroleum to Beyond Petroleum – to highlight its commitment to clean energy. Okay, the company is currently under investigation by a grand jury over the spillage of 1.2 million litres of crude at the Prudhoe Bay field, the largest ever in Alaska's North Slope region – which doesn't exactly scream cleanliness. But don't worry, because 'recently appointed head of BP's US operations, Robert Malone, has made cleaning up the firm's public image a top priority' . . . Er, surely cleaning up the oil should be the top priority?

BP has also recently explored buying large chunks of the controversial, some believe semi-criminal, Russian oil group Rosneft, whose flotation would – according to lawyers representing the Yukos oil group – turn the London Stock Exchange into a 'thieves' bazaar'. If they are right, this would potentially see BP embracing the brave new world of money laundering and gangsterism. Money laundering? That's definitely moving beyond petroleum.

So what of that carefully sculpted ethical petrochemical image? A company source explained: 'If you took all your decisions on the basis of reputational risk, you would never do anything.'

Sometimes never doing anything might be preferable. Like all of us, the oil giants' minds are heavily concentrated on the melting polar ice-caps, the crumbling ecosystems, the livelihoods destroyed. Unlike the rest of us, though, their response has involved making immediate plans to start drilling for newly accessible oil under the North Pole: 'Come on guys,

let's get Klondyke! Let's pump all the oil out . . . and burn it!'
And no one in the boardroom lets out a sustained yell of
primal pain then throws themself out of the window, leaving
tufts of bloodied charcoal wool suit on the shattered glass as
they fall 40 storeys to the pavement below.

All told, asking that lot to save the environment would be
like getting Dastardly and Mutley to join your campaign to
save pigeons: you could never be sure their hearts were really
in it.

Other corporate websites you might enjoy include:
justmakethechequeouttolarry.com and
fuckinghellthechinesearecoming.org

'Work hard/play hard'

I once saw a trailer for *Relocation Relocation Relocation* in which
a bionically smug young professional couple said: 'We need
our weekends to get over our weeks and need our weeks to
get over our weekends.' So I watched the programme and,
fuck me, they said it again!

They were right, though. Because their lifestyle did closely
resemble that of Mötley Crüe in their mid-80s Sunset Strip
prime. Rather than, say, a stupendously unquestioning twentysomething couple who frequent a few late-licence barclubs after
a week spent so far up their boss's arse they could clean the
inside of his hat.

The general public is working longer hours, drinking more
booze and snaffling more drugs than ever before (a recent
survey discovered the average UK citizen now ingests more
cocaine than a Colombian cartel boss dropping by on The
Eagles in 1975). We work stupid hours and then relieve the

stress by hammering our bodies with toxins, and – unlike, say, a Victorian chimney sweep whacked up on gin – we think this equates to radical high-living rather than just alternating between the twin modes of droney worker and droney consumer.

Soon, if New Britain gets any Newer, we will all be obliged to work and play so hard that the two will need to be combined. Young professionals will be standing around in All Bar One of an evening typing up reports on their palm pilots while chugging back bottles of Turning Leaf and eating Marlboro Lights. Young workers will conduct presentations from the middle of the dancefloor in Fabric, throwing shapes and Es in every direction and showing flow charts on a projector normally employed for 'psychedelic visuals'. Staff appraisals will be carried out in the ladies' toilets while racking out a line on the top of a filthy hand drier.

World according to Clarkson, the (not the book)

Here be the manifesto of I, Jeremy Charles Robert Isambard Denim Clarkson (hon. PhD/pie):

I have no clean pants. I cannot work the washing machine.

No to pesto! Say no. To pesto.

Over a lifetime the average man wastes 394 days sitting on the lavatory. That's 56 weeks. They are the happiest and most peaceful 56 weeks of a chap's life. I love being on the lavatory more than I love being on holiday.

Hold on a minute.

One of my special stares.

I'm actively encouraging you to call me a bad-tempered,

fat, balding slob with a gay car and a fondness for vulgar home appliances.

Hold on a minute.

That tall bloke with the long hair whose name nobody knows. Not even me. James, maybe? Anyway, I control him. He keeps a tiny little paint-brush in his car to wipe dust off the switches, and on one occasion he dried his underpants in a mate's microwave. (He had a spare pair; he wasn't naked.)

A man who looked like Robert Plant once gave me a lift to the local pub in what was undoubtedly a Renault Scénic.

I asked a squaddie in Basra why he had joined up. 'Because I wanted to kill people.' Now he isn't even allowed to hit anyone with a stick.

Being Surrey, of course, the pub had been bistrofied. It was also spinning round quite a lot. And then the next thing I knew I was in a bed.

X

X, the letter, at the start of words where it isn't

You don't have to be Lynne Truss to be annoyed by this – and I'm not; I don't look anything like her.

Take that bastard Howard. He keeps asking: 'Who gives you xtra?' No one. No one gives you 'xtra'; there's no such fucking word. Get many points for it at Scrabble would you, Howard? No, you would not. It would be disallowed.

Or Virgin Megastore Xpress. What's even Express about it? It's just small: the staff don't fucking roller-skate around on coke, doing everything in a goddam hurry. Also, surely a smaller version of a 'Megastore' is just a 'store'? The 'mega' bit means it's a larger version of what you're calling a small version of a large version. Your basic unit here is a 'store' – which is what this is.

So if you think you're saving letters by dropping the 'e', you're actually using loads more than you need to because of all this other arrant nonsense. Branson: you want your fucking head looked at, man.

Xenu

The Church of Scientology's theory of Xenu, its highest level of wisdom, must be imparted only to those who have ascended to the zenith of human development (that is, people like Tom Cruise). This is because lesser people trying to process the revelations may die; that is actually the stated reason. But we will now reveal to you what OT (Operating Thetan) level Scientologists pay probably hundreds of thousands of pounds and devote many years of effort to learn. Be brave. Gird thyself, or turn away, damn you . . .

Basically, humans are made of clusters of spirits (or 'thetans') who were banished to Earth some 75 million years ago by an evil galactic warlord named Xenu. Suspecting rebellion due to overpopulation, Xenu – ruler of a galactic confederacy which consisted of 26 stars and 76 planets (including the Earth, which was then known as Teegeeack) – duped citizens into attending 'income tax inspections', where he drugged them and shipped them off to Teegeeack. They wore clothes 'which looked very remarkably like the clothes they wear this very minute' (wrote L. Ron Hubbard), and were shipped in planes which were exact copies of Douglas DC-8s, 'except the DC-8 had fans, propellers on it and the space plane didn't'.

Through the Scientology process of 'auditing', the thetan – who has lived through many past lives and will continue to live beyond the death of the body – can free itself of 'engrams' and 'implants' (the accumulated crud of ages) and thus recover its native spiritual abilities – thus gaining control over matter, energy, space, time, thoughts, form and life. This freed state is called Operating Thetan.

How are you feeling? Dead yet? Do you still want a free stress test?

Scientology claims to be the 'study of truth'. Which is almost amusing. The Church was founded in 1954 by L. Ron Hubbard. Tired of his unsuccessful attempts to be a pulp writer (he had also previously flunked college and was discharged from the US Navy), he told acquaintances: 'I'd like to start a religion. That's where the money is;' and 'If a man really wants to make a million dollars, he should start a religion.' So he started a religion and got rich. The richer the Church got, the more Hubbard could deal with his own stress – ultimately de-stressing by cruising around the Med in his own liner with lots of foxy women in uniforms attending on him. (Since Hubbard's death in 1986, the Church has been run by David Miscavige.)

How did Hubbard discover the 'Space Opera' that is the Xenu revelation? The revelation came to him in 1966/7, when he conducted a series of 'audits' on himself to unearth what he believed to be his hidden or suppressed memories, using an EMeter (the primitive lie detector used by Scientology in its stress tests/'intensives'). In a letter of the time to his wife Mary Sue, Hubbard said that, to assist his research, he was drinking a great deal of rum and taking a cocktail of stimulants and depressants ('I'm drinking lots of rum and popping pinks and greys'). His assistant, Virginia Downsborough, revealed that he 'was existing almost totally on a diet of drugs'. Well, it was the mid-60s: everyone was at it. But you wouldn't let 'I Had too Much to Dream (Last Night)' by the Electric Prunes become the basis for a religion, would you?

The Church now claims 10 million members in 159 countries and more than 6,000 churches, missions and outreach groups. Volunteers sign contracts donating a 'billion years' of labour. Scientology charges for virtually all its services: intensives, the little chats about your engrams, can, according to

Janet Reitman in *Rolling Stone*, 'cost anywhere from $750 for introductory sessions to between $8,000 and $9,000 for advanced sessions'. Being registered as a religion, of course, means the Church is tax exempt.

Anyone thinking critically within the Church is marked down as a Potential Trouble Source. Anyone trying to leave has to go through a year-long 'route out' process, during which they are put under immense pressure to stay. Critics outside the Church have been intimidated with litigation, and also by more direct, old-fashioned methods.

Katie Holmes was, of course, famously told by the Church to remain silent while giving birth to Tom Cruise's child (lest the trauma induce engrams in the baby). A spokesperson for the Church claimed they actually meant the delivery staff, and Katie could make the occasional noise if she absolutely needed to. Oh, that's okay then. Except that the average woman would probably appreciate a few words of encouragement from delivery staff during labour. It really hurts.

But what do we non-Scientologists – or 'common, ordinary, run of the mill, garden-variety humanoid[s]' (Hubbard) – know? Who are we to question the right of people to be blackmailed, brainwashed, separated from their families while having their heads filled with horseshit about aliens? Each to their own. Or, as Kabbalah-worshipping freak Madonna put it: 'If it makes Tom Cruise happy, I don't care if he prays to turtles.' Thus speaks the voice of reason.

Y

YBAs – the biopic

How could anyone possibly make the amazing, soaraway story of the mid-90s 'BritArt explosion' even more deep and interesting and worthwhile than it already was? Well, you could turn it into a Hollywood film.

Amazing news: a big-shot producer behind *The Others* is indeed planning a Young British Artists biopic, to be co-produced with Damien Hirst, which is great because Damien Hirst's got a very impressive track record in film, having made the video for Blur's *Country House*, which was great.

ACT I SCENE II. INT. NIGHT

[*11.30 P.M., London, England. At their studio inside the top of the Big Ben tower, London, England,* THE CHAPMAN BROTH-ERS *(wearing traditional English artists' clothing of a smock and beret) are gluing model vaginas on to Airfix Messerschmitts.*]

DINOS CHAPMAN: I'm telling you, JC, it's got to be over a hundred.

JAKE CHAPMAN: It's fine. Ninety-two toy Nazi soldiers with cocks for ears is perfectly sufficient. It's your fault for putting them in the microwave.

DINOS CHAPMAN: And another thing: we're supposed to

be dark but hilarious conceptual artists – so why did you get Messerschmitts? You should have got Fokkers [*laugh track*]. The word Fokkers [*laugh track*] is intrinsically hilarious.

JAKE CHAPMAN: With the Messerschmitts you get a cool Nazi pilot with a grimacing face. Stick a cock on that and we'll have our own room in MoMa before you can—

[*Massive commotion as the door flies open and* DAMIEN HIRST *and* SARAH LUCAS *burst through brandishing machine guns. Both are sporting traditional English artists' clothing of a stripey top and beret.*]

DINOS CHAPMAN: What the fuck do you two want?

[*More commotion at the door as* TRACEY EMIN *falls through it, accidentally spraying machine-gun fire across the ceiling.*]

TRACEY EMIN: Ta-da!

[TRACEY EMIN *falls over.*]

DAMIEN HIRST: Jake, Dinos – the art world needs us.
TRACEY EMIN: I'm pissed.
JAKE CHAPMAN: Gilbert and George can find their own fucking dog. I'm sick of it.
DAMIEN HIRST: It's more serious this time.
SARAH LUCAS: It's Saatchi.
TRACEY EMIN: I'm from Margate, you know.
DAMIEN HIRST: He's been sending minions out from his fortified island kingdom in a disused volcano on the Thames.

SARAH LUCAS: They've been buying up shit art that's a bit like ads only rude. They want to parade caged pseudo-subversive crappy artists like tame bears on the South Bank – in the old City Hall, where that bloke with the newts used to do, you know, the thing. It's a final assault from Thatcherism.

DINOS CHAPMAN: What are we gonna do – get down there and bust his ass?

DAMIEN HIRST: No – we're going to sell him a load of our shitty art and make huge vitrines-full of cash.

JAKE and DINOS CHAPMAN: Hurrah!

SARAH LUCAS: Do you want to see my melons?

TRACEY EMIN: Let's go for a drink.

[*Fade.*]

Youth Alpha

Youth Alpha is essentially the Alpha Course – that is, learning all about Jesus in a subtle, touchy-feely, Shloer and cheese sort of a way – only for much younger, much more impressionable people. If the Alpha Course gets God into adults who, for whatever reason, find themselves feeling coldly adrift in a world that doesn't care, then aiming it at teenagers, all of whom, virtually without exception, feel coldly adrift in a world that doesn't care, is the getting-God equivalent of shooting fish in a barrel. Or even loaves in a barrel.

Young people are attracted to Youth Alpha by youth-centred methods such as cinema ads, text messages and people talking to them about Jesus. Once enrolled, they first participate in discussions based on the Alpha book *Questions of Life*, which mostly features questions about the Lord Jesus. Then, on a weekend away, they are shown a video about the Holy Spirit, and are invited to receive the Holy Spirit.

Not having seen the video, I can't help wondering how they depict the Holy Spirit. I hope they have used some serious CGI effects and it's not just shiny-eyed Alpha leader Nicky Gumbel with a sheet over his head going: 'Woo-oooh!'

Who is Youth Alpha aimed at? 'The main deal is that if you are interested in getting some of life's big questions sorted, and want to work out what you believe, then come along.' It helps if your 'main deal' involves listening to people talking about Jesus. The 'big questions' will definitely veer quite markedly in that direction. You won't be doing a compare and contrast on, say, Rousseau and Lenin. It will be mostly Jesus under consideration. Primarily, if not exclusively, this will be a Jesus situation centring heavily on the teachings of Jesus (that is, the mythical Christian Jesus who ascends to heaven and all of that; not the historical Jesus, the Jewish anti-Roman revolutionary millenarian – just so that's clear).

Some Christians, though, believe that the Alpha Course, while incorporating a lot of Jesus (as I think we were discussing previously), doesn't focus nearly *enough* on Jesus. The website for Ian Paisley's European Institute of Protestant Studies features a discussion piece by the Rev. Paul Fitton, asking: 'The Alpha Course: Is It Bible-Based or Hell-Inspired? Does its teaching rest solidly and squarely upon the authoritative rock of Holy Scripture or does it teach error in the name of Jesus?'

Now this might be disappointing news for young people attending Youth Alpha courses and labouring under the misapprehension that they are learning all about Jesus, but, sadly, it turns out that the course is more Hell-Inspired than Bible-Based. That's got to hurt. Like hell.

On the plus side, they do provide snacks, although the Rev. Fitton doesn't go into that side of things much.

Yummy mummies

Don't just lie there! It's been two hours since you've given birth Get on that treadmill now. Or you're never going to 'snap right back' by the end of the frigging week.

Society expects! Or, at least, a certain part of vile London moneyed tosspot society expects. Before your newborn's first month, you must be playing *Bartok For Babies* while baking organic muesli bars in your 4x4. If you do not spend on your child in its first three months the same as the average yearly wage, then your child will be ugly and stupid. And who wants that?

The capital is now so crazed with the desire to produce 'alpha children' that some toddlers are even going to Japanese classes. One recent article reported that one two-year-old had reportedly been taught Roman numerals, French and Latin. At nursery, instead of mixing with other children, she just stood howling – possibly in disbelief at the quality of her peers' conjugation. I wonder what's the Japanese for 'teenage nervous breakdown'.

Z

Benjamin Zephaniah

Many 21st-century office workers pass the hours spent in a room listening to someone spouting self-aggrandising bull-crap by playing the popular game Business Buzzword Bingo. Now fans of anti-Establishment/anti-colonial doggerel can join in the fun – with Benjamin Zephaniah Bingo. Points are awarded every time you hear the poet utter the following:

- 'OBE? No BE!'
- 'You know, I was a bad boy . . .'
- 'No way, Mrs Queen!'
- '. . . so they put me away in Prison!'
- 'Who turned down their OBE? Me! That's who! Me! Not you! Me!'
- 'Maybe you didn't know . . . but I've just come back from . . . AFF-REEEE-KAAAAAA!!!'
- 'Me? OBE? OBE? Me? Naaaaaaaah!'
- 'I would just like it to be known that I sincerely hope I will never ever be considered for the role of poet laureate. That is not the job for me. Did you get that? No poet laureate am I!'
- 'Oh yes, Mrs Queen, I'm so grateful. Not!'

Zion train

It still hasn't come.

Z-list celebrities as fuckwit pundits

Just before the 2005 general election, the *Guardian* had a news feature rounding up predictions of the result from sharp political minds like 'Steve Harley, lead singer of Cockney Rebel'.

'What will happen in the election?' we asked. 'If only we knew what Steve Harley of Cockney Rebel thought. He had a number one in 1975, you know. So clearly he's going to know about all this. It had an acoustic guitar solo.'

The *Independent* has gone one better and given a column to Tracey Emin. When not crapping on about how she had a hard time growing up in Margate, her mum or her cat, Emin squeezes in passing mentions of current affairs, such as the question 'I'd like to know how much has been spent on the war in Iraq . . . I wonder where you get information like that.'

In newspapers, Tracey; the people who are paid to write in the newspapers which people read in order to learn information make it their business to find these things out and tell us – otherwise what they are doing is WASTING EVERYONE'S FUCKING TIME.

Z-list celebrities saving the planet

Saving the planet is one of the major challenges facing the planet. Luckily, the celebrities know the score and are fighting – literally fighting – to do their bit. It's almost – *almost* – enough to make you think.

Here's Gaynor Faye, in a short newspaper Q&A, asked what she wishes people would take more notice of. 'The environment,' she answers, no doubt quick as a flash. 'I do as much as I can, but there are so many things we're doing that are destroying the world.' Answering a question about what she does in moments of weakness, she reveals, 'Go shopping and buy too many things which sit in the wardrobe.' In a nutshell, her philosophy is this: 'Live for today and have no regrets.' Live for today, don't care about tomorrow. While doing as much as you can for, er, tomorrow.

Eco-tourism is a big deal: we can see the world without ruining the world. Asked about it by *The Times*, writer and philosopher Alain de Botton contributed a small essay about . . . himself. 'I am drawn to large empty spaces, particularly deserts,' he began, before going on to explain absolutely nothing about eco-tourism. 'Travel offers a constant lesson in humility,' he concluded.

Following Al Gore's rousing example, Leonardo DiCaprio's environment film reveals an interest that dates back to the filming of *The Beach* – yes, the Danny Boyle film that was marred by protests from environmentalists after the production team uprooted indigenous plants to widen the beach. The beach wasn't wide enough for *The Beach*, you see.

Then came the news that *Dirty Dancing* star Patrick Swayze was so devastated by people destroying the planet that he cries about it all the time: 'I cry frequently at the way we're destroying the planet. We are heading for disaster until and unless we do something about it.'

Guess what he's planning to do about it. That's right: make a documentary. Don't laugh. A man is dying here. There could be hope. If only governments would stop ignoring the advice of Tracey Emin. In March 2006 the *Independent* asked a series of minor celebrities/public figures if there was hope for the planet. Emin said: 'We need more research and development in the things like electronic cars. Research is desperately needed in so many areas in this country but is ignored by the Government.'

Yeah, that's really sticking it to them. Sadly, Emin continued: 'It is not just governments who have responsibility – it is people like myself, who are aware of what they are doing wrong, yet still do it. Much more needs to be done to let people know what they are doing.'

So, unless I am mistaken, when asked for your opinion on how we can avoid Armageddon – as well as calling for research into 'electronic cars'; which would be hard because there's NO SUCH THING – you are forthrightly demanding that more needs to be done to tell people like you what is going on. If only people like you could be forced to listen to what is going on, then – and only then – will you properly be made aware of the problem. Essentially, your opinion is that you – at some point soon – must be made to have an opinion.

But if you are a Z-list celebrity and you find yourself being asked your opinion on global change, and your opinion is that you must be forced to have an opinion, because people, like you, don't do anything, you might actually first consider getting an opinion. Otherwise, what you are doing is WASTING EVERYONE'S FUCKING TIME.